Fictocritical Innovations

A Millennial Perspective

Pawel Cholewa

FICTOCRITICAL INNOVATIONS

A Millennial Perspective

Pawel Cholewa

ibidem
Verlag

Bibliografische Information der Deutschen Nationalbibliothek

Die Deutsche Nationalbibliothek verzeichnet diese Publikation in der Deutschen Nationalbibliografie; detaillierte bibliografische Daten sind im Internet über http://dnb.d-nb.de abrufbar.

Bibliographic information published by the Deutsche Nationalbibliothek

Die Deutsche Nationalbibliothek lists this publication in the Deutsche Nationalbibliografie; detailed bibliographic data are available in the Internet at http://dnb.d-nb.de.

Cover picture: © Liam Baster, 2020. Printed with kind permission.

ISBN-13: 978-3-8382-1543-3

© *ibidem*-Verlag, Stuttgart 2021

Alle Rechte vorbehalten

Printed in the EU

TABLE OF CONTENTS

ACKNOWLEDGEMENTS

I gratefully acknowledge the funding received from Central Queensland University through the UPRA Program that supported this research. I also respectfully acknowledge the expertise and guidance provided by Professor Stephen Muecke in the final stages of my PhD dissertation.

Some sections and fragments of this book have previously been published in TEXT Journal, Idiom 23, Stoned Crows & Other Australian Icons: Prose Poems & Microfiction, Colloquy and narratorAUSTRALIA.

Professional editor, John McAndrew, provided copyediting and proof-reading services of my PhD dissertation, according to the guidelines laid out in the University-endorsed national 'Guidelines for Editing Research Theses'.

Various names and identifying details and characteristics of locations, people and institutions have been altered or invented for creative, legal and confidentiality reasons.

Book cover art/photograph "Pink Lake" courtesy of Liam Baster.

To Wally, for stoking the flame.

To Tris, for settling the embers.

To friends and family, for your care, conversation, content, humour and patience.

To Andrea, for being a second conscience, and for just helping me to be a better version of my self during much of this process.

To God, for not existing, therein providing me the independence and freedom necessary to rely on more innate and tangible things.

To all the blurred, pivotal or indirect influences.

To the multitudinous chaotic selves manifested in these writings: may this work bring you some closure and a sense of unified peace and consolidation.

TABLE OF FIGURES

LIST OF TERMINOLOGY

Creative self: Originator of creative folio(s)

Analytical self: Writer of theses

Folio(s): The (creative) fictocritical work written by the creative self

Thesis/Theses: The theoretical analyses (of the creative work) written by the analytical self

Section(s): A thesis and its accompanying folio

INTRODUCTION

This book has been adapted from a doctoral dissertation submitted to CQUniversity in 2019, and conferred in the same year. The study containing the two separate elements of creative work and analytical exegesis, was positioned within the creative writing field of fictocriticism, and stems from earlier 'experiments' in autobiographical writing and experiences of travel and growing up in Australia as a first-generation Polish-Australian male. Touching upon episodes of diaspora, family, education, and questions of 'self' and 'identity' that have arisen as a young creative artist living in an increasingly digital age, the exegesis of this creative work is both intensely personal and clinically theoretical. The creative pieces are thinly veiled personal accounts which, in turn, provide a framework for various thematic constructions for a developing sense of self in relation to the experiences under discussion. The reason for structuring this dissertation in four theses is due to the flexible, yet "inimitable" (Gibbs 1) needs of the fictocritical genre and form and because the discussion demands some definable limitations.

Initially, this exploration was influenced by Josie Arnold's "The PhD in Writing Accompanied by an Exegesis" (2005), where she discusses the dichotomy between traditionalist or conservative modes of constructing a PhD, versus the more creative types of work that challenge preconceived or traditional templates of the exegesis and artefact model. This is where my interest in experimentation comes to the fore, and it offers a space where unique conceptualisations of creative/critical 'academic' writing are disseminated and introduced to provide new literary insights. Arnold references Nelson, Deleuze and Scrivener and their desire to 'catastrophise' or rebel against the type of 'straight-jacket' that is "the traditional thetic/exegesis" (38). This is where fictocriticism comes strongly into the equation, offering as it does, a revolutionary, experimental and metacognitive way of researching and writing in the synthesis of new and original thinking.

To reiterate, and to properly prepare the reader for what is to come, I assert that fictocriticism deserves further academic attention and investigation, and what I believe to be the most interesting and/or challenging aspects at the cutting edge of the debate surrounding fictocriticism is its unclassifiable nature and its potential technological innovativeness. During the course of this explorative discussion, I canvas many different positions in the fictocritical debate, almost all of which are vastly interconnected (or vastly disconnected), depending on how they are examined. I contend that the central motifs, mission and contribution of this book is in its exploration of fictocriticism's chameleonic nature and its growing (futuristic) tendency towards electronic mediums. The first three sections of this study intentionally and gradually synthesise these complex issues and build towards the overarching notion that four individual theses are needed to detail the separate folios of the emergent argument and to provide context for the creative writings. The fourth thesis coheres the various arguments.

Fictocriticism can be described as a hybrid-style of writing that is both fictional and critical, a genre of writing that is naturally theoretical, personal or personalised and professional, (Schlunke and Brewster 393). It has been considered a 'buzzword', on the fringe of mainstream literature, 'meta' and postmodern in nature and form, format and execution or delivery. It has also been referred to as "a refusal of any steady border between genres" (Trottier 1), a mode (or collage) of thought "gently flapping, between experience and interpretation" (Kerr and Nettelbeck 109), "a textual no-man's land" (Dawson 139), "a writing of compounds and mutations, a hybrid writing which is not just any one thing, but *not* any *one* thing" (White et al. 10-11), an "inchoate category" (Schlunke and Brewster 393) that allows or permits one to really disperse oneself and the 'I'.

This book involves two very distinct and different perspectives, each of which has a unique 'voice' and persona: the four-part creative component is recounted by a self-conscious creative informal self in four folios; while the four theoretical theses, which dissect the creative folios and explore the fictocritical strategies, are written with the more clinical and formal voice of a literary scientist, referred to as the analytical self. It was necessary to develop a sense of estrangement between these two personas, to split the author and researcher, (myself, Pawel Cholewa), into these two diverged voices. This is done to be consistent with, and to further the notion of fictocriticism being "double-voiced" (Kerr 93).

Double-voicedness is a key feature within the context of fictocriticism, and it requires some expounding. Double-voicedness is about subtext: the voice on top and the voice on the bottom, or the voices of the writer speaking side-by-side. They are the yin and yang of duality within the context of writing. One is generally creative, the other critical. One is about poeticism and storytelling, the other is about critique, social commentary, philosophy or concrete theory. They can be integrated, work in tandem, or contrast and reverberate off one another dichotomously. They are the tangible and the intangible, working with, against or through one another.

My separation between creative self and analytical self, in the folios and theses of this work, makes this literary technique and function very obvious and literal. This deliberate estrangement of personas, the development of a schism between creative self and analytical self, also enables the subtleties of double-voicedness to be better seen and more clearly recognised in the creative folios.

For obvious reasons, it is generally quite difficult to write about oneself. If my 'self' is going to be interesting, it has to be vulnerable to change. The analytical self in the theses, recorded in the third-person, is armour-plated in dealing with new emerging problems and innovations of fictocriticism. The creative self (or selves), most often in the state of confessing in the first-person, can be guarded at times, but change dramatically over the course of the work. The creative self is not safeguarded to the point that it is immobile. The point of this is to remove the armour carried around with us. The narrative arc, as well as the multitudinous perspectives in the writings, show this. Both diverged selves, just as my own complete persona, change through the process of this exploration. I am not the same researcher or creative writer as I was at the outset of my PhD in 2013, nor do I necessarily hold to the same views and opinions I held between the ages of 25 and 30

(2013–2017); these views and opinions are more so in the creative act of venting/catharsis.

To assist in comprehending the complexity and nature of these 'selves' and their (correlating) diverged sections, a brief list of the terminology used in this book, is provided prior to this introduction, on page 13. It may be easier to think of fictocriticism, not as a literary genre, but more as a way to process thought—"a strategy for writing" (Kerr and Nettelbeck 4). The majority of explanations of fictocriticism, my own attempts included, are inconclusive. They either overcomplicate the idea, or the language used to describe it is too figurative or metaphorical. Hazel Smith's explanation in "The Erotics of Gossip: Fictocriticism, Performativity, Technology" (2009) is well-balanced in that sense and probably the best description found so far to explain the concept:

> fictocriticism juxta-poses creative and academic writing environments, and breaks down their separation and autonomy. Fictocritics may, for example, insert, imply, or elucidate theoretical ideas within creative work without feeling the pressure to transform those ideas into entirely fictional or poetic texts. Such texts can take many different forms, but may often be experimental and discontinuous: for example, fictional or poetic sections are juxtaposed with theoretical interjections so that they reverberate with each other. Or, fictocritical critics may attempt to disrupt the formality of the academic essay with strategies such as crossing of genres, collage, non-linearity, wordplay, anecdote, or use of the first person. (1001-02)

The initial and primary appeal of fictocriticism was its resistance to having any kind of authority dictated over its form, a creative structure that aspires to the convenience of being inherently freeform (Gibbs 310): "There is no specific way to write fictocritically" (Naismith 24). Fictocriticism is referred to as a genre that is about "personal journey and storytelling" (Hancox and Muller 149) and that "the form is part of the message" (Flavell 186). It is an unorthodox writing technique because of the level of literary iconoclasm. To offer any deep level of critical explanation or attempting to cage the creative work within any kind of accepted writing parameter goes against the grain and meaning of its intention as a literary form of writing or 'device'—a tool for the erratic construction and personalised investigation of journal-like 'meaning' (Flavell 29).

When fictocriticism appears in anthologies, articles, in the introductions of theses and the like, it is usually something that is *explained* fictocritically, which is typically personalised, abstracted and mixed in style, genre, form, etc. Yes, "ficto-criticism is indeed a slippery and contradictory category" (Flavell 126). But this is what makes it such an exuberant and stimulating mode. Furthermore, it is particularly useful in being able to construct a fragmentary narrative that is in part abstract, creative and autobiographical but then also a narrative(s) which features some critique regarding the explicit themes or issues addressed. Fictocriticism allows a writer to ebb, flow and move through and between these different primary voices to render a richer narrative.

A detailed review of the literature surrounding fictocriticism and its predecessors shows that there are terms that exist in other countries that have a suggestive fictocritical air about them. In Japan there is *Shishōsetsu* or the 'I-novel', a confessional form of writing that promoted transparency and textual interconnectivity between writer, narrator and narrative hero in early twentieth-century Japanese fiction (Layoun 158). *Shishōsetsu* encouraged authorial presence and 'sincerity', just as fictocriticism encourages authorial involvement and engagement in its 'storytelling' form (Layoun 159).

In the writing of Québecoise women there is fiction-theory or *fiction-théorique*, as seen in the works of Nicole Brossard — someone who "has had considerable impact on the development of creative-critical writing in English Canada", having influence in the development of a "very specific creative-critical style" on the margins of Canadian culture (Flavell 215).

Paul Dawson, an Australian academic, in "A Place for the Space Between: Fictocriticism and the University" (2002), states that the North American version of fictocriticism would be called "confessional criticism" (145):

> confessional criticism is … indebted to the post-structuralist critique of critical and philosophical modes of writing as metalanguages, and the

> subsequent rejection of the epistemological relationship between these modes and an unquestionable truth. If the disinterested and impersonal prose of academic writing can no longer provide access to knowledge, then the intellectual as political subject becomes the only enabling motivation of critical activity. (Dawson 145)

Essentially, both confessional criticism and fictocriticism aim to distance and liberate criticism from its "parasitical dependence on literature" (Dawson 146).

There is also "autocritique, the new belletrism, experimental critical writing, narrative criticism, and literary non-fiction" (Flavell 106). Autocritique is a complicated form of self-criticism — a "trendy 'I' that beams out at the reader from the 'personal' critical essay" (Flavell 274). The new belletrism is another conceptualisation of autobiographical criticism identifying "American ficto-critical moves as a return to an earlier form of the essay (before its appropriation as an academic genre and reincarnation as logical formal writing)" (Flavell 108). Experimental critical writing has been best summed up and expressed by Marianna Torgovnick:

> When writers want to be read they have to be more flexible and take more chances than the standard scholarly style allows: often, they have to be more direct and more personal. In a very real way ... I could not think myself as a writer until I risked exposing myself in my writing. I am not talking here, necessarily, about full-scale autobiographical writing — though I am not ruling it out either. But I am saying that writerly writing is personal writing, whether or not it is autobiographical. Even if it offers no facts from the writer's life, or offers just hints of them here and there, it makes the reader know some things about the writer — a fundamental condition, it seems to me, of any real act of communication. (25-27)

Narrative criticism is a formula of narrativity used to tell a story (Walker 559). And literary non-fiction is "the inclusion of a personal voice into a book of non-fiction" (Flavell 26).

Other possible influences on fictocriticism include gonzo, travel writing, writing-between and beatnik novels, some of which continue to (re)appear and exist today. There is also evidence of the incorporation of experimental, personalised or fictive writing in academic disciplines such as:

> cultural and literary studies, film studies, performance studies, law, history, philosophy, visual arts, and even beyond the humanities into some areas of

the sciences. *A View from the Divide: Creative Nonfiction on Health and Science* (1999), for example, suggests that even the most purely scientific and objective disciplines are not immune to the ficto-critical turn. (Flavell 104-5)

In 2007, Denis Byrne's *Surface Collection: Archaeological Travels in Southeast Asia*, an archaeological travelogue, told through stories in the first-person, was published. This further demonstrates the emergence of fictocriticism in different disciplines, bridging discourses and creating new approaches to writing in the way 'straight' informal theory or 'normal' fiction cannot do. Here is an example from Byrne's book:

> Standing at the window of the second-floor room in the National Museum where I was reading through piles of old reports and archaeological site records, I could see, looking across a stream of traffic and a dusty park, a corner of the Spanish wall and the confusion of rooftops and low facades that lay beyond it. There, in 1571, Miguel Lopez de Legazpi had laid out a gridiron of seventeen streets on the site of what had been the palisaded fort of Rajah Suleiman. The Rajah's small brass cannons, while perfectly adequate under previous conditions, were little more than a joke to the Spanish, and they easily drove him out of his stronghold. Intramuros's defenses were elaborated and modified over time to produce a system of immense stone walls complete with moat, seven gates, several bastions and ravelins, and a large fort in the northwest corner guarding the river mouth. (1-2)

All the foregoing discussion shows that a kind of fictocriticism can both fall into, under (and evade) a plethora of different categories, and at present there does not appear to be a unified, cohesive accepted understanding of the form.

Fictocriticism was first taken up in Australia in the 1990s, stemming from Canada (Flavell 3-4). "Anna Gibbs reminds us that [fictocriticism] appears well before this in the writing of mostly non-academic women responding to the new and 'provocative' texts emanating from France then later Canada from the 1970s onward" (147). Fictocriticism's emergence in Australia is thought to have been prompted by way of "French feminist interest in a new kind of writing defiant of phallocentrism" (147). Some of this French feminist experimental writing is often referred to as *écriture féminine* (Hancox and Muller 148).

The first article to have the term 'fictocriticism' appear in it in Australia was Stephen Muecke and Noel King's "On Ficto-Criticism" in 1991 in the *Australian Book Review*. Muecke and King's tentative two-page article acts as a discussion—even a somewhat casual conversation—between the two academics, in curiously trying to decipher what type of writing much of Roland Barthes' work, such as *Mythologies* (1957), *Roland Barthes* (1975) and *A Lover's Discourse* (1977), and Don DeLillo's novel *White Noise* (1985) actually are. Muecke and King claim that Roland Barthes' texts "simply cannot be called criticism, but [they] cannot, for that matter be called non-criticism either" (14). And that *White Noise* is "at once a quite traditional novel (in terms of structure) and yet one of the sharpest meditations on the postmodern available" (Muecke and King 13). Thus, they emphatically decide on the possibilities of fictocriticism as a postmodern way "to simply [tell] stories" (Muecke and King 13), and as a relief from heavy theory. They even disregard the need for systematically accurate referencing at the end of the article, claiming "No need for bio details—they're in the text, but also we want readers to be a little uncertain about our reality" (Muecke and King 14). Overall, the article paints fictocriticism as providing a refreshingly non-convoluted, un-bureaucratic perspective on the possibilities of (academic) writing in a way that is still rich, provocative and engaging.

Helen Flavell's important and unique 2004 doctoral thesis *Writing-Between: Australian and Canadian Ficto-Criticism* provides a thorough description, explanation and history of the term. What is so good about Flavell's work is that it is likely to be the first thesis to look at fictocriticism as a style/genre through a more theoretical lens: "Through my application of Deleuzian theory I encourage a productive use of the literary machine, extracting from the ficto-critical text its revolutionary force" (Flavell 40).

Elements of fictocriticism are also perhaps comparable to the idea of *jouissance*, which can be inferred from a reading of Barthes' *The Pleasure of the Text* (1973) and French feminism, in the discourse(s) of Julia Kristeva and Hélène Cixous, for instance (Spivak 166). *Jouissance* has been interpreted or connected to concepts such as "bliss", "fully-tasted pleasure", "orgasm" and "perversion" (Gallop 566). And it is a mode or an amalgamation of these things — an excited and stimulated sensation in which a feeling and/or sentiment of sexuality can be interconnected with a blissful intelligence and engagement with the text, whether in the act of reading or writing. And so, an ecstatic jubilation would come under that mode also. Like fictocriticism (and a lot of metafictive devices), *jouissance* is simple enough, though something that one needs to actively engage with in order to understand and appreciate.

Due to the amount of purely fictocritical discussion(s) that needed to take place throughout the research process, much of the 'higher' theory has been expounded in the creative folios also. This, in many ways, is complementary to fictocriticism's double-voiced and subtextual (Rubenstein 37) nature. Still, a deliberate methodology pervading this body of work is all about splitting my cognitive awareness into two parts: one as creative self, the other as analytical self.

Occasionally these two writing approaches (creative and theoretical) are quite challenging to separate as there is a large amount of overlap between the two. This experimental study contends that this is a strong characteristic of fictocriticism though, and there are a myriad of academics that discuss the potential of literary research to be developed in this manner too (Barrett 2004; Kroll 2004; Nelson 2004; Brewster 2005; Arnold 2005). That is a discussion for another time: however, it is a possible avenue for future research and innovation.

Also, I initially assumed that my very early research and work was fictocritical because a concrete and consistent explanation of it could not be located elsewhere. I found it difficult to understand the methodology properly without this concrete, unequivocal definition. It created a severe mental block in the work. Thus, at the end of 2017 a decision was made to alter my doctoral project into a literary 'experiment' which would produce an industrious, working definition of fictocriticism as a literary genre. In essence, my doctoral dissertation (and subsequently this book) construct a definition of fictocriticism itself through the creative writing experiments that would push the methodology's boundaries. This process and feedback formed a renewed and re-focused line of research questioning that was definitive: What is fictocritical fiction? Is there a definition of it that is agreed on by all fictocritical academics? And which of my experimental pieces succeed or fail in this vein? Other similar questions then include: Does fictocriticism work well within both academic and creative writing practices? Does it work in a hybridised manner? Is it a methodology that can still be innovated? Has, or how has, fictocriticism changed over the years to become more concise and dynamic, regimented, or has it become more vague and obscure? By 'doing' fictocriticism, what problems does it solve? And do the 'experiments' in fictocriticism presented in the different (creative) folios of this book innovate upon the form successfully, and also show pathways for future research, or do they fail? This exploration, by its conclusion, aims to demonstrate which pieces succeed, which pieces fail, or which elements of pieces succeed fictocritically and which elements fail fictocritically. Also, if fictocriticism can be better categorised and synthesised, what boundaries and rules could sustain it as a legitimate form and methodology in academia in the future?

Questions that are left unanswered, or open to debate, but demonstrate the potential to take up this scholarly research baton and continue studies in fictocriticism and other hybridised forms of writing, also relate to the potential of academic writing/research to be developed in a different (more engaging) manner (Barrett 2004; Kroll 2004; Nelson 2004; Brewster 2005; Arnold 2005). They are possible avenues for future research and innovation. Autoethnography, for instance, has been taking up an innovative methodological-pedagogical approach for itself for years (Ellis and Bochner 2000; Holt 2003; Canagarajah 2012; Méndez 2013; Anae 2014); Theses One and Two of this text contend that autoethnography and fictocriticism are cut from a similar methodological cloth.

Fortunately, some of these broader questions and theoretical concerns have begun to be addressed. In 2017, a thorough theoretical exploration into fictocriticism entitled *Fictocritical Strategies: Subverting Textual Practices of Meaning, Other, and Self-Formation* was published by Gerrit Haas. This occurred more or less during the final stages of my doctoral work. Hence, it has been both gratifying and validating to find a relatively recent work with a similar theoretical focus, despite fictocriticism often seeming dormant or veiled in the literary fringes of academia.

It is, therefore, at least necessary to summarise *some* of Haas' goals and intentions and how they may or may not relate to this study. Haas calls for "a *systemic* conceptualisation of fictocriticism that can hope to capture its various historical strands as well as possible forms to come without stifling its subversive potential … a defining general pattern at work" (12).

What *this* book calls for is the (re)discovery and categorisation of distinct fictocritical innovations and/or traits. Put excruciatingly simply, Haas seeks to locate an overall theoretical pattern in fictocriticism, whilst my book aims to find some of its 'new' distinct patterns. Both Haas and myself observe, dissect and scrutinise the same literary form from two different angles: Haas from the macro, and myself from the micro.

Haas and I are in total agreement about fictocriticism being capable of more than "marginal relevance" (16), feminism's antecedence in fictocriticism, and we are carefully considerate and respectful of our reliance on Flavell and Muecke's research and writing in this area (12). Haas merely grinds at the 'genre' in a different way:

> In many ways the precise connection between these two aspects of fictocriticism—between genre-subversion and marginal/ised speaking positions, between the text-discursive and the wider discursive, between the fictional and the ethical, theory and criticism—is the main subject of this thesis. (Haas 9)

It is necessary to reference Haas' work, and where my own experiences and experiment(s) enter into the discussion or forefront of the debate surrounding fictocriticism. It is clear we must both be on the right track. Haas' book is purely theoretical, whereas mine is about innovations, primarily based in response to my own creative works. Haas' primary text sources for his study are vastly different (Haas 49-51). Also, due to the predominantly creative focus and field of this book, and the reliance of the theoretical work/theses to reflect back on the creative work/folios in a symbiotic way, I have experienced certain spatial limitations, or to put it more positively, my theoretical focus, methodology and process has had to be fine-tuned, tempered. Hence, this book's predominant focus and/or expectant anticipation of innovative 'technologies' or "electric fictocriticism", as coined by Simon Robb (100), entering the changing medium of reading, writing, communion and the reader-writer relationship in this field. Haas only alludes to this in passing in order to focus more greatly on the "wider discursive and cultural applications" (22) at hand.

Haas does actually propose a list of "textual markers" (30) for fictocriticism, and a reasonable, though pattered and mechanical "working definition" (59) of fictocriticism in his book, though he does not believe these "characteristics" are especially relevant or absolute due to their inconsistency "across the spectrum of fictocritical texts, which take a diverse range of experimental forms" (30). Thus, he does not offer distinct innovative markers either, which this book does. Hence, his working definition and "textual markers" fall short of actually defining the genre as it exists today. These markers can be considered relevant, particularly in relation to identifying and classifying my work.

The four main folios in this text are made up of fragments, stories, experiences and snapshots from my life, and placed or positioned into these four folios of specific interest as a working schema from the perspective of a Polish-Australian millennial between the ages of 25-30. The year each piece was constructed appear in parentheses beside their corresponding title to reflect the narrator/protagonist's age at the time of construction, and generally all occur during the second decade of the twenty-first century. The significance of these four areas are that they are the factors that have most vividly made up my sense of an identity. These four areas relate to me, but also largely to the contemporary landscape of today's *zeitgeist*, and are themes that appear in fictocriticism often (Muecke 2008; Raine 2009; Hancox and Muller 2011; Morgan 2012; Robb 2013).

Thesis One, "Examining the Fictocritical Value of Journeys: The Author Meanders", is about journeys. This thesis, and the corresponding folio, questions if it is possible to innovate upon fictocriticism or if it is the 'ultimate' innovative genre, suggesting that there is a paradox between the theory surrounding fictocriticism, suggesting how 'freeform' it is, and how non-freeform it still seems to be due to its lack of theoretical boundaries. The theme of journeys is used as a strategy to convey the methodology of fictocriticism overall, as an untapped way of writing both personally and theoretically, with a unified and engaging double-voice. Attempts at pushing the threshold and parameters in differing experimental creative works advocate for what fictocriticism could be, and ask if it can be reinvented into something more stable, yet still evolve into a mode of writing that is engaging, identifiable and prominent within the academy.

In this section's folio, the tropes of travel provide a critical vehicle, focusing on the restlessness of the creative self's need to travel both physically and metaphysically, and look at the creative self's experiences within different zones (locations, contexts, environments) with differing comfort levels. Most of these journeys occur within Australia, though some take place in Europe, South America and North America, but these locations are rarely made explicit within the narrative. The motif of the horizon is often used as a symbol for restlessness and the creative self's constant need for motion and momentum. The fictocritical theory used in this thesis prominently features Stephen Muecke and Noel King (1991), Donna Maree Hancox and Vivienne Muller (2011) and Hamish Morgan's paper "What Can Fictocriticism Do?" (2012). Philosophies and approaches from Roland Barthes' *Mythologies* (1957), *Roland Barthes* (1975) and *A Lover's Discourse* (1977) are considered too. Multiple-authored fictocritical works in *The Space Between: Australian Women Writing Fictocriticism* (1998) are explored, as well as unique proto-fictocritical texts like Mark Z. Danielewski's postmodern and metafictive writing in *House of Leaves* (2000), Stephen Muecke's *Joe in the Andamans: And other Fictocritical Stories* (2008) and Josephine Rowe's semi-autobiographical *Tarcutta Wake* (2012).

Folio Two is about family. This folio provides a (manufactured) context for my 'self' from the perspective of a first-generation Polish-Australian male, against the backdrop of a rather nationalistic and/or 'authentic' Polish (and migrant) heritage, background and legacy. The creative sequences in this folio aim to delve more deeply and metaphorically/symbolically into these issues and concept(ion)s, in a much more detailed and vivid way than could be established through a purely rational critical narrative. It articulates 'skewed' traditional Polish (and migrant) views, beliefs and attitudes and the conflict(s) created in a multi-generational family, via a constructed 'persona' called Lou. This thesis aims to find innovation in the contextualisation of fictocriticism. Most notably, in its antecedence in postmodernism and "metafictional strategies" (Waugh 22), its autobiographical characteristics in memoirs (Gaita 1999), anecdotes or use of the first-person (Smith 1001-02) and storytelling narratives (Muecke and King 14; Morgan 2012) primarily within the context of Polish and Australian landscapes, to provide a cultural context or diaspora in the history of some Polish/Australian (migrant) writing, and contextualising the author's European-migrant ancestry and biased millennial voice, in a memoir-like narrative.

Folio One and Thesis One can be seen as diluting or bleeding into Folio Two and Thesis Two. They are both exegetical about my creative work (and comparing it to similar works) *and* they make their own distinct arguments. They (the folios and the theses) are alike and are about the nomad, who simultaneously cannot find his place at home with family, and who cannot escape himself abroad in the tangible and intangible pursuit of travel either. Hence, these sections remain inescapably hybridised in a way that I hope readers will not dislike.

Folio Three is about education and how the creative self was formally educated. It recalls specific experiences of being a Bachelor of Arts and Education (Secondary) undergraduate student at university from 2006 to 2010. The majority of the anecdotal, creative or abstract prose inserted into this folio relates to the narrator rebelling against some of his tertiary experiences, in a state of angst, hopefully creating a more compelling psychodrama within the narrative. It is where the idea of 'purposeful purposelessness' is most clearly introduced as a storytelling technique and narrative framework. The state of flux the creative self experiences in this folio stems from and identifies the same restlessness and exuberant anxiety, which arise from the culturally conflicted background of the first two folios, and which continue to pervade thematically into this folio and throughout this study overall. It utilises and adapts modes of fictocriticism inspired by Drusilla Modjeska's *The Orchard* (1994) and other elemental fictocritical writings and theories by Anne Brewster, Katrina Schlunke, but primarily Anna Gibbs and her uninhibited enumerative, rhythmic, poetic and splicing approach to writing. Thesis Three uncovers some concrete and unambiguous traits of fictocriticism in its connections to education and pedagogy (Modjeska 1994; Brewster 2013), its similarities to more established academic modes like autoethnography (Walford 2004), its phraseology (Gibbs 311; Brewster 2013) and its observable need for a clear "narrative point" (Gibbs 2).

The title of Thesis Four, "Solutionism: Fictocriticism and the Digital World", is derived from concepts by Evgeny Morozov (2012, 2013) and his wariness of technology. This sets a tone for this thesis' corresponding folio and fictocriticism's meandering inconclusive ways. The 'experimental' writing focuses on the disengagement contemporary society has with political news and information because of a preference for other, less intellectually challenging forms of entertainment offered by cable television, streaming movies, Netflix, digitised porn and the whole YouTube phenomenon. These 'arguments' also encompass the negative impacts of the Internet and social media sites such as Facebook, Instagram and Twitter. Thesis Four investigates some of the precise adaptations and changes that have occurred in fictocritical writing over time, particularly in the new millennium, contextualising the methodology in a more modern, technological, or 'robotic' era. This thesis shows how some of the fragmentary and freeform writings of Anna Gibbs, Marion Campbell and Alison Bartlett for instance, located in *The Space Between*, later began to exist in other tangible, less ambiguous mediums and forms, and how the vision of early pioneering fictocritics such as Anna Gibbs, Drusilla Modjeska, Amanda Nettelbeck and Heather Kerr, gradually evolved from their vague, unencumbered, yet highly 'meta' fictocritical beginnings, to the more deliberate and industrious "electric fictocriticism" (Robb 100) of the twenty-first century.

All of these folios incorporate different experimental writing techniques, including first-person narrative, prose-poetry, flash fiction, travel writing, vignettes, stream of consciousness, memoir, autobiography, fiction, creative non-fiction, autoethnography, song lyrics, mantras/meditations, narcissistic critique, storytelling, double-voicedness and soliloquy. The folios also use different voices, personas or narrators depending on what the folio and thesis are trying to portray and uncover. Yet all of these approaches can tentatively fall under the methodological umbrella of fictocriticism as the genre has quite a broad (possibly limitless) scope, particularly for experimentation. Still, the folios arguably becomes progressively more fictocritical as the theses develop and sustain their arguments about fictocritical innovations and discoveries, and as the creative self uncovers subtextual layers and improves upon the necessary critique in the folios. In this 'confused' way the folios are not entirely elegant or aesthetically pleasing. They incorporate their own mistakes and inconsistencies throughout the narrative, just as Mark Z. Danielewski preserves his mistakes and crossings out throughout *House of Leaves* (114-15).

In these creative works, however, I at least attempt to (consistently) employ the fictocritical solution to the 'failure' of the formal omniscient and/or masterful position, the view from nowhere, because now it is more accepted that knowledge is situational and contextual. Again, this partly stems from the feminist influence of fictocriticism, with its emphasis on the personal being political. Other solutions (and innovations) will be examined within the context of this exploration's theses, as I/we progress through them.

Regarding viewpoints, because of the massive variations in my creative pieces' lengths and styles/forms (there are many), not every narrator or scene in every one of the creative works is permitted a concrete (physical) description. This is done to save space and time. After all, for the record, basically all of the narrators/personas are more or less 'reflections' ('ghosts') of the same being/author (me) anyway. Also, as indicated by Haas, one of the common fictocritical markers is "minimal characterisation and dialogue" (26), which I tend to agree with (overall). That is not to say that my creative works do not feature dialogue and character description at all. These traits feature very prominently in the folios on family and education in particular, but dialogue and character description are not the focus here, as there are many other bases to cover, and more importantly to 'play' with, in order to uncover the breadth of fictocriticism's potential, and what possible innovations lay dormant within it.

Taking this broad approach further, occasionally some of the creative pieces are left 'seemingly' unfinished, to indicate where the creative self could (or does not) elaborate on a concept because it would make it less or more fictocritical. This makes aspects of the folio work open-ended. An argument against this approach could be that it demonstrates a lack of texture, and intellectual resources, in the writing. Though it is this book's contention that the creative folios certainly did not need to be completely polished pieces of work. In fact, aesthetic and commercial sleekness was deliberately resisted so that the work would be more experimental. This became the plan and methodology following this study's first draft. This restructuring or deconstructive process became part of this book's reviewed and renewed goals. This would ensure that this 'experiment' in fictocriticism was more official. And in reviewing the creative self's work the analytical self is then able to better take on the responsibilities of a literary scientist in the more theoretical theses.

The open-ended nature of the 'experimental' creative folios make it so the works cannot be considered pure memoir or autobiography as they are, in essence, abstract(ed) and fictionalised accounts. Though they contain obvious elements of these forms, particularly Folios One and Two, where pseudonyms and leeway are given to the expression and dramatisation of real people, places and events, the creative work(s) do not subscribe to any one genre exclusively. The creative works must be considered a fictocritical 'experiment' because of the blending of so many differing genres and forms. Most importantly, the folios must be fictocritical because, as a whole, they are essentially half-creative, half-critical.

Finally, by 2018-19 my literature review found that there are only a small number of theses devoted to a personally exploratory and/or specifically fictocritical, critical or 'fictocritical-esque' hybridised methodology. These include Monique Louise Trottier's Masters thesis "If Truth be Told…" (2002), *The Holocaust at Home: Representations and Implication of Second Generation Experience* (2004), a North American doctoral dissertation by Susan Jacobowitz about the literary experiences, identities and representations of second generation Holocaust survivors (iv); Brent Jason Royster's "The Construction of Self in the Contemporary Creative Writing Workshop: A Personal Journey" (2006), Jeanette Weeda-Zuidersma's "Keeping Mum: Representations of Motherhood in Contemporary Australian Literature—a Fictocritical Exploration" (2007), "Between the City and the Bush: Suburbia in the Contemporary Australian Novel" (2008), a North American literary doctoral dissertation by Nathaniel David O'Reilly, Emily Naismith's Honours thesis "Emily Coughs: A Fictocritical Exploration of the Self via Social Media" (2009), Danuta Raine's "Essaying the Self: Ethnicity, Identity and the Fictocritical Essay" (2009), Jorge Villalobos' "My Name Is/Mi Nombre es: Developing Internal Voices in a Quest of an Identity" (2012), Robin Hely's "Project Neurocam: An Investigation" (2013), Lissi Athanasiou Krikelis' "Postmodern Metafiction Revisited" (2014) and Ania Walwicz's 2016 PhD "horse: a psychodramatic enactment of a fairytale". As can be seen from these titles, they are similar to this work in that they are literary, often fictocritical, autobiographical, a form of storytelling and they explore personal(ised) themes, yet these themes or autobiographies are not simultaneously Polish-Australian, male or about the primary themes addressed in this study: journeys, family, education and technology.

The works listed above relate to specific aspects of these individual writers' lives, ideas, beliefs, identities, philosophies and experiences that make them *them* (i.e., motherhood, love, religion, ancestry, social media and cystic fibrosis, a Mexican-American upbringing, and so forth). These documents are unique to these individual people, though none are like this exploration because none of them are me. None of them feature a crossover or dense tapestry of interests or experiences that specifically include a fusion of travel, education, a hybridised Polish-Australian background and living in the digital world. And that unique fusion, in the combination and sequence of four experimental folios, is one of the ways that make this experimental fictocritical exploration unique, amongst a set of existing 'fictocritical-esque', personalised and explorative works that are already marginal, fairly radical or unorthodox in their format and structure, and certainly relatively few in number.

From this point onwards, my cognitive self will be split in two: when referring to my 'self' or the multiplicity of my various 'selves' that feature in the creative folios, 'I' shall be referred to as the creative self; I will then shift to an alternate clinical persona known as the analytical self in the four theoretical theses, critiquing the creative self's writings for their merit and fictocritical innovativeness. And when referring to my other, full, self, i.e., both my creative self and my analytical self together (i.e., the complete 'Pawel Cholewa'), in moments where both intersect and are relevant/applicable, I will simply refer to my collective person as the author. This (somewhat) goes without saying, but not to worry! Context shall make this clear enough, to be sure.

Henceforth, until we (you, the reader) and 'I' reach the conclusion of this work, the creative self shall be methodically divorced from the analytical self.

SECTION I

FOLIO ONE: Journeys

"At Some Point Reality Needs to Become a Part Of ..." (2013)

When I first moved to Rockhampton from Melbourne in the pursuit of my doctoral studies in 2013, I tried extremely hard to engage in the culture and lifestyle of a more rural part of Australia, a different part of the world to me, obviously, since I was coming from a much 'cooler' (both figuratively and literally) cosmopolitan city like Melbourne.

Here I was on the cusp of a great insight and discovery, and he was on the verge of divulging that unforgettable truth to me, and in his sixty-five years of wisdom and experience and rural understanding he would have finally been able to eloquently and concisely convey this epiphany in a way that was both relevant to him and to me. We could have adopted this and used it as a mantra; pseudo-intellectuals and wannabe academics would have quoted him for years, though if it just weren't for his incomprehensible state of intoxication, and the other intolerant gentleman he was with.

Bleary-eyed, inarticulate, stumbling and fumbling over words and blending, churning syllables so the dribble just ran from their throats, grunting and sighing, breathing and motioning in a vague proclamation and representation of broken 'dialogue'.

And in between these moments of intermittent comprehension and the incoherent babbling drool of language, I sat there, eyes fixed, glued to the barstool, and listened. I listened and I sat there transfixed. I had no idea what especially I was trying to look and listen out for, but I felt that this was extremely important. This was communion, and a completely genuine integration with a new place, with a real emergence existing in a chasm within myself.

Everything I thought I heard him say, or everything I thought I heard him primordially express, or that I was perhaps projecting myself into, listening and looking through with rose-coloured glasses, was a wish and a hope to somehow hear the things I intrinsically wanted to hear. This only happened 'yesterday' and I'm still not sure, but the mantras and detail and relevance poured from him in torrents, like a rush of blood to *my* head: "You're a realist, not a purist"; "the most important thing in the world is to be able to express ourselves", he would say, though his own voice would rise and fall as he choked, spluttered, burped and hiccupped over his own subdued and subverted sentimentality. "At some point reality needs to become a part of …" he said, and abruptly stopped before he could ever finish. And I waited for the closure of that patently grand statement that would not come, anti-climactically. But often closure does not come, we do not receive it, and some of us, like me, are left waiting, on pins and needles, for years to come, in a state of wonder, contemplating what could have been. Most likely nothing, and he probably was merely drunk, not knowing himself what he was actually saying. But you have to wonder about the potential meaning and honesty that could have been there, in that moment. I suppose often some things are better left unsaid, if only for the pure allure and mystery of the moment; that in itself, and for oneself, can become a source of prolonged marvelling and quiet solitary contemplation or re-hashing.

Maybe it's because this moment and scene were so novel to me, and that is why it was so special. I don't really know too much, though what I do know is that both of these men seemed intuitive (in a raw bucolic way that I hadn't really come across before), one to the light, and the other to the dark. The other one had barely spoken, but he saw, cock-eyed though he was, the darkness in me almost instantly: "this is the kind of bloke who would shoot you in the leg and walk off!" he surmised, with a shrieking upward inflection of pitch and tone heralding out those last two words. And he was right, which frightens me, because I know I'm not exactly altruistic any more.

I'm here, this is now, it's new, and yet it is part of something older, more mature, settled, stubborn and fixated than what I can really grasp or understand. It's subjective, but it has no context, so I have no ideas that I can really cement in anything. I'm simply meandering along in this new environment, drifting within a kind of dam until hopefully my foot can latch on to something, at which point I can start simulating and generating algae in a pool of water, a pond of my own.

These are the babbling truths and confronting conservative value systems that I need to start developing on my own, integrating with, appreciating and understanding if I'm to grow at all here from now on. The need to go off and analyse what a fool hasn't been trying to say probably won't serve any purpose but to further distance and isolate me from the truth I am trying so conscientiously to uncover.

And having gone off and walked, tangentially and diagonally across pathways in sober gardens, I have very little to no grounding as to what can possibly happen from this point onwards. Lost and disconnected I repeat my steps and try to adopt a humorous approach, chuckling at the same jokes and commentaries; the greenery and comedy of it all will save me as I keep pacing conservatively, never sitting mindfully, patiently or still enough to produce any grime of my own, and yet I'm infested with 'this' knowledge, and that I might ground myself, and refuse to take charge, in confidence.

A Daze to Come True (2014)

For I find myself just wanting to wander around, from place to place, not really doing much—ambling. If I had to choose or describe a vocation, it would be this. Observing things, not with a keen eye, or not the most important things, but merely the vague and the mundane, as they appear or as they come to me. I may turn down a street or an alleyway, into a random building, a café or a restaurant egged on by a gust of wind, a flutter that ushers me this way or that way. I don't want to learn, to repeat history, to experience the most ecstatic, trying so hard to sap the best juice out of the best experience possible. This is exhausting. If I miss something, it doesn't exist. If I don't do something, it never happened. For once, I simply want the spectral gaze of my daze to come true.

A Literary Mitosis (On Form) (2014)

Why do I hyphenate and parenthesise and marginalise so much with a '/' or brackets — with everything else I write coming with an 'and/or'? Sooner or later a frustrated reader/reviewer will be driven to lecture or criticise me for this, so I will take it upon myself to beat them to the punch. I'm surprised I've evaded this issue for so long, particularly since it's literally staring me in the face almost every single day in the form and format of what and how I write. I guess the most obvious criticism is that it shows a lack of control and mastery over language, an inability to decide on a word or make the right choice because, perhaps, I do not understand the full and proper connotations of every word I select and write with, and why should I? When so many words have apt and adequate synonyms and so many dictionaries define their definitions definitively, yet differently and minimally. So, I make the decision to choose both or either/or. For who am I to choose one word over another? So much of this rambling intellectualised jargon about 'I' and integrity and intuition and influence and (un)originality is about the inability to grasp and control everything and one's expression, whether it is predetermined, (pre)influenced, fatalistic, prodigious, integral, philosophical, or/and so forth. So, I guess I've naturally or organically decided over time to use and utilise a form that *looks* and *appears* to be rigid when in fact it is loose and lucid at best. One thing says more than only one thing using these devices and interwoven formats. I want this writing to have connotations and implications and insinuations, saying more with less and expanding upon vocabulary and linguistics, using tools that shorten and sharpen and cut to ironically elaborate and engage and grasp, breaking and branching out onto or into more by making more out of clasping, fastening but also separating, distinguishing and dividing — a literary mitosis.

The Mission Man (2014)

Though it can also be a speedy transition; a mission of sorts. For I am, can be and have been the mission man, where things irregularly flow from one to the next.

In fact, there is no flow, so much as there is an immediate changeover. As much as I love the 'in-between', I attempt to eliminate as much of the time between the 'in-between' as I can, in order to be moving on to the next thing. The very *next* thing is always the thing to be most excited about. And as much as I wanted to come *here*, then and now, I am disgusted with this place in this moment. Not to mention, I've already been here. And I didn't like it the first time. So why would I enjoy it the second? A persistent delusion of insanity and self-sabotage and the setting up of oneself to fail in the perpetual moment — the moment that is (unendingly) out of reach in the very near future. I was tired of being *there* so now I am *here*, and as soon as I am *here* I want to be *there*, right now. But I immediately destroy that precious 'in-between' as soon as I arrive in the constant and ongoing now-moment because I decide right away that the next thing will be better.

Unable to grapple with the overly ambient or vague concepts in 'self-help' books like Eckhart Tolle's *The Power of Now*, I — the mission man — liken or align myself more so with the notion of Jack Kerouac's falling (failing, or flailing) star idea in *On the Road*: "I like too many things and get all confused and hung-up running from one falling star to another till I drop" (113).

Because, as the psychologist Daniel Kahneman indicates, there is a "conflict between your experiencing self and your remembering self" (238): the experiencing or "current self is the one experiencing life in real time" (236), the remembering self, on the other hand, has to make "all the big decisions. It is happy when you sit back and reflect on your life up to this point and feel content" (237). There is a serious imbalance between these two different selves and the reality that is formed in one's mind about one's life as a consequence of this imbalance (238). These two differing selves or perspectives have to be a well-balanced combination of one and the other. "You have to be happy in the flow of time while simultaneously creating memories you can look back on later" (McRaney 238-39).

Conversely, Tolle would argue that there is only the self that exists in the now, and that anything that has happened no longer exists, and anything that will happen does not exist yet, and so both past and future are seemingly irrelevant to one's sense of contentedness and joy (in the now). I, the mission man, though, tend to lean towards a more Kerouacian approach. I feel helpless in my restless pursuits, endeavours and desires to travel and constantly move, neither fully satisfying oneself or the other, in my tenacious impulsivity.

The funny thing is this makes me stuck in an altogether different kind of 'in-between' anyway!

I'm walking, no, running—I am on a mission. There's always something that needs to be arranged, organised, done—not felt.

The present-now-moment 'stayers' watch me, befuddled. "Why can't he just relax?" they say or think to themselves.

"But I'll stray from a straight line. I'll just stray 'til I'm gone" is what I think to myself in response to their glances, statements and questioning looks.

Like an eccentric ass, I roam and stumble on in a daze, as the figurative apple (of life) swings on a string in front of me.

An Apple on a String Swings in Front of Me (2014)

An apple on a string swings in front of me, dangling in suspense and freeing me from homogeny (a lie)? I look forward through the fence and see the grass is greener, but blurred in my insistent periphery is that laborious fruit compelling forth my effort and greed and corrupted desires, incorrect in all the right ways, to others.

The Island (2015)

Motions frustrated, the predictability of it now. The stagnation follows the same recourse over and over again. Before, now, then after. So obvious, like a mathematical pattern, perfect and (in)solvable in its eloquence.

Majesty. The initiation of social and flirtatious interactions are always perfect. To his friends he comes off as a professional, superficially only, really. The internalised monologue—the soliloquy stews on itself—outwardly, blaming everything else. He could pacify and nullify, reach out to change, became a gamer like the rest, 'sarging' with false pretences and smiles turned 'true', like the phantom of prowess and the cavalier in us all.

The blame could go further back, to varying circumstances, orbiting incessantly in the streams of imperceptible consciousness.

Staring at voluptuousness, enjoying it, and then turning back to the luminous phosphorescent screens of blankness and nihilism. Sigh and sigh again; he almost has a panic attack. The intuition is there, deep-seated, and probably wrong. Not knowing how to address addresses, then signing off charmingly, poetically, over-the-top in his formality.

Sculpting, perfecting, working at the self—that could help— or, otherwise, it's all in the countenance, the personality, the self-sabotage or the self-aggrandising.

One intact, in the bag and on her way, while the other (lesser) sits on pins and needles, sick. So, he is sick, sickens himself, stooping lower and lower every day. A sickness, an unrelenting perversion to want and to need and to desire desire. But really the craving is quite neutral, natural, simplified. And, so, the sickness is a systematic perversion pervading and invading everybody else's personal space.

Apologies.

But forgiveness comes, eventually, tainted by a pity and a need to justify spirituality in the eyes of the on(c)e true beholder. Once resolved, again, back to the screen, back to the phosphorescence, back to the addressing of addresses, of formalism and an awkward charmless countenance on pins and needles and desiring of desire 'til nothing else remains. Retire, leave, exit the room.

Find comfort in the isolation which really is ultimately preferred but external pressures force a forcefulness onto everybody else: let's break down and break apart these connectives and relationships one by one for the sake of a nothingness that saturates the heart and soul forming and creating and inspiring a restlessly racing beat on a drum, out of key, out of tune, out of time with the intuition that is needed to perform the actual task.

An analogy of the tactless man as an island:

The shore vainly folds over and under the veil
Wave upon wave sustained in the name of a tidal game
Now the stage is set for all to witness the journey, the whim
Destitute and resolute he flounders precisely and 'wins'

The Spirit of the Times (2013)

zeitgeist

The amorous subject feels uncomfortably well adjusted to a collective state of stagnant (dis)reality from which he attempts to escape via an exalted and explosive cocktail of self-destruction and personal liberation.

1. We are a self-destructive generation and gradually face a state of deterioration that is completely subjective and totally ill-equipped for our little cluster. Whether we face war, booms, love, or the advances of technology, we all suffer endurably and unwontedly. We fiends must face the facts, but not before the next generation take over, and we vainly attempt to spill our irrelevant advice onto them, and they shelter themselves from it in their erratic displays of angst and self-destructive peacocking portrayals of vulnerable yet violent independence.

2. My dreary eyes wonder and anticipate the future and all other future *zeitgeist* generations that are yet to come and yet to churn the minds, spirits, and bodies of thoughtful thoughtlessness, thinking tirelessly about *all* and *everything*. I wonder about these people, and what they'll look like and what they'll say about us! It's so damn cyclical! We are but another generation and we will not be the last. And we stand at a precipice of wonder and fear and glory; for humankind will always maintain a sense of self that can be best described as frivolously in love with life, regardless of the endless adversity that clouds our endeavours.

3. We ponder in the grey morning in the heaving wooden cabin at the centre of a modern medieval city, having been followed by a bout of drunkenness and confetti brain cell celebrations, and ironic devastations. We sit there and drink stale beer and talk with excited tongues about the word *zeitgeist*. Time and ghost—a Germanic infusion—an

intoxicating cocktail that ensnares and captivates our senses in the most compulsive and reactionary form of excitement. We stand at the edge of reason and jump straight into this fleeting, transitory, yet pivotal moment. We engage and commit to it completely.

4. We sink into a state of exhausted and exalted delirium in which we try to comprehend the bitterness of the sour morning in order to transcend our meagre mortal bodies and become captivated by our own excited notions. Wide-eyed and mad we collaboratively communicate with one another.

5. For we are absolutely and completely engulfed by the system of ethics, attitudes, and morality which we are symptomatically prescribed at an early age—we are nurtured to adhere and abide by certain principles and perspectives from the most impressionable and foetal age. It is the fatal syndrome and entrapment within a skewed field of vision in this postmodern era.

A Sentimental Cynic (2013)

The most frightening and simultaneously liberating thing I can imagine is the sensation derived from absolute and complete loneliness and isolation. I have experienced such a moment. Trapped in the void of my own imagination and excessive thoughtlessness, I found a critical and pivotal form of transcendental clarity. What if there was such a thing as eternity and it was accessible from the arch of the brow and the scope of the mind? And yet there I was, lying sprawled across the floor of a room — the physicality of the situation was real, lucid — and I realised that if I attempted to step outside its doors, I would float into an endless vacuum, and I would be totally alone and my actions would have absolutely no consequences, and I would become and enact my previous lives, up to and including the most recent, in which I had animalistic qualities that I now fail to adequately grasp. Yet I now have total familiarity and reciprocal appreciation for the potentiality of these possibilities. And I was immersed in silent contemplation, and there was so much peace and clarity in this isolation. I began to writhe violently on the floor and engaged in all the rigid-less and residually resonating bodily movements and behavioural motions that would either be deemed unfit, or unnecessary, or unreal or impractical in everyday life. There are actions like this. There are movements like this. The body has the subliminal and subconscious capacity to move of its own free will, and when it does it is devoid of any other responsibilities previously committed to the ego or by the ego, or vice versa, or to the confines of the earth and the upside-down topsy-turvy shelter of the ground beneath the souls of our feet.

The body is malleable and permeable and has the ability to be liberated by the mind's insidious concentration — to become another organism: a seal, a lotus flower, a parasitical insect hovering over the treetops and mountaintops and yoghurt tops of the containers, tinned cans, atmospheres, ultraviolet rays streaming from the neon lights and hidden messages and fetishes and uncontrollable impulses that are contained and limited by reason, or, in other words, logical and systematic restriction of the wandering ghost of TIME and IT.

And, thus, I am aesthetically free in the centre of this room — this kitchen smouldering with crystalline clarity — in the centre of the universe in which my actions and bodily behaviours have no other consequences but are made primarily for the purpose that they are MADE and that is all. They serve no other function, and that is settling. For it is rare to behave in a way that does not dictate foresight or reminiscence or hindsight or nostalgia — it is rare to behave in such a way that simply fulfils the purpose of IS and DOES and nothing more. And I am satisfied and content in this room with walls and if I do choose to leave through THAT door in the corner, I will enter THAT vacuum of space, and that is my personal prerogative. That is my impulse — my choice.

Yet I notice that there is someone else physically present in here, and he is pouring orange juice, and he is pacing and marching powerfully. Power-marching and pouring juice — these are the fruitful juices of our quenched labour: self-sufficiently satisfying and reciprocating the vitamins and minerals evident in this fantastic room with a doorway that leads to infinite self-satisfaction and SPACE and TIME. The duality becomes clear: action and reaction — onward forward momentum and speed.

I peered out of the window in the room. The sky appeared to be moving, though it may have been the room itself. Or perhaps time is in a playful projection of sky and stars that occasionally dance around and explode into an image of ultimate infinity, and what some saints or mystics or believers might refer to as God, who was reincarnated in the night sky, stemming from a cluster and combination of bright shining mythical lights glaring and projecting their past tens of thousands of years into the future and into the current contemplative contempt-filled contemporary world. Stars — they are the real philosophers — the time travellers of future incomprehensible destinies that we simply cannot fathom — our potential is too unrefined to compete with such forces of grandeur that live and breathe and swell and implode in the restlessly racing night sky.

Yet my dreary eyes continue to wonder and anticipate the future and all other future generations yet to come and churn the minds, spirits, and bodies of thoughtful thoughtlessness, thinking tirelessly about all and everything. I wonder about these people, and what they'll look like and what they'll say about us! We are but another generation and we will not be the last. And we stand at a precipice of wonder and fear and glory, for humankind will always maintain a sense of self that can be best described as frivolously in love with life, regardless of the endless adversity that clouds our endeavours.

Yet we shelter ourselves and themselves and yourselves and all selves that are mimicked and mimed and translucent and adjacent to their own sense of self. This room — this cluster of collective experience and truth and 'Dharma' and IT and TIME — as insightful as it all may be, it cannot be enacted or produced in any artificial way. It is too unreal, too unorthodox, too strange and alien and foreign and unpredictable. Our collective selves cannot REALISE the now. It is too much of a frightening thought. As frightening as the ironic fear and timidness in which I initially approached the trajectory of this projection room. It is frightening and liberating. Simultaneously, of course. But it is reason and logic that will always be victorious. Those sinners have a firmer 'understanding' of the realities of perception and its rigidity as something that is ingrained and anchored and clawed into the now-frozen streams of our conscious mind. And, so, we continue to shelter our 'selves' in our erratic displays of angst and self-destructive peacocking portrayals of vulnerable yet violent independence — a continually restless battle between mind and matter and what actually matters in the mind.

'Til Morning Came (2013)

There are certain times, points of the day, that instil a sparse consciousness—a recognition had many times before by many others over the course of human history. This is time, and these are times felt and to be felt by others, in obscurity or promiscuity, vanity, selflessness, or loneliness.

Last night I lay awake 'til morning came, and the sun shone through the cracks of my drawn curtains, and I tried to ignore the slight rays. Throughout the night I kicked and churned and writhed around in bed, making an absolute mess of my doona covers, and the pillows, which I held tightly or kicked violently yet fervently, here and there. I scrunched them up and held them and punched them or pinned them down in a mangled jumble of ecstasy and softness, and pleasure. And eventually a romantic kind of calm ensued from this incensed love.

Over the course of the night and the hours that dragged by, I thought about my relationships with the various people in my life. I was sentimental, yet I pondered my interactions with these folk, these friends and family, these associates, these charming entities, in quite a detached way. I thought of 'us' as a whole, an organism and my place (with)in that organism, and what I actually mean, what my place is among all these collected perspectives?

A change definitely came about in me. I considered my regrets and played out the storylines and the narratives of how things would have been and could have been in some of my relationships if I'd known what I do now. I thought about how different the story would have turned out, how much closer I would have been with some that I am now estranged from, and how much more distant I could have been with the ones I am now closer to—the ones I do not need, respect or appreciate any more.

The tragedy in the matter is that it is almost impossible to reignite a flame with the people lost in plights of stupidity, or gradual, graduating, deteriorating detachment. And it is just as impossible to disconnect with the ones clamped to your lifeline or stuck like mosquitoes in the sap of a tree, oozing alongside you, until hardened and stuck in place by time, sort of like that determining scene in *Jurassic Park* (1993).

So, you cut yourself down and leave the broken forest, town or city from whence you came, and still that sap trails along with you, stuck to your side uncomfortably, lukewarm, despite the recognition you just do not have any fondness for it these days.

Last night my cynicism was nil.

Today I am tainted by the everyday monotony of my rambling groans, droning on as usual.

Last night I was affectionate to all. I considered the avenues and possibilities of love that I should direct outwardly. I thought about my dedications to one or the other. I considered putting my trepidations aside, and the doubt that is always there. I considered lying in bed with a multitude of partners and telling them truths, all true, but unique and individualised, personalised to all of those lovers, physical or not.

I considered kindness as a new form or brand of my personality — something that only really ever existed with traces of sarcasm that are way too ingrained to tolerate or are perhaps in the process of becoming so. I considered replacing my cold, hardened (now flabby) body with hope and a sense of fulfilment that others may intuitively recognise and take for themselves. I considered blossoming in the fecundating pool of dreariness and misery, closed off from others, looking upwards at the sky and the stars, and protected by further aggravation that others cannot see. I thought about changing superficially, and how that change might somehow lodge itself into deeper sensations, reviving them with the promise of goodness, genuine excitement and yearning.

I thought about reparations, justice, and community once again. I considered the importance of optimism and its effects on the self over time, time and time again.

I thought about these things — I considered them — I even believe in some of them now.

Normally there would be a 'but' in there somewhere, and even now I am searching for the problematique, but for now there is none. There is just relief.

Tears (im)practically came to my eyes as I contemplated the love I sincerely and genuinely do have to offer, but a hardened shell of contempt shields me from what I actually want. 'Self-sabotage' is my motto; I have nothing to gain from this but a resolute sterility that no one cares about, or that anyone wants to touch. Why bother then? It is more of an effort to hide behind this shield than to care and subsequently not have a care in the world.

Herein lies a 'slice of (my) life', influenced by not so much a feeling or a sensation but an attitude towards a betterness/bitterness, an attitude that can act as the driving force … an attitude that can, over time, be acted upon, fulfilling the ideals and desires I have released here.

Alter yourself, or enforce alterations, and the result will be an inevitable compromise of an attitude that could sanctify your spirit and the will to save yourself or myself (again); that is an important lesson I have learnt about myself.

Now run.

When looking into the essence or "quintessences" of human nature, perhaps experiencing enlightenment does not always necessarily have to stem from a "long" and "immense" period of time and derangement of the senses, as Rimbaud (9) insisted. The human response does not always have to be a passionate one, when confronted with ultimatums, the pinnacles, 'fight or flight' scenarios, radically menacing or dangerous environments and situations. How the individual reacts and copes when at the very precipice of fear or terror or anger or lust or revenge or whatever, is to find deep-seated internal precipice. And when something mundane, trivial or tedious does occur, what does that mean and what can we derive from it, symbolically and metaphorically, when one is reacting or feeling or thinking with a full heart and mind right then and there? I am not sure, but is that reversal of emotion and transcendental clarity an impossibility? In a sense, that is one of the things I am trying to *realise* here: the everyday, relatable or not, triggers of a soul/psyche in a consciously settled reality ... in motion (walking, running, accommodating, associating, traversing, travelling).

"There's a Road Train Going Nowhere" (2013)

When the following was written, I sporadically divided most of my time between Brisbane, Rockhampton and Melbourne, where I tended to do a lot of driving along Australia's eastern coast and the National Highway. In doing so I frequently saw the turn-off for the town of Tarcutta in south-western New South Wales, on the M31, and I thought of Josephine Rowe. Every time I wondered if I should make the turn and try to vicariously see what she romantically saw in that rural area, inspiring her to write the short story, and the *Tarcutta Wake* anthology. Perhaps I'll come across the same old broken-down and decrepit 1940s style automobile stuck in the branches of a dead (Snow Gum) tree, as is portrayed in a black and white photograph, on the cover of her book—an apt iconic portrayal (or perhaps a borrowed Americanised image). In any case, the image of the car in the tree conveys a rustic and quixotic type of imagery. I wanted to try and convey that same kind of imagery, if I could …

We begin to drive westward, departing from Townsville and into the night. A sense of energy, excitement and apprehension circulates within and around us. We grow silent, but why? Is it difficult to leave the comfort of the coast, perhaps? The coast made sense. It has always made sense. It is difficult letting go of that logic. Trees thinned, and ranges flattened into the secluded plains and scrublands that now grow more and more unfamiliar in their destitute simplicity. The echoes from the crashing surf and bustling city centre and the general roar of the population subsides and penetrates no longer. Our silence turns into contemplation, turns into meditation, turns into a respectful isolation, and still we continue to drive onwards, breaking free from the edges of the world as we drive further away from its fringes.

Music is playing. In fact, it has always been playing in the car, but we have only just realised that. We are waiting for something: something big, ominous, threatening perhaps. We'd all heard stories about road trains leading up to this journey, but none of us had ever actually seen one, and nobody wanted to be the one who had to tackle a road train within the insignificance, vulnerability and (dis)comfort of our automobile. The music grows louder, or maybe merely seems louder. A throbbing and cyclical bass line, and in the midst of a wailing and harmonious yet dissonant harmonica growls the vocal sensibilities of a young impassioned Peter Garrett, proclaiming: "There's a road train going nowhere." And coincidentally, right at this moment, the road train manifests itself. The great mammoth of Australian pride and industry, transportation and solidity looms out of the darkness. A beast foreboding, forbearing and ingraining itself into the earth around us, trembling, shaking, determined it growls rising up from the horizon before us. Lights. A dark shape lurching ever so carefully forward as we hurry or scuttle towards it. Eyes sparkling, lustrous and moon-shaped, our irises recede into the background of our minds. It is a giant, a titan of production and productivity. Rogue and nomadic in essence, it knowingly owns and rides that road.

Australia is one of the only continents or countries to have road trains in use. The only other countries that have and use them are Argentina, Mexico, the United States and Canada (as far as I know).

A monochromatic sheen coats its body, its armour. Too many wheels and too many metres long. Signposted in black and yellow, a fair warning is given to the oblivious, to the naïve and to the overly ambitious. A blackened, darkened cockpit. An anonymous driver never to be seen by others on the road, except for perhaps other drivers of other road trains and the 'other' of more metaphysical realms. These are the dominating species. They control the habitat of these barren roads. We must be respectful to them or perish.

Shrubbery flies in front of and behind us. A kangaroo leaps. Cicadas chatter and chime away somewhere and everywhere in the distance. But the ratios of the animalistic and natural world are all skewed and wrong in comparison to this towering object. So grand, so large, so overwhelmingly powerful it dominates the night sky creating a black hole of some sort unto itself. All the powers of the world seep into it. The night turns light by comparison. I think I can still see the sun gleaming somewhere off in the distance, but I can't exactly pinpoint it—the road train is silhouetted by the powers of the world.

But where is the road train going? Is Garrett correct? Is it going nowhere? It's certainly not stuck or stationary. It has motion and momentum and speed, yet it continues to drive into nothingness, into the outback of absurdity and delirium, into nowhere, in fact. It goes because it needs to go. It propels and projects itself. Its purpose is grander than what we are simply led to believe. Its journey and travels are both the means and the ends of its existence. Through universe and time and change it persists and endures as an icon of Australian industry and power.

Across the great red plains of the Australian outback the road spirals into the centre of an old prehistoric world now dried up. The road train conquers, controls, manoeuvres this road. These road behemoths were built to exist here together; an enforced harmony with our indigenous history and our industrial and multicultural present and future; an uneasy synchronisation, unified by the smoky black tires that the road train attaches itself to the road with, gliding, soaring further into the tranquil inverse universe that is the National Highway.

Very close now. We are right behind it. It shudders. No, we shudder at the prospect of having to somehow actually 'pass' this titan. No, no one will do it. Respect the giant. Leave it be. It owns the road. It owns the night. It owns itself. We will not overtake the road train this night.

After long absences from living in Australia, when I have lived in Poland for instance, the Australian landscape does change and look very different to me. It becomes fluorescent, like the brightness and contrast has been turned way up on a television screen or monitor. I find myself squinting a lot more due to the intensity of the sun reflecting against the burnished surfaces of Australian flora and fauna. Normally, when I am residing in Australia, the landscape of the bush seems quite barren, bleak, brown, light green and grey. But from a European or migrant perspective, and depending on which season a migrant is travelling from their country to Australia in, the landscape of Australia can appear quite different and distorted through compromised eyes.

The imagery employed by many Australian writers, including the contemporary Rowe, and going back to the beginnings of white Australian writers in the works of Lawson and Paterson, all tend to grapple with the conflict or contrast between the bush and the city, nature versus industry, an old world versus a new world.

The "bush" and the "city" were symbols that somewhat negated each other (Whitlock 197). "The city and the country were established as separate moral universes" (200). This conflict, and the Australian art and writing that has come about over the years highlighting it, creates "a staging point for immigrants; a haven for the drifter, the outcast, the man or woman with a past; a twilight zone of rootlessness and anomie" (194). "So we will never arrive at the "real" Australia. From the attempts of others to get there, we can learn as much about the travellers and the journey itself, but nothing about the destination. There is none" (Whitlock 25). This is highly relevant for me, and my endlessly dispersed selves.

"The Writer on Holiday" or Clockwork (2014)

Pure sentiment and a godliness that comes from the rejuvenation and reunion of soulful companions, a band of brothers separated by time in the form of years, and space in the form of long, cross-continental distances:

And yet, still and quietly, in sequential rushes of euphoria:

Tidal forces churn again
To flow aside the current trend
I walk for miles
I wonder through hazy trials

Change the course of modern men
To race against the clockwork bend
I run for miles
In exalted, exhausted strides

Now look for truth beyond the fair,
Where I alone become the heir
I walk for miles
I wonder through hazy isles

Rekindled vigour, an energy formed through bonds and heartfelt leaps of faith: bounding, cyclical, beautiful, ecstatic, genuine. A short-term breeze and a rather cool summer in which the warmth has been reduced and absorbed by men who have taken a break, a holiday from themselves, and instead embraced themselves and one another.

In Barthes' *Mythologies* there is a chapter entitled "The Writer on Holiday" which states that a writer on holiday may stop working or physically writing, but that he never stops "at least producing" (30). The writing or the thoughts and processes continue to exist in the back of the mind. One doesn't choose when inspiration comes — ideas and thoughts that often and sometimes happen to permeate and invade the conscious configuration of the self. The "writer is the prey of an inner god who speaks at all times, without bothering, tyrant that he is, with the holidays of his medium. Writers are on holiday, but their Muse is awake, and gives birth non-stop" (Barthes 30). The creative writer definitely takes their work home with them, and also away with them when they travel, where they inevitably suffer from a pestering doom, a conscience that is incessant and insatiable — an unrequited will.

In her piece "Hemingway's Typewriter" Robyn Ferrell's says, "The writer has a vocation, not a job, so that even while on holiday he is working, whether he is reading or taking notes or doing nothing. Indeed, to go on holiday is to work, for the writer, since all his experience is writing *in potentia*" (27).

There is a reinvigoration that occurs *after* a writer takes a holiday (from journeying). The physical writing is fresh, but it is never very far from the mind. Writing occurs and often changes or becomes different when self-discipline is removed from the context of the writer's personal, emotional or social life.

A Train Ride to Russia in 2007 (2015)

Transient populations roll by and roll on, sideways, somewhat and partially slanted and always in the upper right corner of my eye, where the sun peaks in the morning and sheds its light through moving windows, pa(i)ned and streaked glass that glows with the coming of heat and clearer uncertainty. No longer arctic — the chill is suffocated by a distance and vaulting horizon, insurmountable and without permission, it glows and rises like the daze of the day(s) to come.

The reawakened eye explodes into new vision. After taking a pill, a minor slumber, and then I'm jolted into sudden awareness by the tittering tracks beneath the train, and behold, a sight; we're heading east. The night has passed in a kind of sobriety when I contemplate the fact that now I have this new way of seeing things. The cabin/room comes to life, illuminated by a new-fangled light. I'm sitting up, while the others in the room are asleep in the same space, but the momentum of the train and the tracks and the grind and progressive swagger and sway projects us onwards.

A different headspace now: the one I was seeking, but I'm always surprised when it ignites, as it seems to come after a dreary, sleepy delirium of some sort. A dream from which I don't think I will wake but then I do, and I'm in another dream inspired by a distorted kind of reality. My eyes now fully open and wandering, I stand up, reach for the door of the cabin and step out into the corridor where more light is shining through — I am looking left and right, and I shuffle my feet a little more steadily, carefully.

I muster up a modicum of grace as I sway to and fro, walking down the corridor towards the rear of the train. I can see from a few metres away, through the small circular porthole in the back door of this last train carriage that there are two fellows, still awake from the night just passed, in the breaking dawn of the day, sharing a cigarette and some conversation, discussing sweet nothings in the sincerity of the morning and the sleeplessness and tiredness that can make us honest sometimes, if only in grimly expression.

I step outside to greet them with my unusual stance, feeling rather peculiar with my new diluted vision. I'm hunched a little as they look at me and roll on with their stammering chat, the last of the beer and vodka, lukewarm and nearly empty in their hands as they take a small sip and a little toke now and then, both of which are going to have an infinitesimal effect in the aftermath of the night just now officially concluded with the heavy rise of a new sun over that vaulting horizon, demanding some kind of rigour and stamina from us ignoble folk who continue to defy convention as we travel towards a new and unknown (to us anyway) east. We believe we are pioneers as we stutter and stammer and take the journey for granted, but we (or I) definitely feel here in the moment, now, more so than I ever have before.

The pill, a sleeping tablet for insomniacs, produced in me a kind of effect that was so difficult to understand and comprehend at the time, a giddily distilled sense of experience, two-pronged in its psychological manifestation; I believed I was in a constant state of déjà vu, whilst experiencing and remembering life and what was going on around me concurrently.

One of the fellows outside, neither of whom I knew, asked me something about what they'd just been discussing, to which I retorted that I didn't know or that I knew nothing, and proceeded to comment on his shoes, which I claimed I knew everything about.

I knew everything about them because he'd just told me about them after I'd asked him. But because the medication, was causing me to recall and experience in the now, simultaneously, I was confused about what was happening and what had already just happened. They both looked at me puzzled also, and I, still hunched and perplexed and amazed at my own ability to predict the ... now, dismissed both of them with a wave of the hand that rudely motioned the smoke from their cigarette away from the small space between us. The wisp of cloud dissipated quickly, as did the conversation, and any mutual interest or understanding we had established.

I looked away, back towards the east. They stalled for a moment and after a short while continued on with their sweet nothings. All three of us out there on the rear balcony of the train were too delirious, either from the night, the booze, or our state of medicated or prophetic exhaustion, to care about courtesy or social sincerity at that point in time. No, it was more anti-social than anything. I knew I was waving at and into people's personal space, dispersing the smoke between bodies, a hunchback in a world apart.

Nevertheless, the east shone with sudden clarity in the midst of this entire anti-climactic ruckus. The train curved left, and I was able to see the glow of the east with much more instilled potency. It was a new primordial world, where I couldn't see beyond the horizon or even beyond the front of the train due to the compacted darkness and shadows of the land. There was no way of seeing the beyond. The world was covered in black and blue. The clickety clack was the only noise I paid attention to. I was remembering and experiencing this at the same time. The horizon stopped us from seeing into the future as we simultaneously moved towards it. All conversations stopped here before they began and were understood and comprehended before a singular utterance was made, or at least it felt this way to me. Everything was coming and going, moving forward and standing still, being seen and being ejected out from the horizon back towards us as we gazed in perplexity and fondness towards it, all in the motion of the moving tracks that we rocked and rolled and swayed over and over again. We existed in the abysmal infinity mirrors beneath our feet, caught in the motion of an unchanging and unremitting Doppler effect.

Déjà Vu Delirium (2013)

Dean Moriarty, in Jack Kerouac's *On the Road* (1957), once said, "the thing that bound us all together in this world was invisible" (191). What was it, though — this invisible "thing"? What was he saying? What was he thinking? The potential for the justification or explanation of this concept is manifold: the intrigue, the intuition, the naivety, stupidity or obliviousness. A benzedrine-fuelled madness stimulated his systematic conceptions of 'time' and 'it' and other tangible or intangible concepts. He was a fool, a holy man, a con artist, a goof and a kicker in the constant tireless and reckless pursuit of kicks. How can this statement be trusted then? What faith or divinity or reality can be accepted in this notion of all notions, if at all a notion? This grand statement of grandeur. "Look no further! The answer is here!" someone (I) sarcastically mimicked and mocked in the background of the dreary soulless landscape. Moriarty's enthusiastic, yet vague comment in turn, and in all fairness, requires a similarly obscure answer.

Travelling tirelessly is an attempt to conquer something, anything, all things perhaps. In any case, the horizon itself is one thing that subscribes to many of these attributes and elements. Constantly unfolding and receding and revealing and reigniting sparks of energy as we propel ourselves forward into it or from it or alongside it. We struggle to surmount it, overcome it, know it, beat it, bear it, to encapsulate everything and gain the cumulative knowledge that both drives us and that we drive ourselves upon. To digress, in an attempt to gain a sense of transgression — to do so at any cost. Coast to coast, take my hand into your hand. And beat on racing forwards and onwards. Doubt. There is doubt. What will be the repercussions of reservation? What is the mirror to this story? What is the opposite of exalted exhaustion and moving for the sake of motion? Deep-seated fulfilment from experience, ownership of doubt, ownership of transcendence, in one way or another. To see and experience the world simultaneously. Well, that's obvious … Stilnox (the sleeping tablet). *Déjà vu* delirium. Enough said. But no, this is something slightly different. The world is spherical. No doubt about it. Stop putting faith in the horizon then. Just because your natural vision and the horizon somehow together are barring you from what you want to see. You can't own them simultaneously in some kind of naïve omniscient and omnipresent synchronisation. And so, hence, doubt. Consequences of reservation and doubt will follow on.

Mirror: invert the latitude linearity of the horizon and this regret will now proceed to pain and slay me and try me for many days to come. It will quiver and waver and defeat me as I progress or do not progress in my day-to-day, hour-to-hour, roll on and roll out and still continue to replicate fate and chance and the struggle to go on.

The opportunity was entirely there, and conscience got the better of me. That wicked demon that instils paranoia and fear and what is quite possibly wrong, on a fundamental level. What can I do now? What shall I do now? Conscience has caused me pain. Conscience has caused me regret. Conscience has ironically caused me mischievous wrong-doing of the worst kind.

Ride it out, wait, be patient, the nightmare will pass and blow over. There will be another time, another opportunity. But not like this one, not like this one (I mutter). This *was* the one, and it is over. And another lengthy chip has been struck and splintered away from the wooden, splayed fragmented character of my body, my being. A being or entity chipped away at until less solidity remains, until less remains, until nothing remains. Shame. It hurts me, but not because of the pain, but because there is now less of myself. A pain associated with a lacking of — of therein, of within, of nothing. Time and the timelessness of the sneaking conniving devil of regret and conscientiousness will inevitably and soulfully and meaningfully break me down. So here are the two options: you commit, fly, ride, stride in a desperate state of fluctuating mortality or morality in which the means is the end and nothing makes sense and the purposeful purposelessness of your journey is foolish but fulfilling; or you doubt, regret, let your conscience get the better of this damn thing, this situation, this mirror, this fluctuating principality that shreds at you in the dark corners of rooms and you suffer and think and ponder like a child, getting annoyed for not having leaped at these opportunities, even though the opportunities were so foolish and ridiculous to begin with. It's silly and ironic to still think this way, and yet still *be* this way too—a counter intuitive paradox, yet human nature is synonymous with this type of (self) resentment and an unrighteous sense of crude entitlement; these things are worth saying too.

Coast to Coast Infrequency (Part I) (2013)

Coast to coast infrequency, continentally settled or perhaps 'submerged', I play the role well, but not well enough to suppress the cravings and desires to leave and situate myself on mirrored coastal plains, snow-coated peaks, to swim in torrential rivers in great seeping valleys, engage depravity and isolation amongst the mass of alienating strangers and to feed my hunger and thirst, absorbing the (dis)comfort and solace made from and in the cusped hands of an inverted host.

The plan was to seek out, find and embrace redemption, to refuel the empty, twittering gauge, to reset the cycle, bring vibrancy back to my sagging face and bring lustre back into my drooping eyes; tired but restlessly racing underneath the same and similar skies of the day-to-day and day-by-day drone, I holler (ever so quietly)! The desire was real, sincere.

Instead, I (counter) intuitively fixate myself in the overly frequented corners, dark places and strobing, conniving lights of discotheques that were made in these watering holes and the artificial oases overseas for the abuse and suppression of personal growth. But these places merely highlight the familiarity and mediocrity of my own coast.

Stagnated and alone, I feel the quaking thunder and the waves swelling and crashing. They physically manifest themselves on the beach as well as in the depths of my brain, the pressure in my skull and the conflicted pains I feel in my mind; my obsessive compulsion, my paranoia, my fatigue, my cynicism, my angst, my jealousy and my spite all bubble to the surface, swelling and crashing in a cyclical rotation that reverses and contrasts the purity and beauty of the waves before my eyes. I sabotage myself, knowingly, consciously – the pattern or patent of my youth.

I lie dejected, finally, by the seaside in the paradise that I sought out. The experience has been violated. No more sincerity spills forth. My original pure intention is all but gone. Instead mere toxicity and chemistry and a sweat tainted by an egocentric and awkward fear courses through my veins and the drains of my silent delirium and the Incan(tantory) street. I dream of the other coast, my coast, the foreign yet familiar tones—herein lies, my quiet defeat, but I will celebrate at home, and to others, nonetheless. The coast to coast infrequency will ebb and flow again.

> [A]n inner compulsion to move on—it was still not clear to him where to—troubled him. (Mann 12)

> Solitude produces originality, bold and astonishing beauty, poetry. But solitude also produces perverseness, the disproportionate, the absurd and the forbidden. (Mann 19)

Thomas Mann's *Death in Venice* can relate to the darker side of 'travel', and the often superficial pretentiousness of it. We always feel compelled to convey the 'travel' experience to others as having been positive or revelatory, whereas this isn't always the case. Instead we often subject ourselves to the grotesque depravity in dark places on the other side of the world whilst we formulate a fake romanticised version of what actually did or did not happen to 'us' over 'there'.

Travel (for a youth) can be about pushing oneself to uncomfortable limits in order to ensure we have ventured as 'far out' as possible, but really all we do is destroy ourselves and forget our experiences. And all we remember is the regret and suffering and frustration, and the need for love and respect in the eyes of others to whom the exact same thing is happening (sometimes) when they are abroad. So, really it is a dishonest farce and façade that we tell ourselves and others to keep the perpetual 'frequency' going, to and from different coasts and shores and lands and continents.

Coast to Coast Infrequency (Part II) (2013)

Coastally and inwardly focused once again
Solitary journeys, an accentuated tic of time spread out
And attempts at deprecating and appreciating the self more
Not so much needing others, and then finding that others gravitate
And circulate more easily and at ease
Jarring attempts at stinted and jolted-stagnant communication
And dialogue still exists
Trying just as hard but for only half the time
A course, of course, of plenitude:
Pick and choose your moments ... better
Is there a need to?
Coughing and scoffing followed by a disarming sincerity
And a smile that could actually change you
The niceties, vice-less and true ...

A casual mantra along the lines of 'being alone, and that being okay/fine' could be applied here in an attempt to gain a psychological stability that stems from a simple desire to be alone and be comfortable with that. Sometimes there is no need to engage and be engaging with others in social settings all of the time — the tired and restless self with an act or need to portray energy and enthusiasm.

The imagery and 'daze' of the coast continue to be prevalent metaphors for a state of mind, being undone.

Ghouls (2014)

The coast seems quiet today, though. Deafened, silenced — no hum. Gentle murmurs, maybe. Nothing is happening. The population has been subdued or otherwise has subsided. Everyone looks mildly suspicious, but no one will venture to voice his or her concerns. It's a weekend weakened, but it seems more like a weak end to the plain planetary cycle. Entire systems have shut down, but maybe this is all a result of the volume being turned down for my own selfish reasons or my own reasoning, unjustifiable dystopia, with eyes reddened and sore from the sensory exposure to my ghoulish thoughtless selves ramming themselves, against the grain, outside my bedroom wall, the night before.

End of the Weekend (2014)

Intense temporary bonds and relationships. Difficult to justify? A steep ascent as opposed to a gradual climb; a disappointed overworked air carries us through to the end of the weekend. Paradise sorrows — it is a tense, terse humiliation that we choose to embrace or to ignore. Others notice it more in us. But that could also easily be the dysfunctional, ill-equipped, undisciplined, stifling goggles that we wear. Stake your future on or in these reckoned experiences, forcing the soul to expand as the dust never seems to settle, and we ignore certain choice cuts, words, shabby looks or commentaries being made, whilst continuously shedding skin.

Going Home (2014)

Canyons of thought whisper through the stillness of their depths and predicate a secondary madness.

You need time to stop, and then more time to stop again, in order to then have the free time to actually think for a while—to process everything: homogeneity. The vagabond sits and stews, desperate to get away from the slow-paced cluttered group.

Something 'funny' happens and some fit, clucky middle-aged women come along asking me to take photographs of them. At least they're not taking 'selfies'. I like this generation. I don't think too much truly fazes (or ever fazed) them. They belonged to that whole Fleetwood Mac era, after all.

Finally, a focus comes in like a stream, and all plans come together as I sit atop this mountain, sniffling, in the sun, momentarily happy because I can see where I am, and I like it. I can also literally see where I am going, headed back down the coast this time.

I am a boy. I grow up in the southeast. I travel from east to north to west, and now I'm headed back down those southern plains, to the end, to the finish. I am "hurtling towards it" they tell me.

This is what I came here for. The end is near. The directions and the internal compass are making some chronic and chronological sense for once. As *you* may know, my personal compass hasn't always been on par with my intentions, directions, focus or attempts at control.

But now we are headed on course together. There will be a detox, there will be sanctity, and there will be closure and clarity and no more destruction. It is time to climb south, downwards, back, finally, before I die.

I may not necessarily uncover a "Key self" (Woolf 397) in these meandering motions, but I may complete a cycle at least, and close a chronological loop in the form of a written …

Tiers and Towers (2014)

To reach the ultimate and final tier—a Babylonian tower, where no one sits or stands. There are but two champions on the tier beneath the final one. One old and one young, and they stand and compete against each other, drawing in/on every single game, for years, until a true victor wins and can ascend to that final highest lonely tier-podium.

To reach the second last tier, one cannot climb there but rather one must walk through its gates and up the stairs hand in hand with a lover, a soul-partner. When one does so, the world is crushed and flattened so that the tiers fold, recess and the next become accessible.

As soon as one enters the second highest level one of the two champions takes you and handles you and throws you around absent-mindedly but in a professional manner, and you swerve and fold and fall and spin back and forth, becoming a pawn in these rolling games that are being played, but/though not being an actual player.

The sky here is always dark and overcast, smoky and steamy and stewing in ominous colours of dark grey and a hellish blood orange tinted with magentas, purples and maroons.

Our visit was not long. The place was nonsensical: the inaccessibility, the foolish champions, the brooding sky, the pointless matches and games.

Though, I have all but forgotten the lowest tiers. This tower is a high one (obviously, as it reaches the skies), and a fall would certainly shock and kill and neutralise. I can't even recall how many levels and layers there were, and what kind of games and players belonged to those lower functioning and neutralised boundaries.

What keeps me here is an intrigue and a fascination. Still, it doesn't hold me there long, but long enough to recognise a riddle being painfully played out *ad infinitum*.

THESIS ONE

Examining the Fictocritical Value of Journeys: The Author Meanders

This entire exploration/study took an initial general stance that in any fictional writing or narrative there would always exist traces of an author's autobiography. However, essential autobiographical writing would often attempt to demonstrate a duality and writerly polyvalency (double-voicedness) towards fiction or metafiction. This book planned to invest the writer's creative self in a series of creative works emotionally and psychologically, through a set of themes that encompassed and embraced various thought processes and experiences experienced at different times throughout the conscious (or subconscious) of a young man's creative writing. The methodology of fictocriticism seemed ideally suited to the storytelling intentions of this erratic, adventurous and juxtaposing way of writing about the 'self' in relation to one's context (Gibbs 309; Kerr 94; Smith 1001-02).

In relation to the complex topic of the 'self', this study makes no claims of discussing the subject as it relates to seminal, historical and philosophical positions, such as Nietzsche's conception of subjectivity or "The Subject as Multiplicity" (Booth 1985), Heidegger's views on selfhood, authenticity and inauthenticity (Mansbach 1991) or Sartre's works on *Existentialism and Humanism* (1947) or *Being and Nothingness* (1943). Rather, the 'self' or diverged 'selves' here relate purely to the creative self and the analytical self and their association and exploration of the four themes in these four theses and folios. Any higher philosophical theories applied in this work are primarily of a literary nature as they relate to fictocriticism.

The fictocritical mode and methodology entered into this project one year into the original PhD study. It was at this point that a major and entirely unexpected writing disengagement became visible, between the abstract, hyperactive and autobiographical elements initially implemented into these stories and those stories having a legitimate undercurrent of social commentary. The creative writing component was fluid, impulsive and the stories were easily written, though it might be argued that such ease might have been, in itself, a warning sign. The social commentary, or the way in which the pieces were to be made fictocritical, was planned to arrive much later, after the creative work was complete; the research or theoretical component of this project was originally hybridised with the creative folios. These two elements had become separate, requiring thematic research components to be injected back into the creative pieces in order to make them more authentically fictocritical and double-voiced. In hindsight, this realisation was the true experimental beginning of the explorative study.

This first theoretical thesis aims to clarify the fictocritical underpinnings of Folio One. With relevant parallels drawn from the Australian landscape, the stories explore the notion of travel and journeys and the way in which other (fictocritical) Australian authors write about Australia's landscape, national identity, context, romanticism or lack of 'settled' romanticism (Fergie 195; Morris 115-19; Rowe 102).

In "Autoethnography as a Research Method: Advantages, Limitations and Criticisms" (2013), Mariza Méndez suggests that writers must risk themselves and become vulnerable and even insecure to free up meaning and form in their writing, to reveal "the broader context of that experience" (281). Statements like this can be considered a truism in almost all writing, including fictocriticism. Indeed, it could be argued that autoethnography and fictocriticism are cut from a similar methodological cloth. Both are generally written in the first-person, and both were considered and investigated as appropriate methodologies when approaching my doctoral project. Fictocriticism, however, seemed to have the least amount of research behind it, and the most untapped potential to develop and grow in conjunction with the development of the creative artefact in this study. Eve Kosofsky Sedgwick's *Tendencies* (1993), Weeda-Zuidersma's PhD "Keeping Mum" (2007), Naismith's "Emily Coughs" (2009), Raine's "Essaying the Self: Ethnicity, Identity and the Fictocritical Essay" (2009) and

Villalobos' "My Name Is/Mi Nombre es" (2012), to name a few, all demonstrate how fictocriticism can help writers become vulnerable, honest and open in their writing, even when that openness involves "personal trauma" (Pattinson 6). This chaotic, "mosaic ... emotive" (Pattinson 6) mood and methodology worked for the creative self when initiating a folio on journeys and the notion of 'meandering'.

This first thesis attempts to engage and experiment with the tools of fictocriticism in portraying a restless train of thought, constantly in the act of (creative) authorial speculation and wandering. There is also little formal editing occurring in the creative work, allowing a sense of the freeform structure so aptly demonstrated in many fictocritical narratives. What this offers the reader is a form of narrated disruption and inconsistency, using incomplete or improper sentences and ideas that do not fully develop or come to fruition. Stylistically, and ironically, this approach demonstrates a 'writerly' impatience, and perhaps displays an unfair disregarding or inconsideration towards the reader. It invites a restless Kerouacian excitement or state of "exalted exhaustion" (Charters, Introduction viii) to the work. Some of the fictocriticism in this study seems to utilise a fusion of various French philosophies such as existentialism and the inspiration derived from a somewhat Rimbaudian way of life to adhere to a form of "lifelike art" (Kaprow 41) in which there was an intertwining of the psychological self in a form of "contemporary performance art" (During 183). This led to the impulsive way in which one's life could be infused with the presentation of art as life, and vice versa. It was only during subsequent discussions with academics that it became clear this approach was insufficient for this purpose and that a much more critical engagement with the creative work was needed.

The way in which the creative work in this text was initially planned was not, in hindsight, fictocritical. When first embarking on this doctoral project the proposal and title of the creative writing was "Investigating the Polarised Characteristics of Autobiographical Creative Writing". This nebulous topic was based upon the author's innocent belief that any form of a narrative, creative writing or novel which has been informed by a writer's own life or autobiography, will by default, trace the tideline of a fluctuating 'spirit'.

Prior to beginning the planned fictocritical creative writing, the author's thinking was influenced by a number of writers and their texts. Initially, there was a desire to create a type of *bildungsroman*, in the vein of Charles Dickens' *David Copperfield* (1850) or James Joyce's *A Portrait of the Artist as a Young Man* (1916), as extracts from these texts may elucidate:

> I am a straw upon the surface of the deep, and am tossed in all directions by the elephants. (Dickens 1053)

> New thoughts and hopes were whirling through my mind, and all the colours of my life were changing. (Dickens 1284)

> the mode of life or of art whereby your spirit could express itself in unfettered freedom. (Joyce 237)

> When a man is born ... there are nets flung at it to hold it back from flight. You talk to me of nationality, language, religion. I shall try to fly by those nets. (Joyce 171)

The poetry of Shelley, Byron and Keats, which is thinly veiled autobiography written creatively, provide a framework for how the creative folios enact various thematic constructions for a developing sense of self. Many of the creative self's pieces such as "A Daze to Come True" (to be referred to as "Daze" from this point) and "An Apple on a String Swings in Front of Me" (to be referred to as "Apple" from this point) have been written in the first-person as an account of a young man in the twenty-first century. Other texts that provide an influential framework for this project are Raimond Gaita's *Romulus, My Father* (1998), *A Million Little Pieces* (2004) by James Frey, *Marching Powder* (2004) by Rusty Young, *Tuesdays with Morrie: An Old Man, a Young Man and Life's Greatest Lesson* (2004) by Mitch Albom and *Shantaram* (2005) by Gregory David Roberts. These are contemporary autobiographies, biographies or memoirs by and about young men in the last few decades. They are thinly veiled true stories and personalised accounts, some sold as fiction, while others are ostensibly fictocritical. It is the form and function of these texts that have shaped the original creative elements of this research.

The first section of this book is about journeys and the movement between places, both real and imagined. It is about interrogating fictocritical stories and theorists and how they relate to the creative works presented in the folios of this exploration, essentially a search for the 'self' and for relatable social truths (Kerr and Nettelbeck 9; Naismith 12; Gibbs 1). Thematically, they correspond to one another as some of the fictocritical pieces selected here are about a quest, ambling, or a contextualising of oneself within a particular zone, that zone often being an Australian landscape (Fergie 188). Moreover, the majority of these fictocritical writings and articles are earlier texts, from the 1990s, and are essentially all Australian because, after all, most fictocriticism was 'coined' and taken up in Australia in the 1990s, though it originally began in Canada (Muecke and King 13; Flavell 3-4).

The philosophies and approach of Roland Barthes in *Mythologies* (1957), *Roland Barthes* (1975) and *A Lover's Discourse* (1977) are also considered, as well as several forms of autobiographical/creative non-fiction and metafictive writing, as seen in the multiple-authored fictocritical works in *The Space Between* (1998), Danielewski's *House of Leaves* (2000) and Josephine Rowe's *Tarcutta Wake* (2012). This book will explore how some autobiography, but more specifically metafictional autobiography, is a fundamental predecessor or catalyst to the fictocritical form (Dawson 141) and how the many different voices from around the world have found a space to tell their stories within the interpretation of fictocriticism.

The first fictocritical piece to be investigated here is Hamish Morgan's paper "What Can Fictocriticism Do?" from *Altitude: An e-Journal of Emerging Humanities Work* (2012). Morgan's paper directly relates to first-person travel and fictocriticism in Australia. It is much more of a story than criticism, which is greatly relevant to the opening creative piece in this folio, written in 2013 and entitled "At Some Point Reality Needs to Become a Part Of …" (to be referred to as "Reality" from this point) as they are both quite similar. Both pieces are about finding oneself or a 'self', passively, outside of one's comfort zone, in a foreign, though still Australian, location. Morgan finds himself writing in Sydney — whilst "Reality" is about arriving in Rockhampton, Queensland for the first time in 2013. Both pieces respectively attempt to absorb the detail and attention paid to 'life' and the generalised tedium, simplicity or 'mundane' rolling by. The thought process undergone when planning this piece dwelt on Josephine Rowe's writing and the detail she pays attention to her scenes in her short story "Tarcutta Wake" (2012) in an anthology by the same name — this will be elaborated upon later as Rowe's writing and depiction of Australian landscapes and imagery relates more directly to pieces in Folio One such as "There's a Road Train Going Nowhere", which from here on will be simply referred to as "Road Train" (Rowe 102). Moreover, the thought processes, which may or may not be conveyed in the creative folios, aim to allude to Barthes' sentiment, also expressed in Robyn Ferrell's fictocritical piece "Hemingway's Typewriter" (1998) in the seminal fictocritical anthology *The Space Between*, regarding how a writer can never in fact be on holiday. For the writer is always thinking and reacting to their environment and the impulsive workings of their inner mind — their writing is, therefore, often on the brink of potential outburst as their mind is constantly moving, or anticipating the act of writing, whether they choose to want it or not (Barthes 30; Ferrell 27).

Both creative pieces "Reality", and more specifically Morgan's "What Can Fictocriticism Do?" (2012), set a superficial scene and an opening 'space' for fictocriticism:

> People stare at me writing. I am a strange presence, still and observant in this free flowing space. Mums and dads walk by pushing toddlers. I look, missing my kids back in Geraldton, Western Australia, feeling a little unanchored in this place. A mother, a young thirty-something smiles at her daughter as some observation is murmured on the little one's lips. The mother smiles in honest fostering of her daughter's intelligence and being-towards-the world, but she also smiles for herself, her own acceptance and love of the mundane extraordinariness of parenting, for those uncanny and strange articulations that form in the minds of pre-schoolers. Concepts get mixed up, or appear as they truly are, infinite and momentary in their assemblage. Love, compassion, the tender human experience, is all mixed up, strolls by, and is an event itself. (Morgan 1-2)

Here is an extract from "Reality":

> And in between these moments of intermittent comprehension and the
> incoherent babbling drool of language I sat there, eyes fixed, glued to the
> barstool, and listened. I listened, and I sat there transfixed. I had no idea
> what especially I was trying to look and listen out for, but I felt that this was
> extremely important. This was communion, and a real genuine integration
> with a new place, with a real emergence existing in a chasm within myself
> … I'm here, this is now, it's new, and yet it is part of something older, more
> mature, settled, stubborn and fixated than what I can really grasp or
> understand. It's subjective, but it has no context, so I have no ideas that I can
> really cement in anything. I'm simply meandering along in this new
> environment, drifting within a distilled dam until hopefully my foot can
> latch on to something, at which point I can start simulating and generating
> algae in a pool of water, a pond of my own.

The deeper fictocritical hypotheses, or "rich synthesis of
rumination, memory, reflection" (Hancox and Muller 149), in the
Morgan narrative comes much later in the work. The creative self's
extract, on the other hand, appears to be almost stream of
consciousness. Morgan later incorporates descriptions and
explanations of fictocriticism in his dialogue with locals within his
piece, where he talks about it being "like a new writing style in the
social sciences, a new way of engaging in the real world reality of
things" and "it observes life but does it through a story" (3). A
fictocritical piece such as his can be analogised to Meaghan Morris'
"Uncle Billy, Tina Turner and Me" from *The Space Between*, which
encapsulates the same sense of nostalgia, whilst being based in
Sydney also. Morgan's extract was identified as a suitable comment
in this first thesis precisely because it does not commence with the
typically double-voiced form of fictocriticism. Rather, it initiates
with "personal journey and storytelling". The fictocriticism and
social observation comes into play later (Morgan 3). Hence, the
piece is more fragmented than layered.

Though fragmentation, of course, is another significant trait of
fictocriticism (King 272; Kerr and Nettelbeck 10; Walker 254; Robb
99). Similarly, this thesis and the stories presented in its correlating
folio, commence with more literal and/or abstract "personal
journey and storytelling" elements, whilst the denser theory comes
into play later. In general Hamish Morgan's piece captures the

essence of both observation and self-analysis within the context of 'journeying' or travelling whilst, ironically or incidentally, sitting still as he writes, or metafictionally writes about writing (1). The sentiment or mood of Morgan's piece is analogous to the one in "Reality" and in the creative pieces in this folio in general. Additionally, in *The Space Between*, Linda Marie Walker's piece "Speed Kills, Comma" (1998) includes similar experimental literary strategies to the ones incorporated in the works "Apple", "A Train Ride to Russia in 2007" (to be henceforth referred to as "Train Road"), "Coast to Coast Infrequency", "Tiers and Towers" and, in fact, most, of the creative pieces in Folio One. These strategies, as demonstrated by Walker, involve the implementation of sporadic, stinted language with numerous parenthesis and words or single letters within words, one-word sentences, incomplete sentences and the excessive use of forward dashes and hyphenation: "standing it (then) in air" (253); "A (col)lapse" (253); "f(r)iction" (254); "a/originating" (254); "It seems End, Fullness. The memory of dream is waking life. The dream, the nothing, rescues nothing" (255); and "Sociably. Body (every) which-way" (256). The decision to write in such an overtly (or overly) concise and objectively jarring way is best explained in the creative self's piece "A Literary Mitosis (On Form)" (2014).

The intention behind this approach was also highly personal/ised and intentionally jarring in order to convey a Joycean effect of the kind of free-association demonstrated in *Finnegan's Wake* (1939) and that text's "literary allusions … dream associations … [a] dismissal of conventions of plot and character construction … [representing the] fall of man from grace" (Coupland 110) in contemporary society. It is a relatively original or unique technique adopted in much of the writing in this book, which explains a lot about the creative self's style. For the creative self has often been criticised for writing in a style which incorporates brackets with words within words, excessive hyphenation, inverted commas, slashes dividing different words or synonyms, and other abstract or experimental writing techniques that could alienate some readers. "A Literary Mitosis" attempts to explain or justify some of these practices. This form (or lack of form) is derived from and also inspired by the lack or disruption of punctuation seen in the exuberant style(s) of Laurence Sterne's *Tristram Shandy* (1759), Henri Michaux's *Miserable Miracle* (1956), Jack Kerouac's novels (1922-69), Samuel Beckett's *The Unnameable* (1979), Pi O's *24 hours* (1996) and Danielewski's experimental novel *House of Leaves* (2000). These texts in particular venture into the metafictive and experimental realms that have helped to inform the work, 'style' and voice of this book. Interestingly, like in the creative self's "A Literary Mitosis", Haas performs/writes in a very similar manner in his *theoretical* explorations in *Fictocritical Strategies* also: "per/form/ative aspects" (8); "in/forms fictocriticism" (12); and "If fictocritical wri*ting* is de/territorialising" (17).

Walker's piece "Speed Kills, Comma" is thematically similar to "Road Train" also, as she extrapolates on the symptoms or effects of being in a car crash (253), whilst "Road Train" is a commentary on the tension felt by the characters of the story regarding a potentially impending collision with a road train in the context of the Australian outback. What "Road Train" does *not* do, however, which Walker's piece *does*, is draw on and clarify its metafictive and fragmentary form and style, whilst doing so fragmentarily, in what Hazel Smith, in "Erotics of Gossip" might call a writing of juxtaposition or reverberation (1001-02):

> The interruption of the incessant: this is the distinguishing characteristic of fragmentary writing: interruptions having somehow the same meaning as that which does not cease. (Walker 254)

"Road Train", however, at least intends to be an autobiographical commentary and meditation on the Australian outback from the perspective of a young Polish-Australian male writer.

Morgan's "What Can Fictocriticism Do?" attempts to explain fictocriticism within the dialogue he shares with a local "woman all heaving breasts, bangles and smoker's cough [that] takes a seat nearby" (3):

> "What are you doing in Sydney?" she asked.

I told her that I was in Sydney for a conference on fictocriticism at The
University of New South Wales called "What Can Fictocriticism Do?"

"What's that?"

"Well, it's like a new writing style in the social sciences, a new way of
engaging in the real world reality of things. Like any good writing, it has
critical depth, insight; it observes life but does it through a story. You know,
it uses things like character, setting, events in order to tell a story, but also
has a kind of sub-plot to it as well; a sub-plot of social observation or critique.
It is a method of writing where you become an actor in a social space rather
than a removed observer. It's not about maintaining critical distance, but
being an active participant with forces, objects, other actors. Like being part
of something, rather than standing apart from what's going on." (Morgan 3)

This is a highly reflexive 'embedding' literary device,
incorporating a framed-narrative method to story-crafting in which
there is a "story within a story" (Herman, Jahn and Ryan 134), as
can be seen in "The Use of Frame Story in Kashmira Sheth's *Boys
without Names*" (Alobeytha, Ismail and Shapii 105-11) and in "One
and 'I' in the Frame Narrative: Authorial Voice, Travelling Persona
and Addressee in Pausanias' *Periegesis**" (Akujärvi 327-58). These
novels alert the reader to the fact that he or she is writing (or has
written) a novel, a narrative of the sort that Roland Barthes might
call 'writerly'. A seminal example of such a work is *Tristram Shandy*,
in which the reader comes to understand that the story is about a
writer writing an autobiography in which the author experiences
almost nothing new. Laurence Sterne uses reflexivity among other
literary devices to illustrate the 'disconnect' between 'real life' and
the life of the subject. There are a number of other notable reflexive
narratives written in the same period, such as Fielding's *Joseph
Andrews* (1742) and *Tom Jones* (1749). It became fashionable in the
mid-1700s to experiment and craft such narratives in different
structures, in turn, surely the precursors to the more recognisable
metafiction seen two centuries later. It becomes clear early on in the
reading of these texts that the authors are fully cognizant of their
experimental approach, an attempt at shaping a chaotic reality into
a reproducible narrative form, especially notable in James Joyce's
Ulysses (1922), American feminist author Marilyn French's *The

Women's Room (1977) and Salman Rushdie's *Midnight's Children* (1980), which won the Booker Prize in 1981.

It was anticipated that the creative writing in this study might be considered equally reflexive in a similar manner as the creative self attempts to forge an autobiographical record of lived experiences in a fictional, self-reflexive form. Other fictocritical texts that share a similar style and structure with *this* book's creative work(s) include Ania Walwicz's "Look at Me, Ma — I'm Going to Be a Marginal Writer!" (273-77), Sedgwick's *Tendencies*, Anna Gibbs' "The Gift" (1998) and "Writing and the Flesh of Others" in *Australian Feminist Studies* (2013). However, what transpired in the creative writing was not quite the intended outcome, as mentioned earlier. The original project proposal deviated into fictocriticism from a basis in sheer abstract autobiographical works. The difficulty was in reconciling that deviation and retrieving the/a necessary double-voiced fictocritical form (Kerr 93).

With regard to Morgan, it is doubtful that the extract from his piece above is indicative of how he expressed himself at the time his conversation was taking place, particularly considering he was speaking to a woman who, based on his own descriptions of her, sounded homeless (3). There seems to be a discord here between naturalistic and non-naturalistic dialogue (Anae 4). However, Morgan's piece is eventually successful in conveying the literary tropes he lists: "character", "setting", "a story", and "social commentary" (3), all of which come in the form of a story about interacting with Sydney-siders, and then later through an anthropological lens: "the study of human cultures ... Like, now, I've been working with these artists as they develop concepts for some public art sculptures in Bayton-West, you know that new subdivision in Karratha ..." (Morgan 6).

The creative self's experimental piece "Reality", on the other hand, has character, setting, a story (though all based around dialogue within one primary scene), but, upon reflection, no real social commentary or research, unless a biased, anecdotal autobiographical account of the drinking/pub scene in Rockhampton from the perspective of a 20-something year-old

Melburnian male counts as social commentary or research. The story works as a piece of autobiographical creative non-fiction with some examination and analysis, but it is not fully-fledged fictocriticism. Fictocriticism demands a double-meaning in order to make the narrative 'work'. Fictocriticism requires a double-sidedness or "double-voicing" (93) as Heather Kerr suggests in her 2013 text "Fictocriticism, the 'Doubtful Category' and 'The Space Between'", in which it does two things at once: observation but also critique. One of the only other things that can be said of both Morgan and the creative works in Folio One, now also to include "Daze" (2014) and "The Mission Man" (2014), is that their sentiment is the same, and they are appropriate 'openers' to use for commencing a text on fictocriticism.

Particularly useful for this discussion is Deane Fergie's experimental piece "Unsettled", again from the *The Space Between*, which has sections that are comparable to "Road Train". Fergie also states that "[popular] texts would have it that the outback is timeless and unchanging" (188) though she, personally, is against the idea. Fergie has a beautifully ambient and otherworldly perspective of the Australian landscape as "a *cultural mirage*. Evanescent, oscillating, shimmering, never quite settled upon" (195), which is reaffirmed in the creative self's works and writings here. Fergie's description could easily be applied to fictocriticism itself and, in fact, to most postmodern writing—that is, the faintness, vagueness, and incomprehensible distortion of it. This book contends that Australia's sense of an identity, for non-indigenous Australians, is still growing and is itself confused and 'unsettled'.

What truly brings together Fergie's fictocritical piece, though, is her final line, regarding her own sense of self, in relation to what she writes about Australia or Australian culture, and which is something the creative self attempts to convey also: "I am apparitional. Evanescent, oscillating, never quite settled on ..." (198). This conclusion is beautifully apt. A similar sentiment and mood is conveyed in, but not limited to, "Daze", "The Mission Man", "Apple", "The Island", "'Til Morning Came" and "Déjà Vu Delirium".

"Coast to Coast Infrequency (Part I)" and "Coast to Coast Infrequency (Part II)" are part of a sequence about trying to find comfort, rest and complacency when travelling in isolation, though they are presented in a polarising way. Like the stories "Road Train" and "Train Ride", both "Coast to Coast Infrequency" parts (now simply referred to as "Part I" or "Part II") attempt to come full circle in an introverted description of a solitary 'self' in the grips of travel, heading west in the evening in "Road Train" or almost dying in "Part I", and then going east in a daze in the morning in "Train Ride" or having a sense of rebirth in "Part II". These polar stories in Folio One psychologically ebb and flow, so to speak. "Ghouls", "End of the Weekend" and "Going Home" are all based on the same journey, which took place in Queensland in 2014. They were written sequentially also. In this sense, the postmodern and fictocritical sentiment does in fact work within these pieces, even if nothing else about them does. Though as this exploration has found, capturing the mood and essence of fictocriticism has been the hardest part.

As Muecke concludes in his introductory "What Is Fictocriticism?" in *The Mother's Day Protest and Other Fictocritical Essays* (2016), "These are some of the things that fictocritical writing can do. What it is, exactly, remains to be seen" (xvii). The paradoxical and contradictory rules, double-voicedness, form and formatting can, and will, be worked out in subsequent sections. That 'unsettled' mirage-like aspect of fictocriticism at least *has* successfully worked in this section's folio though. More importantly, *this* thesis and folio (Section I) considers the activities of moving, journeying, ambling, looking, searching for the unknown, grasping, trying to find, figure or uncover something rather abstract. This is significant because this first thesis and folio, like the last thesis and folio (Section IV) of this book, are both about uncovering fictocriticism's obscure methodological origins in metafiction, autobiography, postmodernism and creative non-fiction, as well as where and how those obscure methodological styles and forms can progress and evolve in the future (Gray 3-23; Hancox and Muller 147-48; Flavell 40, 106, 215; Dawson 145). Hence, the 'abstract' nature of the creative self's stories are both theoretically *and* thematically abstract. They elucidate "a claim to the real and to truth" (Morgan 8). And perhaps the Rockhampton-based story "Reality" could be seen as comedic. Nevertheless, as the first creative experiment in fictocriticism presented in Folio One, it fails to encompass the greater movement of duality, the feeling of there being two levels of narrative: one superficial and visible; one subterranean and intimated.

The creative self's piece "The Mission Man", however, does support some claim to being a fictocritical work, due to its analyses of Jack Kerouac's *On the Road* (1957), Eckhart Tolle's *The Power of Now* (1997) and David McRaney's *You Are Not So Smart* (2011). There is some research incorporated as a double-voicing, which reverberates against the narrative relating to not being capable of living in the moment, or feeling like an erratic, restless entity, which is a relatable concept for human beings (Kerr 93).

Roland Barthes is mentioned frequently in fictocriticism too and is very warmly appreciated by pioneering fictocritical Australian and international academics since the early 1990s. He seems to be treated as a predecessor or 'godfather' figure of fictocriticism. He is fondly cited in Noel King's "My life without Steve: Postmodernism, Fictocriticism and the Paraliterary" (262), Kerr and Nettelbeck's *The Space Between* (4) and Monique Louise Trottier's Masters thesis "If Truth be Told..." (2002). Paul Dawson in "A Place for the Space Between" (2002) says fictocriticism is "a mode of critical writing which echoes the work of Barthes and Derrida" (141). Robb Simon in "Academic Divination is not a Mysticism: Fictocriticism, Pedagogy and Hypertext" (2013) states "[central] to current theorising of the fictocritical is Barthes' *A Lover's Discourse*" (98). King claims that Barthes, along with Derrida, "[blur] the distinction between literature and literary-critical commentary" (270), which is the precise underlying mood of fictocriticism, and exactly what many of Barthes' texts (*A Lover's Discourse, Roland Barthes, Mythologies*) are.

Barthes' *A Lover's Discourse* (1977) was one of the most influential postmodern and metafictional works that led to the construction of the creative pieces "The Spirit of the Times" and "A Sentimental Cynic" in this folio. Furthermore, the "automatic writing" (144) style that Barthes alludes to in "The Death of the Author" (1977) led to the kind of writing experiment performed in this section, which is much more impulsively written, or Kerouacian. In fact, it would be appropriate to introduce the works of Jack Kerouac at this point, particularly seeing how he was a nomadic traveller himself, yet it would be more suitable to survey the fictocritical, or pre-fictocritical, theorists and texts to maintain a focus on the research question(s) at hand: Does fictocriticism work? Can it be innovated on? And do the experiments in fictocriticism presented in the different folios of this book innovate upon the form successfully, or do they fail? Still, it will be necessary to mention the works of itinerant authors such as Kerouac, Arthur Rimbaud and Josephine Rowe in this thesis, at least in passing, to contextualise the bases, inspirations and themes of travel and where some of the creative work stemmed from. The point being, these early 'travel' writings by the creative self had minimal restraints or limitations put upon them. Many were written before this literary experiment officially began. They are uninhibited. Thus, they also reject many fictocritical 'norms', if such things can be said to exist.

The method for this creative enterprise, in the creative self's pieces "The Spirit of the Times" and/or "A Sentimental Cynic", involved reading passages and excerpts from Barthes' *A Lover's Discourse* that were most relevant and closely related to the definition of the word *zeitgeist*. However, it is important to note that Barthes' descriptions were used as a source of inspiration for the content of these works, and not necessarily for the style or form he utilises in his work. As previously mentioned, a more spontaneous, Kerouacian or "automatic writing" (Barthes 144) style was used in order to separate the physical action of writing from the mind.

In "I am engulfed, I succumb ..." (10-12), Barthes describes a morning scene in which he suffers from "an insipid notion" (10) where he craves a state of mind in which he can be hypnotically engulfed. Similarly, morning scenes are included in the creative self's pieces "'Til Morning Came" and "Train Ride", in which the unknown protagonist/creative self is engulfed by the idea of being totally entrapped within a frenzied lifestyle that is indicative of the self-destructive generation or era to which he belongs. In Barthes'

"The Intractable" (22-24) the following extract was particularly useful for establishing the state of exalted exhaustion conveyed in descriptions such as: "dazzlement, enthusiasm, exaltation, mad projection of a fulfilled future: I am devoured by desire, the impulse to be happy" (Barthes 24). A similar effect takes place in "Talking" (73-74): "releases, nourishes, ramifies it to the point of explosion" (Barthes 73).

The notion of 'pigeonholed' in "Tutti Sistemati" (Barthes 45-47) most vividly and accurately captures the essence of the idea of *zeitgeist* in that people are compartmentalised systematically into a place from which they cannot escape. This was demonstrated in the description of the spirit or predisposed frame of mind of our generation(s). This idea also occurs in "In the loving calm of your arms" in which Barthes describes 'us' as "enchanted, bewitched" in a foetal-like "infantile embrace" (104).

Finally, from "I am crazy" (120-21) and "Identifications" (129-31) the notions of madness and identification stimulate an exercise or "experience of depersonalization" (Barthes 121) in which a state (or description of a state) of obscured delirium could be shared or identified with another person within a moment of transcendent clarity. Hence, the incessant use of the collective 'we' as opposed to 'I' in the creative self's descriptions. The collective 'we' was also believed to be more relevant to a word such as *zeitgeist*, which seems inherently applicable to a group of people or a whole.

Even though *A Lover's Discourse* (1977) primarily revolves around the concept or psychology of love, it can be applied to broader issues or ideas such as those raised by the prompt *zeitgeist* or the uninhibitedness that stems from journeying or travelling. After all, this was an introspective creative piece that happened to indulge or result in the exploration of concepts such as universality and togetherness, and that too reflects a kind of love. As King notes and concludes in his article, fictocriticism comes back to the value and dynamism of "intertextual collage, bringing together fragments" (272) in writing and its uses in the academy, for fictocriticism and for writing overall. That is especially what this section on journeys is: fragmentation, collage, a searching and 'finding' of a 'self' before the more concrete themes of the subsequent folios emerge.

A useful metaphor with which to conclude this first thesis is that of the 'horizon'. Naturally, the notion of the horizon ties in to any kind of writing about travel or journeys. This could even be considered a truism, that is, striving for the unattainable in the quest for the unknown. This should be a feeling that is had by any traveller or voyager. The 'horizon' metaphor features distinctly in the creative self's pieces "Road Train", "Train Ride" and "Tiers and Towers". The Greek term horizon means "a bounding circle" (Fitzsimmons 1). It is also a paradox, being a boundary and "a line which is never reached" (Fitzsimmons 1). It is a constant. Furthermore, in Muecke's *Joe in the Andamans: And other Fictocritical Stories* (2008) he says of travel:

> The pleasure of anticipation is sweeter and more imaginatively varied than the consummation, but tickets eventually have to be used, we come sooner or later face-to-face with the jetlag, the hassles, the 'thick of things' and the tropical weather really starting to get irksome. (26)

The creative self's horizon-oriented stories mentioned above dramatise the idea of being caught up within something that is moving whilst being still — paradoxically also, just as a Doppler effect causes one to only hear a present fraction of a 'now' (moment) as something fast passes one by at a specific point. And "yet whilst the future is embodied in the horizon and the continual need to trek towards it, the present seems accessible only by apostrophising the past" (4). "At the moment of arrival, the horizon was before us; at the moment of departure, it has become us" (5). "The horizon is all — the past, the present and the future" (Fitzsimmons 7).

The way in which Folio One was initiated, the plan behind it, and the cautiously-grasped model of fictocriticism that was initially held, turned out to be something less than fictocritical. Thus, the horizon is also a suitable metaphor for fictocriticism's literary potential overall. The subsequent sections will attempt to further uncover (or discover) ways in which fictocriticism can be innovated on, if it can be innovated on at all, or if any attempts to innovate on it are as futile as any attempts to physically surmount a horizon, as the creative self attempts to do in "Road Train", "Train Ride" and "Tiers and Towers". The next section, for instance, will also look at texts like *House of Leaves* by Danielewski, as well as fictocriticism's roots in metafiction, and if those roots can possibly nurture more fruit as the fictocritical and academic seasons change.

SECTION II

FOLIO TWO: Family

Guise (2014)

There exists a connection to the pet, to the animal, that has never been felt for the girl. Constantly bombarded with photographs transposed electronically and a shiver down my spine, a flutter through my heart, every time. Animals, normally, I could not care less, but this one is different, and the projections enforced onto him by the voluptuous girl resonate. A deep affection is had, seated somewhere, still and stagnant and then jarred and jolted once again into life by a force unrecognised.

Humans; saints, sinners, others—I could not care less, belonging to the rigid and misaligned surface lingering and existing between the two sides or faces of the coin. Somewhere no one looks normally, rolling along surfaces, never scraped or scratched. Rather, it is the edge that scrapes and scratches nonchalantly, but generally 'chooses' not to. The side, the space, the 'edge', this fourth, almost metaphysical dimension is unaffected, by and by.

A distant family member was injured recently. Loved and somewhat lost with age and strict sincerity, always with the best intentions but misaligning the moral groundings of her children's children, and now all disconnected, personally dishonest and askew, all completely different because all had been exposed to different dosages at different times or peak periods. Whether male or female, placid kid, teenager or young adult, an infectious effectiveness was transferred to these siblings, all of which have an eye/I that is disintegrated and somewhere else. So, they too struggle with identity and go looking for it in places, delving into it with a false modesty, but an intensity that strikes and truly tries to delve itself into the skins of others. Ticks and leeches, and not necessarily always others but into cliques, clicking and clacking their tongues and cheeks, riding and striding, walking and talking along with warm bodies that frown carefully and cautiously behind palms and hands and glasses and food and alcohol, gluttonous with irrevocably empowered pride.

I am neither relating to people or to animals, necessarily, but to a pet with a humanised projection projected onto it. It would be nothing by itself, but a need exists to distinguish and to separate through layers to others, and to feel, see and understand through another's eyes, and to connect and love with an animal, a pet, anthropomorphised. A rare opportunity to love without scarcely being recognised, absorbing the love of another (person) without ever being caught in the act of reciprocating the sentiment at all.

Brought up and raised by a bleeding heartfelt ghost ... a growth accumulating and pulsating, a generation of exponential force and a generation of brothers and sisters, using the pet, the animal as a guise to both hold, and withhold truisms, be strangled by clenched fists of radiating and infectious effectiveness for deep-seated, heartfelt and long-winded frustrations, transitory and cyclical in their power and poisonous poise, poignant and rich in traversed and trained trails (or travels), exhaled and exhumed by the blood on the steps of some place before us.

Kwiat Dwóch Puszcz (2017)

… I suppose you can just call me Lou for now. Whatever. Who gives a shit. I am, at present, a dual citizen, and thus own two up-to-date, yet very distinct and contrasting passports that are both used fairly frequently: a Polish one, carmine in tone; the other, Australian, and navy blue in colour. I believe their colours could be considered emblematic of the countries and cultures they represent, but more on that later.

My life is mostly an Australian one, girt by 'ocean'. My (Polish) family, on the other hand, all essentially live in a Central/Eastern European country grasping a crook of the Baltic Sea, known as the Republic of Poland. My family there have always been proud and historically, or perhaps legacy, oriented. It has often seemed to me that Polish people's engagement with and understanding of their own difficult history, even in relatively recent years—with WWII affecting my grandparents and then communist times affecting *my* parents—have forced many of the twentieth-century generations in Poland to account for their bitterness and stubbornness as a cluster of citizens. Though I have always felt detached from this type of mindset.

When I was a kid visiting my *dziadziu* ('grandfather'), in his hometown of Rudnik in Poland, where he lived all his life until the day he died, he would sometimes tell me about how he used to transport the wounded in a horse-drawn cart, mostly at night, to and from the forest behind his home during WWII.

"How old were you at the time, *dziadziu*?" I would ask.

"Oh, around ten."

"Must've been scary?"

"Scariest time of my life, the things I saw at that age."

He, Kazimierz, rarely elaborated, whilst sitting stoically on his preferred stool in my grandparents' kitchen, his back arched against the wall, contemplative and sombre, gazing, but not really looking at anything in particular.

Kazimierz wrote a novel over the course of his life. He once showed me various drafts of it when I was younger, and my dad eventually persuaded him to publish it in 2003, right before he passed away. *Kwiat Dwóch Puszcz*, Granddad had called it, which loosely translates to *Flower of Two Deserts* or *The Flower of Two Forests*, a *puszcz* meaning a kind of deserted valley within a forest.

I cannot read *Kwiat Dwóch Puszcz* because my Polish isn't good enough. I can speak Polish, I can understand it, and I can write a little, but my abilities are rusty, and the longer I spend away from the 'Motherland' the worse it gets and the greater the disconnection and disassociation from my ancestry and heritage become.

"Why do you think *dziadziu* didn't try to publish it sooner?" I asked my dad when I was in Poland over Christmas last year. "He spent such a long time writing it. Years. Decades actually. But he didn't want to get it out there?"

"Your *dziadziu* was an uncharacteristically humble and modest man … maybe even a little too naïve and disenchanted with life. You probably know that he was quite sincere and religious, but he struggled with Catholicism, I think. Kept quiet about it. In any case, it took me years to convince him to publish his novel. He finally let me do it though, provided I would organise everything for him."

"But he published it under a pseudonym, right? Why? You don't think he wanted the credit, the legacy? Do you think being Catholic had something to do with that, being a humble and modest man that is? All the Polish people I know, including our family, don't seem quite so humble and modest. They're generally annoyingly loud and proud."

"Yes, everyone in our family here was quite agitated with *dziadziu*. *Ciocia* Bodgana was actually yelling at him."

I laughed. "Of course she was. But *ciocia* is probably the most vocal and bible-thumping Catholic in our family, isn't she?"

"Well, it's just that *ciocia* Bodgana is the one who keeps everything in line in her home. But her protests didn't have much of an effect on your *dziadziu*, particularly in his later years. Despite my dad's mild temperament, he was quite obstinate in his own quiet way, and always did what he wanted in the end. And *dziadziu* said that he wanted to release the book under the pen name Dominik Mak, which combined and dedicated three names: his father Dominik, his wife, your *babcia*, Maria — Ma — and a little bit of his own name, Kazimierz — 'k'."

"Oh, okay. Intriguing. What's his book about?" I asked.

"It's about a group of children who share some experiences during WWII in the forest behind *dziadziu's* house in Rudnik. The children reunite several years later as adults, to recall and reflect on what had happened to them in that place at that time."

"So, you think *dziadziu* may have written it about some of his *own* experiences during the war? It could have autobiographical elements?"

"Yes, I think that's a possibility. It's quite detailed and romantic in this respect."

"Amazing." I wondered about the novel. "I wish I could read it."

In the lengthy saga of adversity in the Polish people's history, their difficulties can sometimes accumulate, stagnating in their hearts and invading and exacerbating cynicism, negativity and pessimism in their sense of ethics and morality. Perhaps then there exists this sort of dichotomy between religious, spiritual and familial values and virtues that is obstinate, one-sided but loyal at least. This dichotomy creates a struggle within a sense of self that is incessantly present and seems impossible to surmount. On the one hand, there is emotional romanticism, and on the other, dark doubt, cynicism and pain, which all teach to unite these two things within their national character and personality, in an ongoing struggle, prevalent and present within the self, that is cyclical and difficult to overcome. This is what I have come to believe, and that is how I perceive things within my family anyway.

Even now when I visit Poland as a young male in my late twenties, the relatives with whom I stay will force me to go to church every Sunday. If *they* have to go, then *everyone* has to go. No one is allowed to stay behind when the family goes to church. Yet it doesn't actually seem as though my family gets much satisfaction out of the exercise. In fact, most people at church in Poland seem sullen and miserable. It's a grim yet intensely focussed affair. They push and shove and pry at one another to get into the mass. The priest speaks harsh 'truths' about reality and modern civilisation and the Poles soak it up.

Poles *have* to go to church. Why do they have to go? Because they just *have* to. There seems to be no other logical explanation. This is perhaps an example of the kind of duality that seems to exist within their character. It is as though there is an invisible force compelling them to attend church and *be* religious—like the invisible force that compelled their parents, grandparents and their entire ancestry to be Roman Catholic before them. They can't seem to refuse and go against the grain of that deep-seated conventional 'wisdom'. So, they keep forcing and pushing and thrusting that religious 'wisdom' upon their children, and their nieces and nephews, and that invisible compelling force grows stronger in their own minds.

"Get ready, we're going to church, Lou," my uncle would tell me on Christmas Day last year when I was staying with him and my auntie in Rzeszów.

"Mmm, no, sorry, *wujku*. Not today. I really need to get some work done," I'd reply tentatively.

"What? Today? On this Holy Day? You must be joking, Lou. Hurry up! Get your shoes on. We're leaving in five minutes."

I would often ask my dad, Mirek, about his views on the matter in these situations; "But you're a scientist, *Tata*. How can *you* still be religious?"

"It's all about faith," would generally be his non-committal reply.

My overworked auntie Bodgana's reaction to my prompts or theological questions would generally be a dismissive, "Just, just read the Bible! It's all in there."

I also tried to have Kuba, my aunt and uncle's son, explain his parents' sentiment and philosophy on our way walking to church that Christmas Day. Perhaps he could rationalise my more Western or liberal ideologies in the face of his parents' obnoxious Catholicism. Kuba has spent some time abroad, and in Australia also, so I thought he might understand me. We're quite close these days. He's only a year or two younger than I am.

"Perhaps they just don't want to have to defend themselves all the time?" he would say to me, as we trudged through the snow on that 'holy' morning, grey clouds overhead.

"That's fair enough, I suppose," I would respond sheepishly. "I guess I can be a little like that with my own views too. I rarely feel in the mood to have to explain or justify myself *all* the time. Still, going to church, and forcing *me* to go the church. The nerve! It seems like they can't break the habit for themselves, like a nervous tic or twitch, so why force it upon others? Their religious-ness seems to itch at and project itself on to everyone around them, regardless of other people's personal or idiosyncratic beliefs."

"It is Christmas though, Lou. It's one of the most important Catholic days of the year. You don't think you can just accommodate your family now and then, on a day like this? Also, my parents, your *ciocia* Bodgana and *wujek* Rajmund, are always stressed, always overworked, bitter and agitated. And though it may not seem like it, they're very excited to see you and to have you here this year. We all are. You live all the way in Australia. It's nice for them that you're here with us. They want to share the experience with you, because maybe you don't get this kind of Christmas in Australia."

I swayed my head to one side and let out something in between a sigh and a constipated grunt. I was feeling frustratingly sheepish again. How do I always overlook the bigger picture? Now that I was walking with Kuba outside, in the sub-zero temperatures of a traditional Polish winter, with the rest of our family in a huddle before us, and the entire neighbourhood in procession on the streets surrounding us despondently walking to church in unison, I did at least feel like I was part of something bigger, and it felt good even. So, I maintain the charade of complacent faith, if only to keep the peace, for now.

When we eventually walked through the doors of the seemingly modern, brightly lit and practically kidney-shaped *Kościół Najświętszego Serca Pana Jezusa* (Church of the Holiest Heart of Jesus Christ) in Rzeszów at noon, it was difficult not to think, particularly with the intensely echoey reverberations of my measured steps, that I wasn't in a much more stoic and historic

European cathedral. To me, the faint pastel-like paintings coating the internal walls, and the bright yellows and powdery blues of the ceiling above, always expressed a sarcastic insistent grimness. *This* eastern European church seemed out of place and character considering the serious and pious nature of the congregation that routinely attended it.

As we took our seats in the cramped and creaky pews, I felt no warmer. The harsh chill from outside persisted inside. It seemed we weren't allowed to be comfortable in the house of God. Still, I thought to myself, let me try to properly listen to the sermon and the priest's homily this time around, at Christmas, at *Kościół Najświętszego Serca Pana Jezusa in Rzeszów*, with my Polish family sitting alongside me, and let me see if I can find some peace or something fruitful in that specific context.

I will try to listen to the priest's reasoning with an open mind, despite having a dismissive and superficial bias towards the whole 'process'. For I cannot view a priest without a preconceived notion or prejudice, no matter how charming, 'righteous' or friendly he may be. I find the institutional abuse, sexually repressed, tax-evading, arrogant and paedophilic nature of Catholic priests that has come into public and political spotlight and scrutiny in recent decades to be an overt sign of their irrelevance in the contemporary world.

The priest who delivered his sermon was red-faced and bloated. Perhaps he was an alcoholic. He had short, dark hair that uniformly coated his crown. His eyes were murky but stern. He never smiled, though he did occasionally grimace. He was often short of breath as his gluttonous belly rose and fell. He frequently took short, snappy breaths from a stomach that would unsteadily inflate and deflate beneath his sharply ironed jet-black cloak.

"Some people think that Christmas time is about presents or gift-giving and materialistic things," he would dictate, his voice reverberating through the glacial cathedral. "Others believe it is about peace and rest, a holiday from work at this time of year. Others still believe that Christmas is about family and cherishing the ones we love around us."

Yes, I'm on board so far.

The fat priest would pause after he had made each statement, allowing the value, truth and 'worth' of what he was saying to sink in.

Thus, he continued, "Christmas is not about these things. Christmas is about Jesus. It is about acknowledging the sanctity of his birth and his vital significance in our lives."

At this point I had to switch off and disconnect from the mass. I wanted to fling and flail my arms into the air, but instead I turned to Kuba to my left and dismissively declared, restraining myself to a whisper, "Well, I tried. I made an effort. That's enough for me now. *He*," pointing at the "mad priest ... of ideology" (Williams 232) lowly, "has proven me right!"

"Shhh!" my auntie snapped at me to my right.

Kuba stayed put, grimaced a little, and whispered to me, "Fair enough, Lou. We'll speak about this later though. Not now."

I remained in my seat fuming somewhat, but even my jittery and fiery mood could not keep me warm from the elements that seemed to have pervaded their way inside the church.

Once mass had ended and the congregation clawed their way out through the wooden arched cathedral doors even more furiously than they had entered it, I could not bite my tongue any longer, and in amongst the compressed crowd I began rambling to Kuba again, in English this time though. "So why did the priest say Christmas had to equate to and *become* Jesus (Christ)? Christmas does not *equal* Jesus! That is not a mathematical dogmatic statement I have heard or come across before being here in this church!"

"He didn't say Christmas *equalled* Jesus though," Kuba replied in Polish. "He was just talking about how important Jesus Christ and his message are at this time of year."

"Whatever. The '*equals*' was implied. He was frothing over that shit."

"Hmm," Kuba murmured, confusedly.

"And why can't Christmas not be about all those other important things also: presents, rest, family, love? Why do we, the congregation, have to sacrifice all of those other real, tangible and heart-warming things that we can actually touch and feel and experience in our lives in service of an undocumented intangible fiction?"

My blood boiled. We were now walking down the side streets back to my aunt and uncle's house and I had much more room to flail my limbs as I marched and composed my arguments in a huff.

"What the priest was saying was that not everyone has family, gifts, loved ones or materialistic things, but the one thing they do have at Christmas is their faith. But," Kuba hesitated, "I do fully understand and see what you're saying. There's a paradox in the Polish style of faith and our culture." He sighed. "This. Is. Poland." was Kuba's sarcastically austere retort. "That's just the way it is," and he sighed again in his own defeatist way. Although he may have been humouring me to some extent, I also recognised the sadness in Kuba—the kind that I perceive in all Poles, something that I tend to pry up from time to time via these obnoxious rants of mine.

It appeared to be becoming dark already, even though it was still reasonably early in the afternoon. That was typical in most northern European countries during winter though.

I had calmed down a lot. I was probably just a little too fidgety earlier at mass. We continued walking.

"Do you think Polish people believe in all that though? Do they take what all priest's say as being written in stone almost?" I asked.

"Yes, I think so. It makes sense to Poles you know, the rhetoric, the dialect. As long as it sounds like scripture, it'll make some kind of sense to them. Also, Poland is a conservative, maybe a short-sighted type of a country. Perhaps they don't see so much beyond what's right in front of them. They're not exactly quite westernised yet. Well, they are, since the late 80s, but then again, they're not. Not really. *Our* generation," he said, taking my shoulder, "is the first one to grow up with fast food and American films and pop music and all that stuff. Our parents and grandparents didn't have a lot of that, really. Know what I mean? They had tradition, inflation, scarcity and of course, church. The staples."

"Yeah, but ... do they still all act, believe and behave accordingly, according to Biblical law or something like that?"

"I don't know. Well, you saw them in there. They don't *seem* happy. Maybe pious? But it's that fierce tradition also, within families? This stuff goes back many generations, not just recent ones. But then as soon as they get out of church it's all a mad rush, and no one ever smiles. You saw this. The dichotomy? The paradox? They're pushing and shoving, and everyone is trying to get out first in the car park. This is Poland. It's what Polish people are like. They're not going to change for logic *now*. Not yet. But ... maybe logic is too harsh a condemnation. Loyalty, tradition, God. These are the truly important virtues, values and concepts to them. More important than any other material or westernised things."

"They don't want to be liberated?" I chimed in.

"They do. They did. The *Solidarność* movement and generation. They did some things ...", Kuba trailed off, "I'm not sure to what extent ... a lot of them left the country in the 80s and 90s I think ... so ... that solidarity is elsewhere now maybe. Not so much in Poland."

In "Life Narratives, Common Language and Diverse Ways of Belonging" (2015), Katarzyna Kwapisz Williams defines *Solidarność* or the 'Solidarity' movement as a group or groups that took their name from a Polish trade union, which gave rise to an anti-communist social movement (2). Many of these "Solidarity migrants" came to Australia "in the wake of political unrest in the 1980s" (Williams 2):

> They were usually tertiary-educated and highly qualified, often with good knowledge of English and willingness to embrace Australia as a second home and face all the challenges it required (e.g. changing professions, or undertaking further education). (Williams 4)

Was my father one of them? I think I saw a *Solidarność* handbook at home in Melbourne as a kid once. I never tried to read it, but I saw a tattered Polish flag on it. It felt like it carried weight. Not a spiritual weight, but a radical one.

Kuba bobbed his head downwardly and lopsidedly, just a tad, when he walked and talked. He always did this. I think Kuba has perhaps resigned to a somewhat pessimistic fate, accepting the fact that if one wants to be a Pole living in Poland then one has to suffer for it. Even though I might be actively cynical, at least I have some vigour and a sense of rebellion in me.

I felt sad for Kuba though, particularly seeing him as this former shell now. He once had so much more energy, vitality and health when he was living with our family in Australia several years earlier. His skin was darker then, tanned. He has now lost that tan, and any glow, hope or optimism he used to be bathed in with it. He is fat and bloated now, constantly wearing a grim contemplative expression, an 'honest' expression. Scabs cover his chapped lips and furrowed face. He's too honest I think, in that he understands the nature of Polish people and occasionally openly talks about it to others. A melancholy soul, suffering within the paradigm of a truth that no one gives a shit about hearing or listening to in his own country, and I force him to open up to me about it. The joy. Maybe I should stop doing this to him. Maybe I should leave it alone. Say nothing. Ignorance is bliss. This. Is. Poland.

A colleague of mine living in Rzeszów is studying law, not because she wants to but because her grandfather wants her to. She claims she doesn't even necessarily like law. She would prefer to play volleyball professionally, which she did when she was younger. This resignation of hers isn't uncommon in cultures like China, South Africa, Italy and Portugal, which are said to "have the strictest parents" (Mayol 1), and where parents or grandparents dominate a child's life and their decision-making process, as a testament to their own vicarious goals in life. But I feel that in Poland it is used as ammunition for complaint on behalf of the individual. This friend of mine, Magda, is quite calm and intelligent about all of this, for now. My father was asking me about her and why she would do something like this. I replied, "because she's Polish, and so that she has something to complain about." My dad paused, and replied, "Polish people are indeed a pack of *smuciarzy*." There doesn't seem to be an exact translation for this word 'smuciarzy' into English, but I'd say it means something along the lines of a 'sad sook'. It is rare for members of our family to admit to this 'sooky' trait in themselves and their own country and culture. But dad and I are fairly well travelled and cosmopolitan, which has had a different kind of impact on our perspectives as opposed to what I perceive to be the more standard Polish viewpoint.

The duality within the character and personality of Eastern European people, from what I know and understand of my own upbringing, plays host to the darkness and difficulties of their very long history. The cynicism that results, coupled with the moral and ethical grounding in and loyalty to Roman Catholicism makes it incredibly difficult to have a character that complements both of these polar elements.

Contentedness is a difficult thing to find for my Polish family. Hence, acts of selflessness or seeming disengagement or disassociation with the self, like that of my grandfather's, in his implementation of the pen name or nom de plume Dominik Mak, or the inability for my Polish family to resist the shackles and tug of insistent conservative religious ideology, tend to go over the heads of some Polish citizens.

Kazimierz also retired too early and perhaps lost some of his sense of worth, integrity and productivity in the end. Both he and my family have spoken of this to me, though it is often hard for me to separate their whining sentiment with what they actually believe to be true on the inside.

I feel that *dziadziu* and I were extremely similar people, though that he never really understood me. There's even a good chance that I will wind up being very similar to him in personality and character. But the language, age and communication barriers never enabled him to see how much I empathised with him, or how similar we actually were. Instead, I think he saw me as spoilt, restless, unappreciative and vindictive, based on the way I interacted with my cousin Kuba. This was a version of my 'self' that he perhaps perceived to be real and true, with his graceful and intuitive heart—a romantic creative (writer's) heart. The coincidental thing is that he was seeing much of himself in me: genetically, biologically, mentally and physically, I doubt there had ever been anyone so similar to him in our family as I. Maybe he didn't like himself though — that could also be a consideration.

He and I were creative types whilst everyone else in our family (within one or two immediate generations anyway) were fairly science-oriented. He and I played musical instruments; he played well on the mandolin, whilst I play guitar. No one else plays an instrument in our family. He was a hopelessly hybridised romantic-realist, a sentimental cynic — as am I. But the fact that I cannot read or understand his work and the fact that he'll never be able to read any of mine is both symbolic and indicative of my disconnection from my ancestry into a predominantly Australianised unknown, of today, and since my birth here in Australia in 1988. My grandfather owned or compiled a family tree going back twenty generations of our ancestry/name, all of them Polish or Polish Jews, or so I've been told, though I've never physically *seen* this family tree or any documentation to support it. And Polish people, particularly my family, are prone to intense exaggeration and melodrama, in my experience. Nevertheless, I am allegedly the first family member in a very long line to not even be European — to have not even been born in the northern hemisphere of this world. I am the first family member to be Australian. Even my two older sisters were born in Kraków, Poland, in the early 1980s.

But I've spent a lot of time in Poland — maybe two or three years altogether, spread out over the course of my life so far — something like seven or eight trips in total, and I would go there almost every year throughout secondary school, during my formative years. I also spent a brief stint there over Christmas and New Year's Eve in 2015-16, which was incredibly sentimental and also very useful to me as it helped me to re-establish my Polish (language and heritage). It also led me to cement many of the notions, concepts and ideas I had about Poland and Polish culture, as they relate to my own perception of 'self' and my family.

I should doubly mention that the notions or impressions I gain of Poland are filtered through my familial experiences, and do not necessarily represent Poland as a nation by and large. Ultimately, they are merely my distorted impressions.

All of the time I spent there was perhaps not enough to forge a real connection to my history or my Polish past, and not enough to understand or connect with it. I mean, there's my family, and then there's the rest of Poland, which could be very different. Maybe we're the only 'loopy' ones.

I don't know. I am still going and grasping for my own way — and since my birth I have assimilated with Australian culture more so than my Polish heritage, but what does that actually mean? An assimilation with mateship, camaraderie, the bush, and whatnot? Gillian Whitlock lists a range of facets or aspects of Australia in the introduction to *Images of Australia* (1992) that could be relatable and/or make sense to most people, or most Australians:

> … a multicultural nation, a British nation, an Aboriginal nation, an "American" nation, an Asian-Pacific nation, a sporting nation, a nation of slobs, a Christian society, a secular nation, an egalitarian society, a racist or sexist society, the land of the outback, the land of suburbia, a workingman's paradise, a banana republic … [and] images which associate the Australian national character with mateship, the land of the beach for example. (1)

According to Richard White though, a "national identity is an invention" (23). And a personal identity or self is a construction forged by personal growth and external influence, and time. My external influence, the landscape I was and am in, Australia, and what I experienced around me growing up was a little different, as would be the case for most migrant families and the struggle or duality of culture they experience; it's not quite black and white — it never is. There is a hefty tug of war happening, a push and pull going on between the assimilation trying to occur and exist in a day-to-day life outside of home, and then what happens to you in the time you spend inside your (Polish or European) house, in Australia.

Whitlock's emphasis for Australia's sense of an identity is to not so much struggle with one's own internalised cultural tug of war, such as the one I experience, or that many other migrants experience, but rather to idealistically disintegrate the cultural barriers between people in order to create a more universal or unified identity. I find her views and interrogation of Australia in

Images of Australia simultaneously hopeful yet bathed in a strangely absolutist light: "Australia is not a society in its own right and can never be understood by looking for a genuine essence" (18), and, so, "we will never arrive at the 'real' Australia. From the attempts of others to get there, we can learn much about the travellers and the journey itself, but nothing about the destination. There is none" (25). "An Australian might still be a Man from Snowy River, but he or she might also be a man or woman from Italy or Turkey, Ireland, Lebanon or Cambodia" (101). "The step beyond multiculturalism is the transcending of national identity ... Human identity must become transnational" (136). "Our aim must be community without nation" (Whitlock 141).

Whitlock's *Images of Australia* is littered with the (often heavily masculinised) imagery, descriptions and ideologies of Australia, which include terms such as "consciously isolationist" (15), "homogenised ockerism" (114), "a community of brothers" (148) and a "traditional" Australia that has "been constructed through positively-inflected accounts of the workingman's paradise, the social laboratory, pioneers and settlers, Anzac heroes, egalitarianism, social harmony, manliness and the bush" (145). The evolution, I feel, of the Australian character and value-system can be inferred from her reference to Russell Ward's *The Australian Legend* (1958):

> *The Australian Legend* ... advances in four stages. Firstly, Ward argues that there is something identifiably Australian, a proletarian "mystique" ... Secondly, this mystique evolved out of bush life, especially out of the conditions of labour and leisure of the nineteenth century nomadic bushmen ... Thirdly, this set of values was transferred to city people by osmosis, especially through the fiction of popular writers such as Lawson and Furphy. Finally, the advent of socialist ideas ... after about 1880 was accepted by these men quite quickly, since mateship—an integral part of the mystique—was a "natural socialist ethos". (Whitlock 14)

Whitlock's understanding of Australia, or the way I understand it, is still evolving—it is not yet fully formed, so the tug-of-war occurring within my 'self' in terms of culture and 'background' is made up of a rich tapestry (a variety of selves) of persistent uncertainty from the perspective of migrant writers.

There is a cultural dissonance here, which opens up an opportunity for migrant writers' perspectives to be highlighted, and for them to speak up:

> From this perspective the experience of migrant groups, as articulated through a still small number of writers, is by no means marginal to an understanding of the construction of an Australian identity … a version of the multicultural perspective has a crucial role to play in current criticism providing as it does, in formal terms, an almost exact mirror image of tendencies outlined in our earlier chapters. (Hodge and Mishra 179)

Bob Hodge and Vijay Mishra's research in their text *Dark Side of the Dream: Australian Literature and the Postcolonial Mind* (1991) also finds a way to vocalise exactly how the internal dissonance and hybridity of being a first-generation Polish-Australian can feel:

> First generation migrants tend to emphasise cultural maintenance, while the second generation moves closer towards assimilation, thus creating a major fissure within the group across generation. But the split is in some respects a way of managing the fundamental contradiction, since the children are assigned the task of making links with the new on behalf of the group, while being required to maintain their allegiance to the old. The second generation has to live with a basic double message, to renounce purity while remaining true to the group. (Hodge and Mishra 181)

For me, my "double message", as articulated by the writing and viewpoints in these works is *sentimental* (as expressed by my Australian-ness) *cynicism* (as expressed by my Polish-ness).

Storm (2017)

My personal growth during my formative teenage years was largely influenced, and occasionally distorted, by my uniquely passionate and unyieldingly obdurate grandmother Maria, who raised my sisters and I in Australia, and tried to teach me to be *more* Polish I'd say (growing up out of context and out of relevance in the south-eastern suburbs of Melbourne, Australia). I think her raising of us sometimes rubbed me the wrong way, and I resisted her in a number of different ways, as so many children tend to do.

Though I was growing up much less Polish than she expected me to be and was becoming much more Australian than she could appreciate or understand. I won't go into the reasons as to why *she* raised us during this time, and not my parents, but she did, and we (my two elder sisters and I) and Maria, adapted to the situation and circumstance as best as we could, or the only way we all knew how to, which was largely through fitful stubbornness, temperamental anger, frustration, and a strict lack of compromise, or that was my perspective and recollection at least. However, my recollection(s) may also have been distorted by my exploding hormones, angst and that inherently rebellious attitude that comes with being a teenager.

One of my grandmother's lessons was to trust no one, and to cheat if I needed to, to get ahead in life. I don't know if it's just my family or Polish people in general, but adversity and circumstance can be quite taxing in poorer, eastern European countries. One must be crafty and conniving when it comes to human competition and success within or among the rat race of life. Polish people would never quite put it this bluntly, I think. Their dialect is one of charm, wit and subtlety, with an expansive language: they have the capacity to talk for hours on the same topic, much the same as I imagine French, Russian, Czech, Italian and North American folk from the Deep South might do. Polish is a passionate language. I remember family members telling me about how exams and testing all worked at school and university in Poland; tests and exams were brief—unrealistically short—forty questions in fifteen minutes—

that kind of thing—rather than time ratios that go the other way around or function properly, realistically, and above all, fairly.

Fairness seems like an outdatedly reckless and foolish concept in Poland, and perhaps went out the window a long time ago. In any case, Polish tests sound like impossible tasks. It seems like they're more than just about challenging students; they're about trying to trip them up and weed out the weak from the capable— those who are unwilling to push the envelope of what they're comfortable or not comfortable with, and what they're actually willing to do in order to succeed or get ahead.

I hear that in their final year of high school, students aren't just tested *on* their final year of high school. They are tested on everything and every subject they have ever taken in their entire schooling life, in a very short space of time. Questions are built upon questions, or questions are simply asked out of context. You're just expected to *know* everything off the cuff. Moreover, there are numerous oral examinations in which students need to rely on their ability to talk, also off the cuff, casually applying a suave and sly style and tone when and where applicable.

My parents, grandparents, aunts and uncles have always encouraged their offspring to try and come up with cunning ways of retaining information, or cheat, in other words. Then they praise us when we 'succeed' in the endeavour. This methodology doesn't translate to Australian audiences where the climate is cultivated to be a little more realistic, possible, and most importantly, ethical. Australia is a Boy Scout. Culture shock. Australians are more inclined to go the other way, in a more Americanised 'no child left behind' manner. I know this from my experiences as a secondary school teacher in Australia.

My grandmother also tried to teach me that there are no such things as friends in life, as one cannot (fully) ever trust anybody. You are essentially (and must be) alone, self-sufficient, because "everyone is always trying to take advantage of you," she would say with a prudent wave of a forefinger, "so you should take advantage of them first before they betray you!"

These days I always feel as though I'm the one taking advantage of something or someone, even when I'm being sincere, because I've been taught to look for that crafty angle within myself. I often see reciprocity, business, trade and even social interactions through that skewed lens.

What kind of perspective should I have at home? And then what kind of perspective should I adopt outside of home? Can they be different, or do they need to be consistent with the desired outcome of my personal character?

Looking before me I can see the slope, the gradient of the hill, as it ascends and is forged with a horizon adorned in quiet black, anonymous and symbolic of the impending doom — a storm is coming.

A tension escalates in my Polish-Australian battle zone of a house, as we prepare for the storm and brace ourselves against the plight and chaos and sinister activities engulfing our anxieties inside and outside our home.

Babcia's Story: My hands hurt. I can't hold my rosary beads properly. I see the humid grey clouds on the horizon to the northwest of the house. I can see a storm brewing, and its darkness cast over the street outside. My grandchildren don't pay me that much attention now that I'm here in Melbourne. I cook and clean all day, every day, on and on, and now these dry hands of mine hurt. I'm often tired, but I still make sure that I work hard and keep to my faith and do what's best for my grandchildren. They're young. I think they'll grow to appreciate what I do and have done for them later on in life — all that I have sacrificed coming here to Australia, leaving Poland and my home behind.

I tell the grandchildren often, "You know your *dziadziu* and I were married, oh, in … 1951. I was very slender in my wedding dress. So … we were married for fifty years. Maybe a bit longer … until he passed away. After your *dziadziu* died, his ghost would return to our house in Rudnik. He was as tenacious in death as he was in life. His father Dominik was the same. It went on like this for months. Almost every night *dziadziu*'s ghost would enter a room to interrupt me. A door would open, and he would stand somewhere. Maybe in front of a doorway. Or the living room. The kitchen. Sometimes just outside the house on the front porch, peering in at me from behind a window. He never said anything. At first his presence didn't trouble me. It never frightened me. Eventually I had enough of it though. What do you want? I would ask him. What do you keep coming back here for? Oh, you stubborn old man. You don't need or want anything from me. You're just stuck in your ways and are too silly to leave and move on. It's time to go, Kazimierz. Leave! Leave me be. Leave me in peace. I'm fine. I'll see you soon. Don't worry. Don't worry so much about us. Look at you. Still you have nothing to say. You know I'm right too, don't you? Just go. It's fine. Move on. Once I said all of this to him he did go. He left finally, stubbornly, sheepishly. But that was Kazimierz. Sentimental, nostalgic, stuck in his own obstinate and obsequious way." I conclude with a self-assured nod, gazing through the kitchen wall. Do they hear me? They don't hear me. They will have to listen one day though. They must remember.

So, it can be hard sometimes. Life is a struggle. And those brooding clouds I see out there make me even more anxious right now.

I try to help my grandchildren as much as possible, but they don't really listen.

"I don't complain that much. I just don't like that there are so many Asians in this country. The people here could learn to speak Polish, couldn't they? It's not like they speak any other languages. It's not civilised. Europeans are better. There's more to the world than just two centuries of English-speaking folk. Ah," I sigh.

> The Polish language has an unchanging, uncompromising endurance, like the (stubborn) people whom speak it. It has, after all, been sustaining the nation's sense of an identity for centuries (Williams 4).

I try to talk to the grandchildren about these things, but nothing ever sinks in. They usually wind up leaving the room or simply ignoring me. I try not to be too resentful or hurt by my grandchildren's (re)actions. A young teenaged Lou plasters both his hands over his ears in 'mock' deafness.

"I'm trying to teach you about God and the world," I tell him and Marta. "God is a very serious matter. There's nothing more important. Not friends or fun or drinking. Nothing else matters. You must only rely on God and family. Everyone else is a cheat in this world—they will only ever take advantage of you, including your 'friends'. So, you must learn to cheat too if you want to get ahead! By the way Marta, you need to be much thinner than that," pointing at her, "if you think you will fit into your wedding dress. When I got married to *dziadziu* I was this thin," indicating a small circle with the thumb and forefinger of both of my hands.

"I was, I was!" I still remember these things well.

Marta's eyes widen. She raises her eyebrows brusquely. It was as though the winds from the approaching storm that day suddenly changed direction, fixing her facial features in place like that for the next twenty years or more.

Marta would become erratic later on in life, I thought, as her relationship with me would eventually grow to become one of reciprocal understanding and a kind of skittish appreciation. She will realise everything I did for her in the end though.

I continue to fondle my rosary beads, gazing through the kitchen windows at the cloudy horizon. I remove my glasses and rub my sore eyes. "I never used to need my glasses. Oh God, what is happening to my eyesight?" I mutter, "Oh well. I'll just take them off when obliteration comes, I suppose. For that and when photos are being taken. I'm not going to look like some tarsier in any photographs I have or see or are seen of myself!" I shudder and shake my head at the thought.

I have to crane my neck a little to look out the kitchen window. "Fire is going to come down from those clouds and engulf this house. I am afraid, for there is little faith here. These children are lost. They lack respect. They don't respect me, and they don't respect God. Oh, God. What am I going to do when this fiery storm comes and engulfs this sinful house? These children are bound for Hell. We will all be in Hell soon enough though. Me also." I moan apprehensively.

I keep my expression stoic as I have these thoughts. A pious and calm exterior is the righteous way. "Yes," I say, commending myself with a curt nod. "That is the Polish way. That is a woman's way."

Tending to the garden I have nurtured and brought to life outside is my refuge, a sanctuary. I take the time to talk and sing to my flowers and plants (that's my secret), but soon all of this will matter no more once the biblical flames engulf this flimsy single-brick, red-tiled house—a home without character that could not possibly hold up against a storm of any kind, let alone a potentially apocalyptic one. "This is not a proper house like the kind built in Poland," I say, fingering the thin walls. But I keep the household clean and tidy nonetheless, for those are the virtues and principles that might save the burdened souls that lack fierce morality in the end.

Lightning flickers, though without any sound. The hallucinatory storm of a delirium and the 'error' of all of our ways is coming.

I believe that I continue to do what is best for them. Even if there is a vast generational gap, that does not mean that my value system no longer has merit!

Another slap of thunder. I sigh and catch my breath yet again, compose myself and ask Lou who is now sitting at the table in the living room beside the kitchen reading, "How did you go on your maths test at school today, Lou?"

Lou groans dejectedly. "I'm no good at maths. I'll never be good at maths. Maths is shit! I can't stand certain kinds of logic that can only ever have one correct answer."

Lou is restless as usual when I speak to him (about anything). He seems to be on the verge of a tantrum. He rocks back and forth in his seat with his right foot jittering—a nervous tic—with plenty more of them to come in his post-adolescent years. He gets up to race to his bedroom in the hopes of escaping the 'banal' conversation with me, knocking over the chair he'd been rocking on in the process. It topples to the thin hardwood floor with a resonating crack.

I mutter to myself.

The storm is here. It's so hard to say if these heartrending visions are real or not. Maybe they are real. What if they truly are? A tremor of fear hits me. I see the house swept up in flames as lightning strikes it, and charged currents travel through the house.

The following morning over breakfast, desiring to know what elements of my perceptions last night were tangible or intangible, I ask my grandchildren, "Did you see the lightning and chaos all around the house last night? There was so much flame and thunder outside the windows. I thought we would all ignite and explode." I try to tell them this jokingly, but I am clearly still a little nervous and on edge.

"No. No I did not," Marta responds coldly.

"Nope," Lou concurs, in between mouthfuls of over-sweetened cereal.

Marta and Lou turn to each other and chortle, semi-sarcastically. They dislike one another, but this form of amusement brings them closer together.

They clearly do not know, realise or care what I am talking about. They dismiss me, but I know. "You do not yet know God. You do not understand real pain and suffering," I tell them.

Marta leaves the house in an ignorant fluster, like on any other given day.

I step outside into the front yard, stoking the phantom embers that coat my garden from the night before.

Be the Tallest Poppy (2015)

My father, Mirek, Kazimierz's son, is a very complicated, charming and intelligent man, knowledgeable and competent about speaking to anyone, anywhere, about anything, for any duration of time, so long as it is in Polish. The tragedy seems to be that his charm and charisma don't necessarily translate to Australian or English-speaking audiences. I've witnessed him be the belle of the ball, captivate everyone at a dinner table and bring a whole lot of Poles out of their overly introspective, embittered self-indulgent slump and have a good time, because of him, and his ability to lift people up and make them happy.

He's a social butterfly in Polish contexts, and he enjoys it too. He always did very well in his oral examinations at school and university in Poland because that calm swagger and pleasant demeanour came naturally to him, and it is what was necessary to do well within these Polish intellectual landscapes. He could have been a poster child for the attitude and personality required to perform and take on the challenges that 'life' or the education system would throw at students in Poland. And he was, and would always be, relaxed in the process.

I often wonder why this perpetually aggravated conduct in Poles is even necessary. Is it armour? Perhaps Polish people are always preparing for the worst, getting ready for difficult times ahead, which, if history (and my grandmother) has/have shown anything, these situations have never really gone in their favour. Through my eyes Poles have often been at a disadvantage, and so they need people — individuals — who know how to conduct themselves calmly and 'perform' when all the odds are barred and jarring uncomfortably against them.

Yet here in Australia, Mirek, my dad, comes off as awkward, vague, flat and is never quite on the same page as others due to his misinterpretation of conversations, or because other people misunderstand him, his harsh, mafioso-esque Slavic accent. And his sense of humour, when speaking English, which is so dry, to the point of resembling dialogue in a Wes Anderson film, and is delivered so quietly, and with such poor timing that people listening are often left wondering if he has a screw loose or if these extended pauses are the result of the onset of Alzheimer's.

Though he does all of this quite happily, positively, because nothing really bothers him all that much. He doesn't care about the opinions of others or what they think of him, especially in Australia. His home and his heart are in Poland with his people and his (extended) family. Social interactions in Australia are but a veneer to pass the time for him, to cover up his true sentimentality, and to not cause a fuss or be hassled too much. Here in Australia he just wants to get along and get by. He has assimilated well with Australian culture. He is, after all, a traveller and relatively cosmopolitan. His trick, as he will sometimes say to me, is that "it's just life. It's not that serious or important when compared to the grand scheme of things in the cosmos". As enlightening as this would seem, it is really just a noble cover-up. Unlike most Poles, he doesn't want to disturb the grain or ingrained sensibilities of others. But also, he is his mother Maria's son, and though he is fiercely intelligent, he has been entrenched in or with those same views and attitudes about 'other' people: nationalism, cynicism, doubt and distrust. Though, unlike most Polish people, he doesn't wear these hostile feelings on his sleeve for others to see. He buries them deep down—a permanently dormant, slow and languid dolefulness, a defeatist approach to humanity, with an exterior that portrays and exudes a general sense of poised happiness and well-being.

> In the Polish context, those who had survived the Second World War came to Australia with the emotional baggage of war memories and experiences. They were later followed by those who managed to escape the Communist regime and its cultural suppression. (Williams 236)

My dad, mum and two older sisters left Poland in the early 1980s, partly due to Communism, but also because of a lack of opportunity there and my mother's desire to travel. They were living in Kraków prior to their departure, where dad had also been living and studying since 1972. dad had completed his studies at Jagiellonian University, the third oldest university in Europe, and travelled to New York where he would complete his PhD in Medicinal Physics at Bradford University.

Once he had successfully completed his doctoral dissertation my father landed a position in the physics department at Marston University in Melbourne, Australia. The family migrated to Australia in 1987. I was born in 1988. I was first-generation Australian. And that was basically that. We weren't especially well-off in those days. Mum and dad were still honing their English skills, and we were living in St Kilda, a bayside suburb ripe with drugs and prostitution at the time—not the bohemian, hip, cool-coffee-café, arty hipster-oriented neighbourhood it is today. I think there were some artists living in our apartment block. In fact, there was a fairly famous one. Umm … Sidney Nolan! Yes, that's the one! Quite true. The reason this excites me so much is because it literally took me several years to remember the fact! But there was not great wealth in the area, by any means, at the time.

What I don't mind discussing here is the dichotomy between dad's professional working and research experience in the United States and his personal sphere in Australia. This dichotomy was further accentuated when dad eventually left Marston University in the late 1990s and travelled and worked in various contract research projects in Japan, Germany and Singapore for a number of years.

In 2008, dad finally returned to Australia after acquiring a position at Martyr University in Melbourne, after many years of collaborative research and working experience in different countries and continents. This, I believe, gave him some wisdom (cynicism) and perspective. Martyr University, according to him, compared to all those different places and institutes he'd worked at over the years, had a few inherent problems/issues.

> Australians have avoided prolonged periods of self-questioning. The result: we are ill-equipped to think about social problems, tend to rely on rules rather than reason (and punish deviance from rules), and resort to piecemeal social tinkering rather than reform when problems are encountered. (Whitlock 19)

Dad had always openly believed that Australia, and Melbourne in particular, based on his and our experiences of living and working here, had a "village-like mentality". I never understood exactly what he meant by this when I was a kid, but I now realise he was referring to a number of things: the way the town is sprawled out (Australian cities are geographically enormous); everyone has a home, a front yard and a back yard, in the suburbs; moreover, everyone has a unique purpose in their professional or vocational sphere, and there isn't allowed to be very much deviation from that, even if it is in the best interests of the project or task at hand. He found this to be true here, and perhaps especially at Martyr University. I, in my less prolonged experience, have also found this to be true, and I focus in great length on this issue in particular in Folio Three on education.

By the time dad was working in the physics department at Martyr University, he was almost 60. He had had a great deal of experience, exposure and expertise, which he'd accumulated over the years. Nevertheless, it seemed as though nothing being done in that department made all that much sense to him: he often claimed they were doing the same research there that he'd been doing when he was working on his PhD in New York around twenty-five years earlier, yet they had so much funding and terrific resources. The problem was that everyone had their role and their purpose (just as they do in a village?). And the staff there were merely going through the motions of work and doing what a department should be doing; working, but without any real innovation. Not much was new. Not much was exciting. He was bored.

Dad would often remark that American, German and Japanese scientists were excited by new ideas and new possibilities. If you suggested something or had an unorthodox new theory they would become enthusiastic, while the working environment would become collaboratively and gregariously elated at the prospect of investigating something new or unique. Everyone would jump on board and would be inspired by the prospect of trying out something new. Something new — wasn't that the whole point after all? Something revolutionary — how else were scientists (or anyone in any profession) expected to break new ground? It wasn't going to happen by diligently following every rule, going through the motions and reinventing the wheel to the point of monotony and tedium — purposeful purposelessness.

Here in Australia, or at Martyr University, you were ostracised for suggesting anything new or experimental. $2 + 2 = 4$, so it could certainly never equal 5. There could only be mathematical certainty. Dad has always been fairly off-the-cuff, and quite improvisational, as I mentioned earlier. It had worked in his favour in the past. Though I suppose that can be quite frightening here in Australia. As Whitlock states, we are punished for deviating from the rules (19).

Raimond Gaita's autobiographical 1998 novel *Romulus, My Father* is a story of a Romanian family's migration to Australia, with a first-generation Australian son (Raimond) growing up and assimilating in Melbourne and country Victoria, whilst describing the life of his own father, Romulus, and his experiences and processes of acclimatisation in Australia. Gaita tells an anecdote in the novel in which Romulus is entertaining a group of Australian middle-aged hippies near Maryborough in Victoria one evening, and the hippies mistakenly take "him for a kindred spirit" (182):

> They responded to my father with the double-mindedness with which some Australians discovered multiculturalism. They responded to his charisma, admired his skills and his peasant know-how, but their tone of voice and the ease with which they touched him and comported themselves in his home betrayed the qualification that it was, after all, *peasant* know-how. (Gaita 182)

Although Romulus, in this story, works on a farm, in the field, in his workshop, with his hands, and is generally described as a more pastoral or practical man, the attitude that these hippies (whom you would imagine would certainly have a more left-wing view of or association with migrants in Australia) have towards Romulus is comparable to the way in which Australians relate to my father Mirek nowadays. The difference being that my father is a scientist—a physicist—a professor and a white-collar professional. Though that same sense of relatability and ease of respectful communication is also lost or strained with him in Australia, simply because my father cannot talk to Australian audiences in the same way that he speaks with Polish audiences. I'm not sure if it's for a lack of trying or a lack of concern on his part, but it's mutual and goes both ways. It resembles a kind of deep-seated dismissiveness of the 'other' — an attitude that one has without even being aware of, even if one is genuinely trying to adopt the (multicultural and sincerely open-armed) attitude he or she is *trying* to adopt. Australians are multicultural in theory, but not in reality or practicality, just as (European) migrants assimilate with Australia but also seem to have some reservations or limitations about doing so in reality. I don't think this back-and-forth will ever work — certainly not any time soon anyway.

As a first-generation Australian growing up quite 'Polish-ised' (and polarised), I find it both amusing and disappointing to witness these interactions (i.e., between my father and his Australian 'associates') because I feel as though I see and hear the entire undercurrent of communication (through body language, eye contact, syntax, and so forth) going on between both parties who are talking and listening to one another, and all of those things that aren't being said, that are being missed, lost or misinterpreted by the other. It is as if both parties are talking to one another through a glass window; and as clear as their speech may be, something is being missed on a fundamental (molecular, philosophical or spiritual) connective level, and most of what they're saying is being bounced back at them, or not received.

Skip ahead to February, 2015, and I am in the United States for the annual Southwest Popular/American Culture Association conference held in Albuquerque, New Mexico. I was speaking to an American there, in passing, about how I wasn't overly confident in delivering my presentation at the conference because I felt that what I would be discussing was too ambitious — I didn't want to come across as "arrogant".

"Why do you say that?" they asked me.

"Partly because of tall poppy syndrome" I replied.

"What's that?" they inquired, genuinely befuddled.

I did my best explaining to them that (over)confidence in your abilities or any kind of boastful arrogance, however minute, even if that confidence is only modestly valid or merited by one's genuine ability or success, isn't held in very high regard in places like

Australia, New Zealand or the United Kingdom. You need to keep your head down or it'll be chopped off. I didn't necessarily believe in my presentation as much as all that. It did actually have some major holes in it, but I tried to explain that "tall poppy syndrome" was part of the reason why I felt nervous about delivering it.

Their response was one of perplexity: "if you've done it, written it, have a good idea that you've come here because you want to share it, collaborate and talk with other people about it, then you need to do it! *Be* the tallest poppy!"

Be the tallest poppy? Wow, I've never heard *anyone* say that before. They were actually advocating for me to push my head up above the rest. "But don't you get it? The tallest poppy gets cut down," I responded in angst.

"Not here it doesn't," they concluded in that self-assured, ignorant and cocky way that only Americans know how to do, whilst paradoxically being oblivious to the fact that they're doing it. No wonder they piss the rest of the world off so much. There are so many layers to this kind of attitude that are both infuriating and enviable at the same time.

This American colleague did not understand the concept of tall poppy syndrome at all. All they took from it was that you always needed to 'go for it' — any chance or opportunity — and try, to have a go. Our conversation was so foreign to me, and what I was saying was so alien to them. America, the bull-headedly dubbed "land of opportunity" — why would they be troubled by a little bit of well-earned success and self-esteem or a sense of worth and significance, when after all, they seemed to see the bigger collaborative picture in all of it? In my opinion, this is what Australians lack. This is why my father felt that he was being ostracised, like a martyr, at Martyr University. This is why we seem to lose, or do not progress with new ideas, and a developing sense of an identity. We'd prefer to meander on in bland complacency and mediocrity rather than attempt something that could possibly be great. And not just great for oneself, but for many — it's a more universally inviting concept, and not explicitly an egotistical one, when one permits it to be. Instead, Australia "levels 'tall poppies' in the name of egalitarianism, and deploys a relentless scepticism against social and intellectual pretentiousness" (Hodge and Mishra 219).

I think part of this problem could be as a result of Australians being petrified of fully forming a new identity. We've always relied on derivative and vague notions of identity from publications such as *The Australian Way of Life*, edited by George Caiger, which "stressed stability and congratulated Australians on their lack of revolutionary heritage" (Whitlock 43) or texts such as Joseph Furphy's *Such is Life*, but no one actually knows, understands or seems to be able to explain what the 'Australian way' (of life) actually is:

> "the Australian way of life" was "something much deeper than words can depict ... it embodied some "inner principle" which, although difficult to define, was related to "the freedom, the security, the justice and the individualism of life in this sunburned, muscular continent". (Whitlock 45-46)

This undefinable principle is, and has been, particularly confusing for migrants, and probably still is confusing, even to people like my father who have lived and worked here, as permanent residents, for decades and yet still don't exactly know how to 'adapt'. Perhaps this is because the country itself doesn't know how, where or what exactly is going on in it either. A Brisbane journalist and commentator, Elizabeth Webb, in 1950 wrote,

> When it comes to The Australian Way of Life every foreigner I have met is completely at sea. To quote one—"What is this Way of Life? No one yet tells me what this is! Yet always they tell me I must adopt it ... perhaps I began to behave like you behave in pubs. I drink beer until I am stupid. Or learn to 'put in the boot' and bash the other fellow with a bottle ... Is this the way of life I must learn? Thank you. No. I stay a bloody Reffo!". (49)

Australia is a very new country—*not* for indigenous Australians, or in a geological sense, but rather for the white *non*-indigenous population that came about as a result of European discovery in the 17th and 18th centuries. And it's very hard to be romantic about it because so much of the 'romantic' imagery is subtle, or banal even. I am also largely referring to the literal landscape, the climate — it is grandiose, but not epic in the traditional literary romantic sense.

Alluding to the quote from Webb above, there is certainly something about the non-indigenous Australian mentality and way of life that seems unfinished or incomplete, like being interrupted whilst speaking halfway through a sentence and being told you're addressing the wrong topic.

How does a country like Australia make its mark when its non-indigenous population is relatively small and young? Moreover, so many national forms of 'identity' already seem to be covered by different countries around the globe. It's like being the new kid at school and trying to fit into some kind of social clique there; is Australia the hipster, the goth, the teacher's pet, the recluse, the art student, the jock or something else entirely? As always, I'm sure it's a little more complicated than that.

Though what else is there to form an identity with? "Most new nations go through the formality of inventing a national identity, but Australia has long supported a whole industry of image-makers to tell us what we are" (White 23). Also, attempts "to create a general "we-feeling" through sport, life-style symbols or indeed through the Bicentenary, have had no enduring success," according to Whitlock (139). Even a cursory examination of Australian cuisine, for instance, is problematic. What is it? Fish & Chips, BBQ's and VB, meat pies and sausage rolls, a pie floater, Milo, Tim Tams, ANZAC Biscuits, possibly some different version of lamingtons? These are all derivatives or mild variations of dishes from the UK or elsewhere.

I am reminded of that 'bit', that melancholy 'gag', from the 1998 film *The Truman Show*. As a child, Truman, the film's protagonist, is very curious about the (meta) outside world; one time he announces that he wants to be an explorer to his teacher and classmates. And the way the producer(s) of the show (within the movie) attempt to dissuade him from leaving the town (or set) of Seahaven is for his school teacher to tell him, as rolling down a map of the world, "Oh, you're too late. There's really nothing left to explore". This analogy can be applied to the non-indigenous Australian identity also; we're too late — there's really nothing left to 'be'. Or, to be more optimistic, we don't have anything we can 'be' or with which to construct an identity just yet. As I've said, maybe we're still too young as a nation. We've grappled in the past with assimilation and/or multiculturalism, but as in the case of the foreigner quoted by Webb, our identity is confused, hard to explain, difficult to grasp, an amalgamation of a variety of different things and different contexts and different backgrounds. We/I have the sentiment, but we don't have the wording quite figured out just yet. This kind of thing takes centuries. Maybe even just one more century for Australia? Let's touch base around 2100.

Though it may not even take that much longer for us. Australia just needs to find a way to respond to a few more crises perhaps (like the way we did in WWI)? Just a thought. And I don't necessarily mean, nor do I support the idea, that we always need (to be going to) a war. I am a pacifist. Maybe what I mean is that we need to respond to a few more of our *own* crises (like the state of COVID-19 within Australia), responding to them in our *own* way, whilst demonstrating (to ourselves) what our national identity is in the process. I only suggest 'crises' as a way in which the process of developing a national identity *can* be hastened. I do not believe 'crises' are the fundamental way in which a nation *should* develop.

On Australian history [Banjo Paterson] acknowledges that there has been no "hot blood spilt" — a commonly held prerequisite for worthwhile history — but Australians do have something to celebrate: "honest toil and valiant life" (Whitlock 208). Again, this view is poetically vague and ambiguous, and perhaps even *desperately* patriotic? Perhaps this is like most, if not all, national identities though?

In my opinion, we (Australians) are much too eager to demonstrate our value and character on an international scale (i.e., our need to be involved in every single war, and never really getting the credit, appreciation or international recognition for it, despite that to largely be the point, based on how I perceive our government bodies to talk, act, 'behave'). Or the way we tend to over-emphasise and accentuate our nasal accents when abroad. I do this too. We're like the younger needy brother amongst other countries, our older and more mature siblings, who know they can always count on us, the Boy Scout, because they can see, hear and smell our desperate need for approval in the eyes of others. They can use us if they wish, and we drop everything and obsequiously run to their aid. Then they discard and throw us away when no longer required, back to our lonely inescapable island-continent.

One relatively recent instance of a domestic crisis of our own was the "Sydney Siege" — the hostage crisis in Sydney in December of 2014. Though the crisis was disastrous, Australia in general, as a first-world nation, is fortunate enough not to have to deal with the kind of catastrophic crises and struggles that various other third-world nations, such as Haiti, Zambia and Syria cope with on a daily basis. Nevertheless, our media and government went into a frenzy over the "Sydney Siege". I'm dismayed and disheartened to say that I believe they saw it in an opportunistic light. *ABC News* stated that the "the leaders of Britain and the United States have been briefed about the Sydney siege situation" (16 December, 2014). British Prime Minister David Cameron had been quoted (on social media) as being deeply concerned. "The White House said President Barack Obama had discussed the siege with his top counter-terrorism advisor" — no direct quote cited from him though. Umm, so why were *they* informed? What was the need for that? Were they going to do anything about it? Because they didn't in my opinion. It was a senseless attempt for Australia to get itself on the 'scene' — to be seen and heard abroad. It was the younger brother saying "Hey! I'm still here. I'm important! I have important stuff going on *too*! Why won't you pay attention to *me*?" It's embarrassing, and I apologise for these provocative comments — they are personally biased opinions after all, and not meant to be expressed as fundamental facts by any means.

And I am not completely cynical about the situation. There were three deaths in total (*The Australian,* Box 2015). And any death that occurs in the name of extremism, religion or any kind of abstracted fictional or wicked supernatural delusion is awfully troubling to me.

Though I think Australia would have gained more respect abroad for handling it ourselves, in our own introverted way, if respect and identity is what we so desperately crave (and will need, in time). It seems counter-intuitive to get something you want by showing or demonstrating that you don't actually want it, but unfortunately that's how the (reverse) psychology of the world appears to work. You get what you want when you're not actively looking for it or pursuing it.

The PR situation in response to the crisis in December 2014 reminded me of someone who would use a brother's death to gain attention, sympathy or popularity at their high school. It's a terrible thought, and a horrible thing to say, but it's in the back of some of our minds, this type of self-centred and indulgent opportunism. We all have the capacity for this kind of thinking. Sometimes these thoughts come to us without us wanting them to come. I know I have, more than once, accidentally laughed in church, at a funeral or when someone has injured themselves. We can't help it. In this century we're wired for horrific (competitive?) thought. "We all feed on tragedy" (Tool—"Vicarious"). This is not just true for our country. I feel it is universal.

Whether or not we act on these thoughts though, that's the fundamental and characteristic difference. In my opinion, that's where honest self-acknowledgement and subsequent integrity (should) take over.

It takes time and patience to grow up. Australia, and we as human beings, should not get ahead of ourselves. An ingratiatingly unctuous or revolutionary stance is what can ironically get us into these professional, vocational/working or social predicaments, like that of my dad's at Martyr University, in the first place. Both growing up as an individual and growing up as a nation takes place within a tough social system and cycle—a kind of parabolic trend. And this is greatly relevant to my own developmental self too. And that is why I generally position my understanding of my developmental formative self alongside that of Australia's developing national identity—it is an intensely reflective and self-evaluative process. I too am in the process of struggling to find my own, and my 'national', identity, whilst living in a country that I believe is also struggling to uncover *its* identity.

The Polish identity, on the other hand, is rich, long and clear (in its sense of 'self', self-evidence and history). But even though I am a full-blooded Pole, I only partly identify as Polish because I have always primarily lived in Australia. Though I do understand that Poland has certainly had a lot of crises, which the Polish people have responded to themselves, independently. The borders of that land have been changed and altered many a time. Poland has even been geographically wiped off the European map in the past, in times of war. My grandfather Kazimierz drew on a lot of this history, tradition and language as well as his own personal experiences of World War II in the construction of his novel *Kwiat Dwóch Puszcz.*

Yet even amongst the most romantic Poles there are also those, as in any culture, who are simply dickheads. When nationalism turns xenophobic and racist, and when pride and self-indulgent overt isolationism or 'lonerism' turns into hubris and petty jealousy, we have to deal with dickheads also: those who speak and act on their thoughts as though they have merit and importance and significance, but actually do not.

The subsequent short pieces anecdotally relate some of this 'dickhead-ish' wickedness that is ingrained, perhaps, in the intensely vehement personality and character of some Polish people in my family, which can be common in our culture, I think, and often makes some of us very quick and prone to having a short fuse and being riled up because of it.

Maybe I have a short fuse? Possibly. An anxious one. Or maybe I just want to whinge about dickheads for a while ...

Daj Mi Pić, Proszę Cię (2016)

Hungover and bleary-eyed Kuba and I blunder through Kraków's *Rynek Główny* on a Saturday around mid to late morning. It's still cool outside, in the very early days of Spring, and my pungent alcoholic breath condenses in the air. I'm red and burning in the face though, my skin dry and lacking hydration.

"Ahh, I'm so parched!" I exclaim. "*Daj mi pić, proszę cię,*" I ask Kuba, yanking his water bottle from him before he can offer it to me. I take a swig. "Fucking gross! Why does everyone in Poland drink bloody carbonated water? It's disgusting! What, was *Auschwitz* not enough for you all? You need to infuse gas into your drinking water too? It's hardly refreshing!"

Kuba ignores me. Right then I have a philosophical flash of insight, turning to Kuba I say, "Actually, you know what I've just realised?"

"Hmm?" Kuba responds.

"I think people are like ... humans. You know what I mean?"

"What?" Kuba turns to look at my self-satisfied grin, holding back a chuckle, he asks, "Are you still drunk or something, Lou?"

"Ahh ... maybe. Probably."

We laugh idiotically and return to our sick and fumbling meditative state.

"That's not exactly what I meant to say. I don't know. I can't remember now. Doesn't matter. Fuck, some of those Polish chicks at that party last night were pretty hot though."

"Mmm," Kuba concurs.

"I wonder ... I got some of their numbers, you know?"

"Don't," Kuba stops me abruptly. "Trust me. They're not going to be interested in you unless you want to get married and have kids. And soon."

"What? That's still the rule is it then, even in this day and age? We're too young for that shit. Ah, whatever. You're probably right. They're not my type anyway. Polish gals. Too alabaster, porcelain, fake. I like the girl next door type," I explain to him, perhaps a little too defensively.

"Mmm," Kuba reiterates as he did prior.

"Fun. Times. Though." I proclaim slowly, just as I bump into someone standing nearby. "Ooh, sor-przepraszam," I say, correcting myself and glancing up at the gruff-looking brown and beige plaid Polish gentleman I had accidentally elbowed.

"Woah, what's going on over there?" We hesitate at the eastern outskirts of the *Rynek*, just near the entrance to *Ulica Sienna*. I point at the crowd gathering close to *Pomnik Adama Mickiewicza*, a statue of one of Poland's most famous literary writers, and ask Kuba, "Is it some kind of demonstration or something?"

"It's a protest or a rally of some sort," Kuba says.

"What for?" I ask.

Rainbow-coloured flags alongside rainbow-coloured flags with black and red crosses through them compete against one another in the frigid air above the heads of two parties — a gathering mob.

"Holy shit! Is this legit?" I ask Kuba, "anti-gay protestors trying to mess with a pro-homosexual rally? Is that what I'm seeing?"

Kuba nodded sorrowfully.

"Protests are not entirely uncommon for Poland. They happen all the time. They're just something to be cautious and wary of. But this … hmmm."

"Out-bloody-outrageous," I say, my eyes widening, cracking.

Both parties shouted and cursed at one another loudly and with equal vigour, sporting slogans, banners and antagonisms. The tension and hostility in the *Rynek* built steadily.

From the north several armoured trucks and vehicles approached the demonstration and parked. A police and riot squad had arrived, equipped with protective headgear, body armour, batons, tear gas, pepper spray, gas masks and riot shields. They promptly formed an ordered protective barrier between both parties.

The tension continued to escalate. Kuba and I took a few more steps back. I had never seen anything like this. I was in awe.

What we saw next would shock, confuse and amaze me for many years to come. A small and thin lone middle-aged Asian male tourist walked briskly through the bustle, between the two protesting mobs and police riot squad, in what seemed to be a simple and innocent attempt to pass through Kraków's *Rynek*. And from where I was standing *this* appeared to be the catalyst to send *all* of the protestors into chaos and anarchy. Both groups lunged into, on and seemingly through the Asian tourist, upon him and upon one another in a clambering battle fuelled by ignorant hate, fear, agitation and overly zealous and hubristic pride. Immediately tear gas canisters began to erupt in all directions and the crowd of onlookers, and tourists were forced to run as quickly as possible, away from the *Rynek* through the numerous cobbled streets and avenues leading away from the pandemonium.

Out of us two, Kuba was the first to react. "Oh, *kurwa!*" he exclaimed.

"Oh, shit!" I shrieked.

There was no time to stare or gasp—there was only a brief moment in which to register what was happening, and that was it. We had to run. We turned on our heels and legged it immediately down *Ulica Sienna*. Behind us, the tear gas quickly spread and engulfed the scene in smoke.

"What!" I yelled as we ran, "Is this seriously happening? Jesus Christ!" I couldn't help but muffle myself, as I scoffed and ran at the same time, losing my breath quickly. I could see out of the corner of my eye that Kuba was alarmed and determined to run as far away from the havoc and get to safety as quickly as possible. We ran for several hundred metres, which only seemed to last a few seconds, and eventually slowed, ultimately turning around again to see the general hubbub that had escalated disintegrate, as stragglers with tears streaming down their face from the residual gas gradually joined our position.

One young, gaunt and skin-headed male approached Kuba from the mass, coughing and spluttering. His chest fell over his knees as he asked Kuba, "*Daj mi pić, proszę cię.*"

Kuba handed the fellow his water bottle, which miraculously caused him to over-straighten his posture, so that he could scull it back. Carbonated water effervesced down the sides of his face. Did that fucked up water not bother him? He was sporting only a plain grey jumper, and panted from relief, squinting into the dull sunrays he himself glared into.

"*Dzieki. Jezu,*" the fellow said.

"You're welcome," Kuba replied politely in Polish.

I remained silent, still in shock, disbelief and puzzlement about the whole situation. How could he have *scull*ed that water?

At least the adrenaline had helped my hangover subside a little. I observed the interaction between Kuba and this random male. There seemed to be so much affection, loyalty and an unspoken, understated understanding between the two of them. It's *solidarność*, I thought.

I think what it really came down to was that solidarity, that empathy. I knew that Kuba was a pacifist and that he resisted violence of any kind — a humanist of sorts — and that on any other day if Kuba and this male had encountered one another it may have even ended in violence. After all, this random 'boy' was a pretty rough looking neo-Nazi type, most likely a soccer hooligan or petty thug of some kind. But there seemed to be a deep-seated connection between him and Kuba when it came to pain and oppression. Sure, he was probably an asshole, and most likely part of that anti-gay mob by the look of him, but he needed water, and Kuba gave it to him, without hesitation — with love. Furthermore, the guy showed Kuba gratitude and was well-mannered. In that moment they were nakedly human with one another. I was astonished.

I wondered if this kind of interaction could happen in Australia? Does our/my Australian history and understanding of one another as human beings at home run extensively and deeply enough? Does it penetrate to the innermost depths, and surge to the surface of our character when called upon, or is it much more superficial? I really don't know too much about that kind of thing. I haven't seen or experienced a similar instance like this in Australia — hateful far-right aggression that is. I know they happen, the 2005 Cronulla riots and whatnot, but are they rarer, tempered?

Now, in retrospect, what I remember seeing of that riot in Kraków's *Rynek Główny* in 2007 was two parties, discordant in their hate for one another, seemingly united by their even more overbearing and dominating, racist and xenophobic hate of foreigners and those who are physically and culturally different to them. Everything else seemed to go out the window as we fled away from the centre of town as well as our own sense of centred selves. Of course, it may have been a coincidence or terribly bad timing, and horrible luck for the poor Asian tourist, but from where I was standing, in that moment, racist hatred and intolerance was the straw that broke the figurative camel's back and exploded the escalating tension on that particular cold morning in Kraków, from heated protest to full on rioting.

I don't know what happened to the tourist or what happened in that town square for the remainder of the day, as I didn't have time to stay and fully observe what was happening—I only had time to scoff and run. And obviously my memory has forced the event to seem surreal, and perhaps distorted it since then, due to personal introspection and reflection over time, but that does not mean that this isn't what happened. Or that this isn't what some Polish people can be like. Underpinning whatever moral or ethical convictions they have is a strict loyalty to one another in the face of, or as a defence mechanism to, foreigners and outsiders, and especially other races.

Even I have been refused service, charged extra or called a "fucking English" by young naïve Polish lads walking by me in their city streets, for my seemingly inadequate Polish-speaking abilities, despite the fact that (a) my Polish is actually quite advanced, (b) Polish is an incredibly difficult language to learn and master anyway, (c) I'm Australian, not English, (d) Polish youngsters often seem to obtusely stress to foreigners the need for them to learn Polish, despite not really accepting anything that is below an 80 per cent standard, and (e) who the fuck wants or needs to learn Polish anyway? It's not a language or economy that is 'on the rise' as far as I can tell. Their attitude, to me, conveys an ideology in which they both want you to try *and* to fail. It can be impossible to please or satisfy them and their paradoxical expectations.

I think that this kind of attitude could be getting a little better each year as a new and much more open-minded generation of youngsters grow up and mature, but that doesn't mean that the old and the ignorant folk or rabble won't take the opportunity to undermine tourists (even at a tourist information centre!), criticising them for their inability to converse in Polish, or hanging up signs in their tavern windows stating their refusal to "serve the English". This can be common, or it can be rare, depending on what you're looking for, which season it is you're travelling in Poland, and which area or which city you are in. But that agitation often seems to be there, scratching away, under the skin, at a perverse sense of disillusioned power and pride.

But of course, I no longer live in Poland, and I have never lived in Poland for more than a year! And this all happened years ago now. As I've mentioned, my time in Poland has been fragmented, and I see myself more as a sentimental Australian these days. So, when I am in Poland I always view it through the lens of that general Australian light-heartedness. So perhaps some of these seemingly coarse and crude attitudes of Polish people are misinterpreted by me when I am in Poland. Who knows? Maybe these scenes that I see are actually manifestations of Polish people's 'tough love', or their mysterious version of affection towards others? Maybe they don't hold grudges or resentment at all, and in fact all this seeming hostility is actually just deep-seated passion and exuberance that will always be misinterpreted by the Western world. Communication barriers are a curious thing in this regard. I should try to keep an open mind about the differences between *mannerisms* and actual *intentions*.

Nevertheless, to my sentimental but cynical eyes, the way I experience 'some' of the (Polish) people I personally know are, well, simply in the form of (contradictory or oxymoronic) dickheads.

Dickheads (2015)

Dickheads possess a kind of sickness, more than likely a defence mechanism of some sort, in their mannerisms. I know a few (Polish) people like this that follow the same course, the same patterns of thought, projected: being vindictive, condescending and patronising all at once, for whatever reason (to take out their own shit on others)? Perhaps it is due to their own sense of worthlessness or reassessing and reaffirming a misplaced sense of worth in an anxious cover-up and in consistent passive-aggressive attacks on others.

Eerily, the word 'dickhead' autocorrects itself as 'sickness' on my smart phone, and so I could consider (through an unnatural or fortuitous sway) the idea of dickheads as being like a virus, but a virus I want to have in my life also? There's a price I pay for befriending a dickhead, or having one close to me, in my life: frustration; betrayal; self-loathing; the inheritance and adoption of cruelty and vindictiveness. What I gain is amusement and a kind of armour and protection (from others and against my own insecurities or sometimes with them). Whether I am myself cold and harsh enough to take that cruelty with me and into me is my decision and a reason as to why I might just have a place for these dickheads in my life and in my heart.

My (Polish) uncle is a dickhead, the epitome of one: a sponge, soaking up 'worth' from others, a sleaze, a closed-minded oblivious and overbearing know-it-all, seemingly and senselessly 'knowing it all' to compensate for the dull monotony of his daily life, an entrapment due to a stricken lack of skill and resources, and too late now to do anything else about it (but be a dickhead). He is reminiscent of the kind of dickhead Robert De Niro plays in Michael Caton-Jones' 1993 film *This Boy's Life*, based on the memoirs of writer and literature professor Tobias Wolff. De Niro's character in the film, Dwight, is always looking, watching and observing, out of the corner of his eye, ready to pounce, demean and criticise his family around him, at any given opportunity, to prove his own sense of self-worth and status, regardless of how trivial the criticism or observation may be. "I know a thing or two about a thing or two," he often remarks.

Similarly, I walk into a room and turn on a light. My Polish uncle follows behind me and turns it off right away, even if it's dark and verging on night time. I make myself a cup of green tea (a pretty standard ritual I've formed over the years), and my uncle conveniently appears to ask me "why"?

"Because it's healthy," I respond.

"Wcale nie jest takie zdrowe" (translation: "*Actually*, it *really* isn't that healthy") he tells me, loudly, obnoxiously and emphatically.

Once he told me not to wear sunscreen during a summer in Poland because "it's not possible to get sunburnt in Europe!"

"Jesus Christ," I think to myself. Where are these contradictions coming from? What is this insistent falseness based on? Next thing you know he'll be telling me the sky is not blue. And now that I think about it, I'm sure he could find some deluded basis and reasoning for that (mis)information also. Some American documentary he saw on television that had been poorly and inadequately over-dubbed in Polish from English had told him it was so, which he would then reference and cite, to everyone else's annoyance, even though he is quite nationalistic and anti-American to begin with, so why would he take this documentary's word for it? These persistent contradictions within incessant contradictions spiral down into a lethargic and disdainful oblivion.

I have a friend who is a dickhead too, and he seems to be taking it out on me. I am rarely utilised as a scapegoat, so I have a hard time coping with this. Though if I were to concentrate on the positives I would see that this friend (this replicated, statuesque, synchronised, geared-up, cogged and clogged formation of a skeletal structure – the ideal blueprint of the mapped-out dickhead) is a natural dickhead. It was his doing, his vision, his choice-making, his process and circumstance that brought him to a state in which he could tee up a partner, a sponge from which he could source strained and residual energy easily, without any real harm, but more like a leech or a grub who roams from one end of the house to the other blankly staring with eyes glazed over, or staring out at the corners, at one wall and then the other and then the other, a little like Huxley's precious John whose "feet [in the end] turned towards the right; north, north-east, east, south-east, south, south-west, south-south-west; then paused, and, after a few seconds, turned as unhurriedly back towards the left. South-south-west, south, south-east, east ..." (213).

But I too have made the choice to have this dickhead (and other dickheads just like him) in my life. Today and tomorrow even it may hurt, but in time his worthless worth will show and shine mildly to me.

I smile a little. I should be patient. I am, after all, an 'unusual' combination of 'all sorts,' I've been told: a social butterfly and a recluse all at once. I should unlock a little of that good ol' unconditional love-stuff, take pity and feel sorry for the poor fellow, who chose this life(style) out of a possible fear and an inadequate ability to realistically and practically cope with the world outside of his cornered wall-space. He doesn't have much. He certainly doesn't have freedom. He has laziness and leisure, which he'll defend to the pitiable death, but he doesn't hold any real swagger or sway by any other measurable standards.

And so what? He takes it out on me sometimes, as well as on others, of course. I could choose to laugh or to cry about it, be sensitive or prudent, or reacquaint myself with that crudely seasoned dickhead spice that contributes to my own palatable freedom, and not his.

So, I acquaint myself with some dickheads. It's not a real problem for me. In my skewed upbringing, I was counter-intuitively taught to trust no one, that there is no such thing as (real) friends. I suppose a response to that was to recognise a dickhead from within my family (i.e., my uncle—one of the two personifications in the construction of this short segment on dickheads) and locate those characteristics amongst 'friends' (and the unnamed 'friend' in this piece would be the second example).

In 2015, I was speaking to my sister-in-law in Poland, whom I only met around Christmas time, and trying to explain the Australian mentality to her—things like tall poppy syndrome and the like. She was very inquisitive, and asked very incisive and open-ended questions that I didn't particularly want to respond to because (a) they required me to respond in immense detail (in Polish) which can be quite taxing for me to engage with already, and requires a lot of effort and energy, plus I was jet-lagged, and (b) because I really got the sense that she wasn't asking because she wanted to purely get an idea of Australia from me. Rather, she was asking to get a general 'read' on me, which I didn't appreciate. Was she being a dickhead? She followed up what I was saying with a response about the Polish mentality. What she said was something I, more or less, already knew, but it was interesting to hear it being vocalised and acknowledged. I would have thought Polish people would've been too proud, secretive or ignorant of their own cultural faults to openly admit their flaws. But my sister-in-law is the same age as me, and part of a newer generation, so she is a little more aware and open-minded about the formative characteristics of Polish people, and their ingrained Polish-isms and/or negative tendencies. She told me that there's a saying in Poland ... something along the lines of "I wish you all the very best, but really, in my mind, I wish you all the very worst" (this phrase rolls off the tongue more pleasingly in Polish). It's a false and heavily embittered mentality. One cannot be allowed to get ahead. Much like our Australian tall poppy syndrome, but without the more safely harnessed optimism that goes with TPS, in Australia at least, it seems.

Was my sister-in-law being a dickhead? Maybe. Maybe not. But I'm merely aware of it (bad news and bad vibes) when it's/they're coming. I'm on edge in anticipation of the dickhead at my door. If gay men have a 'Gaydar' then I have a 'Dickhead-dar' or a 'Dickhead-ar'. Much like George Costanza of Seinfeld has a "sense" for "cheapness" in "The Reverse Peephole" episode (aired January 15, 1998). At least if I can identify what a dickhead is then I won't be misled, manipulated or led astray if I befriend one.

I have, not all the time, but every now and then, sought out a dickhead; I identify one on a superficial level (i.e., exhibiting many of the characteristics of my uncle) and let myself get to know them. They become my friend. And I'll put up with their shitty attitude and behaviour if I need to. The strategy and the idea has been that timeworn, traditional, militant approach of keeping your friends close and your enemies closer. These dickheads have been a reminder of what I don't want in my life and what I don't want to succumb to. It's training and conditioning – building up a tolerance for what I cannot and will not want to tolerate within myself. Plus, there are some positives that come with having a dickhead in your corner: amusement and as a potential defence from other dickheads.

In any case, I've grown less and less drawn to dickheads as time has gone on. There is less and less of a need for them now as I've unlearned a lot of what I 'learned' from my grandmother and broader European ancestry during my formative years. My intuition is more 'normalised' and fine-tuned, and I know now that I'm a much better judge of character than I was before. I also know that friends do in fact exist in reality. This didn't take me that long to learn, really. I have a fairly active and social lifestyle, like my father when he is in Poland, and I suppose that would make me more cosmopolitan, or at least more egalitarian with regards to the kind of camaraderie and mateship that exists within Australia.

That doesn't mean I'm not careful. My familial contexts, upbringing and relationships have taught me to be more than careful with people. Today my friends always tell me that I approach every new social situation in a cautious and calculating manner. I don't notice this too much personally – I probably just phase into autopilot (self-mode). All of this, within the context of my family, makes for a slightly more difficult social path, but at least it has been an intensely reflexive and introspective path, which has helped me to gain a deeper understanding and appreciation of myself in familial relations.

THESIS TWO

My Family and other Fictions: Fictocriticism Creates New Subjectivities

This second thesis explores the antecedents of fictocriticism, its literary context in autobiography, postmodernism and metafiction, and how some texts such as Danielewski's *House of Leaves* (2000) serve as excellent illustrations of ways in which fictocriticism could still be an innovative genre. This section explores the perspectives of different generational, cultural and diasporic migrant writers who utilise their protagonists or antagonists to disconnect from any sense of family or prefer to meander recklessly, in texts like *Loaded* (1995) by Christos Tsiolkas and *The River Ophelia* (1995) by Justine Ettler. Interestingly, both Tsiolkas and Ettler's 'could' be considered thinly veiled autobiographies, and a rebellious 'guise' for their authors. Hence, the name of the opening creative piece in this section is "Guise" (2014). Other Australian novels like *Romulus, My Father* by Raimond Gaita referenced here are memoirs that are entirely (auto)biographical, and attempt to understand their migrant heritage, history and cultural background. This thesis also considers autoethnographical texts by Katarzyna Kwapisz Williams and fictocritical writing by Danuta Raine, both of whom have Polish familial roots. The Polish short stories "A Cynical Tale" (1958) by Michał Choromański and "The Cruel Sunday" (1981) by Tad Sobolewski are explored too, primarily within the context of the Australian landscape, to provide even more of a cultural context or diaspora in the history of some Polish/Australian (migrant) writing. Most of these texts belong to the baby boomer generation or Generation X (1946–1981). After extensive research, the almost inescapable conclusion is that there have been no creative studies/theses written fictocritically or autobiographically by a contemporary millennial Polish-Australian creative to date. Even though that, of course, is a tiny demographic, this study does stray into relatively new and unexplored territory in the fictocritical, autobiographical and creative sense. Of course, it is worth mentioning Ania Walwicz's 2016 PhD thesis, "horse: a psychodramatic enactment of a fairytale", as she classifies herself as a first-generation Polish-Australian, though Walwicz is in fact a baby boomer.

This section, especially, examines the experimental voices in first- or second-generation Eastern European-Australian fictocritical/autobiographical writers. And from that perspective, the focus of the creative folio in Section II is on family and diaspora.

In writing the first piece in this folio, "Guise", the creative self was influenced by a theme of detachment, similar to that which is presented in Joyce Carol Oates' *Zombie* (1995) and Danielewski's metafictional postmodern masterpiece *House of Leaves* (2000). This idea is not so much related to fictocriticism as fictocriticism is anything but detached, though "Guise" as a stand-alone experimental piece, functions as a transitional work between the first section on journeys and this second section. "Journeys" is about the self wandering and meandering outwardly, whereas this section is about engaging with family on an intensely personal level. "Guise" is like a musical interlude, severing any sense of attachment between the two sections, as each section is a distinctly different fictocritical experiment.

The serial killer in Oates' *Zombie* experiences a fundamental disconnect, unknowingly, in his lack of empathy towards other people (Oates 8). He kills his victims in his desperate sense of longing to turn them into brain-dead docile sex slaves (Oates 169-70). In Danielewski's *House of Leaves* the character Johnny Truant feels a connection to the 'pet':

> I sure as hell wasn't thinking about Johnnie's tits or her lips or the positions, the absurd positions, we could have made together. I was thinking only about the Pekinese, its safety, its future. The Pekinese and me: a contract of concern. (267)

Comparably, "Guise" alludes to having a greater connection to a pet, the creative self's girlfriend's pet (dog), which is something quite alien to the remainder of this experiment. Yet "Guise" functions as a transposition from the indulgent meandering of "Journeys" to a folio that is entirely about an invented semi-autobiographical protagonist-persona called Lou and his relationship with his family. "Guise" serves as a way of disconnecting from people, others, family, relationships and various human ties, and sharing a state of 'otherness' and an unperturbed unwound disengagement from people, with an animal. Thus, this section begins in a way that attempts to create an unfeeling disconnect from the section's main theme, family.

Segments of Thesis One, as well as the Introduction of this book, alluded to metafiction's antecedence in fictocriticism. The reference to *House of Leaves* serves as a similar disconnect or detachment from fictocriticism, for *House of Leaves* is extremely metafictive, but it could also be considered exceptionally fictocritical. So much so, that it demonstrates ways in which fictocriticism could be innovated on in the future. Some ambitiously multi-faceted and collage-like features of *House of Leaves* include its multiple genres, including horror, non-fiction and journalism, documentary, romance, satire and postmodernism. It has varying fonts, almost endless formatting styles and multiple narrators tell elements of the same story through different perspectives. *House of Leaves* could be considered pseudo-encyclopaedic in this respect. These kinds of examples are practically infinite in *House of Leaves* as most of its pages are structurally or thematically different to the ones that precede them. *House of Leaves* is endlessly ironic in its postmodernity: certain footnotes have footnotes (137), some pages only have one or two words on them (224), there are sections in different coloured fonts and crossings outs (114-15), and sometimes the use of excessive purposeless detail or extrapolation is used in confoundingly writerly and unreadable ways, whilst the word 'house' is always written in blue:

> Sonny Beauregard conservatively estimates the special effects in The Navidson Record would cost a minimum of six and a half million dollars. Taking into account the total received for the Guggenheim Fellowship, the NEA Grant, everyone's credit limit on Visa, Mastercard, Amex etc., etc., not to mention savings and equity, Navidson comes up five and a half million dollars short. Beauregard again: "Considering the cost of special effects these days, it is inconceivable how Navidson could have created his house.". (Danielewski 148)

In "Haunted House—An Interview with Mark Z. Danielewski" (2003) he states,

> I didn't write *House of Leaves* on a word processor. In fact, I wrote out the entire thing in pencil! And what's most ironic, I'm still convinced that it's a great deal easier to write something out by hand than on a computer. You hear a lot of people talking about how computers make writing so much easier because they offer the writer so many choices, whereas in fact pencil and paper allow you a much greater freedom. You can do anything in pencil! (McCaffery and Gregory 117)

Danielewski's comment here is relevant to fictocriticism and *this* book for two reasons: firstly, because it demonstrates the necessary innovations experimental authors can take in order to truly create a performance within the construction and form of a written text; and secondly, that software and technology cannot always be the medium writers, or anyone, rely on when creating some works of art. Danielewski's statement suggests that, in his case, technology was a hindrance and a limitation in the creation of his art. Technology was something to be wary and sceptical of, and that it cannot always be relied on. In Evgeny Morozov's book *The Net Delusion: How Not to Liberate the World* (2011) Morozov asks the reader, "Technology is the answer, but what was the question?" (306). Similarly, through Danielewski's experimental construction and form he poses the same rhetorical line of questioning—a line of questioning that will be continued in Thesis Four. *House of Leaves* "is a text about a text about a text; about obsession with text" (Fathallah 195). Its patchwork, mosaic-like construction and varying undertones can be considered a satire on academia (Woodcock 2).

 This is Derridean and deconstructionist, and as mentioned by fictocritical scholars like Paul Dawson in the previous thesis, fictocriticism is, after all, "a mode of critical writing which echoes the work of Barthes and Derrida" (141), whilst Noel King claims that Barthes, along with Derrida, "[blur] the distinction between literature and literary-critical commentary" (270). Thus, *House of Leaves* is Derridean, and thus, also fictocritical. As with Lynne Woodcock's (2) idea in "The Comic Gothic" (2009) that *House of Leaves* satirises academia, which is further validated by Judith May

Fathallah (195) in *Fanfiction and the Author: How Fanfic Changes Popular Cultural Texts* (2017), and in this book's assertion, this satire is most prevalent in examples of the text's footnotes having footnotes (Danielewski 137), so too is Derrida's "entire philosophical movement … devoted to an opposition towards opposition" (Brennan 290). Furthermore, that unconventional, non-conformist and strikingly non-academic "opposition" is even further endorsed in the very first pioneering fictocritical article in Australia, "On Ficto-Criticism" (1991) by Stephen Muecke and Noel King, which goes as far as to disregard any need for accurate, if any, referencing at the end of the article, claiming "No need for bio details — they're in the text, but also we want readers to be a little uncertain about our reality" (14).

This tapestry of deconstruction, satire, non-conformism, opposition, and even incorrect, sarcastic or non-existent referencing demonstrates the raw potential of fictocriticism. Though, being such a rule-breaker, it is understandable why fictocriticism's impact in the academy has been sporadic. Still, perhaps it is time for a change. With new technologies, software and the Internet being so readily available, perhaps universities should focus less on correct referencing, and more on the proper flow of writing and ideas, even if that uninhibited writerly flow goes against the bureaucratic tide.

House of Leaves inspired works like "Guise" and "A Literary Mitosis", because of its playful experimentation with, and 'freeing up' of, language, form, content, style, thematic obscurity and abstraction, formatting and multiple-genre use. Though unfortunately "Guise" and "A Literary Mitosis" are not nearly as adventurous or radical in their form. Danielewski plays with presentation in his novel a lot though, in his inclusion of illustrations (570-71), photographs (572), images of paintings (660), models (661), film stills (662), diagrams (421) and scrapbooking (Danielewski 582-83).

Similarly, Ross Watkins and Nigel Krauth's 2016 paper "Radicalising the Scholarly Paper: New Forms for the Traditional Journal Article" looks for ways to overhaul the construction and form of the academic journal, whilst also trying to make it engaging and unorthodox, and they are very successful in doing so. One of their most effective techniques is their inclusion of coffee ring stains throughout the paper to represent a juxtaposition of email communications and informal thoughts between the two writers interjected and reverberated into the text of the paper (Watkins and Krauth 1, 2, 7, 8, 17). These visual and communicative inclusions resonate with Hazel Smith's excellent explanation and definition of fictocriticism in her "Erotics of Gossip" article previously cited.

Watkins and Krauth are metafictive too, exploring the idea of the coffee rings in the past tense, as though the paper being read has not yet been constructed, challenging the reader's preconceptions about thinking they are reading a paper in the present (17). They self-satisfactorily recognise the effectiveness of this technique too, in their final coffee ring-framed comment: "Ross, I love the coffee cups. Let's do them" (Watkins and Krauth 19). "Radicalising the Scholarly Paper" has similarities to Danielewski's metafictive and illustrative inclusions in *House of Leaves*, though the former is less extreme than the latter. Still, it is difficult to recall any other fictocritical paper 'performing' like this. Perhaps fictocriticism, and the academic journal in the broader sense, is already in an act of evolution, or perhaps it always was and still continues to be. Though Watkins and Krauth address their process of construction in the most present of tenses (10). "A Literary Mitosis", "Guise" and "'Til Morning Came" do this also. As do many of the pieces in the creative folios of this text. The creative self includes examples/figures of scrapbooking in Folio Three, for instance.

Danielewski includes abstracted and heavily parenthesised ways of writing, similar to those adopted in the creative folios, and like other fictocritical writers such as Linda Marie Walker do, in her piece "Speed Kills, Comma", which was mentioned in Thesis One: "so perfect(ly grotesque) and all at the age of" (Danielewski 267). This jarring way of writing is again best explained in the creative self's fictocritical piece "A Literary Mitosis (On Form)" — its point is to disconnect from conventional ways of writing or formatting cohesive sentences in order to make the reader work and feel uncomfortable when engaging with the text.

It is probable that there are very few creative/theoretical works written fictocritically or autobiographically by a 'millennial' first-generation Polish-Australian male living in the contemporary world. However, there do exist creative, semi-autobiographical works by Polish migrants to Australia or the United States from the baby boomer generation. Two examples investigated in this thesis are Michał Choromański's "A Cynical Tale" from *Ten Contemporary Polish Stories* (1958) and Tad Sobolewski's "The Cruel Sunday" in *Ethnic Australia* (1981). These stories provide a distinct cultural context for Polish migrant writers in Australia or the United States. However, they belong to an older generation, in which English was not their first spoken language. This exploration cannot strictly relate to them in too specific or direct a manner as the author of this study is a millennial born in Australia, unlike the other immigrant writers. In fact, the creative folio in this section expresses quite a different generational rejection of more traditional Polish value systems. Hence, why the persona of Lou was dubbed in *"Kwiat Dwóch Puszcz"*, "Storm", *"Be* the Tallest Poppy", *"Daj Mi Pić, Proszę Cię"* and "Dickheads" as a thinly veiled semblance in which to bellow a series of intensely biased but contemporary opinions about Polish culture. Many of the comments the characters in Choromański's story make are indicative of the kind of Polish bitterness, hysteria and single-mindedness the characters in this section's folio make: "ideas have no age" (67); "It's true, there's an evil spirit in the house … The Devil!" (105); "God pity me," Eva moaned" (Choromański 108).

According to Lou in Folio Two on family, these emotions are part of the national cultural image, and possibly even more so in his family image: however, there may exist a tradition of exaggeration and hyperbole in the works of Polish writers such as Choromański and Sobolewski, as this exaggeration and hyperbole is certainly a trait in this section's folio. These intense Polish personality traits are heavily criticised by Lou throughout his narrative. The kind of dialogue and monologues that Choromański and Sobolewski implement are also adopted in Lou's narrative: however, their frantic and grumbling nature, such as those taken up by the grandmother in the "Storm" story, are accentuated, exaggerated or entirely fictitious, to create a discord between more traditional Polish narratives and the creative self's contemporary and unorthodox rebellious ones. In "Storm" the grandmother clutches at her rosary beads, staring out the kitchen window, whilst anticipating some kind of delusional apocalypse. Coincidentally, a similar kitchen scene occurs in "A Cynical Tale" (Choromański 105). This coincidence was of course, not intentional.

In Sobolewski's "The Cruel Sunday" the disgruntled Polish peasant and protagonist Kubiak tells the Australian owner of a farming property:

> [Poles] have a long and heroic history ... May I tell you, Mr. Stanley, that my country was the real refuge for several countries for all those persecuted like the Jews, the Unitarians, and many others? Our country was the first to have a ministry of education in Europe; from the 16th century our democracy went so far that we had even the kings elected? Our soldiers fought on all fronts in defence of freedom and democracy, and our General Kosciuszko as well as many other Poles helped the Americans gain independence? Did you know that? (172-73)

Kubiak is portrayed by Sobolewski as "happy" (173) at smugly seeming to have "unruffled" Mr. Stanley, and then "bitter" (173) at the unexpected lack of respect he receives from him. *All* of the pieces in Folio Two (*"Kwiat Dwóch Puszcz"*, "Storm", *"Be* the Tallest Poppy", *"Daj Mi Pić, Proszę Cię"* and "Dickheads") with the exception of "Guise" (a transitional work) aim to shed a different, more unflattering light on traditional Polish values from a young Polish-Australian male's perspective. A perspective on a culture that, as conveyed by the left-wing Lou, is overly smug, arrogantly proud, single-minded, extremely religious, lacks change, self-reflection or compromise, is resentful, stubborn, cynical, defeatist, annoying, deliriously hysterical, oppressed yet all the while proud.

These pieces are semi-autobiographical, though told through the persona of 'Lou' in order to create an exaggerated (fictitious) and jarring cultural tension. They have a unique perspective, different to any other Polish literature that preceded them. They highlight the perspective and bias on why Polish attitudes are too conservative, outdated and one-sided. This second thesis proposes that perhaps the reason there are no first-generation Polish-

Australian works like this thus far is because these millennial creatives have potentially become too disinterested in and disenchanted with Polish culture. They want to separate themselves from it as much as possible. In Katarzyna Kwapisz Williams, a Generation X academic's "Life Narratives, Common Language and Diverse Ways of Belonging" (2015), she claims to be ambivalent about her Polish background ... she does not have a Polish accent but feels inescapably ingrained (or displaced/lacking in a personal identity) in Polish culture in Australia (1):

> I felt ambivalent about the question of my own national belonging even though I did not consider the possibility of renouncing it ... I found myself in an impossible situation: I did not want to be perceived as an outsider, but I also rejected being an insider — a migrant at a new home — and questioned the possibility of being a bit of both. (Williams 1-2)

Danuta Raine's short fictocritical piece "Essaying the Self" comes very close to this section's background, context and intentions overall. Raine writes fictocritically about who she thinks she is as a Polish-Australian: "I have been a hyphenated Polish-Australian all my life, and I still don't have any answers. Sometimes I belong, and sometimes I don't" (4). "When I come to myself, to my work with family stories, I sift through these voices. These fragments and unknowings, the elements of both memory and history" (Raine 1).

Coincidentally, the word "meandering" is used twice in her text (Raine 4, 5), which suggests a way of thinking similar to both Lou and/or the anonymous travelling creative self/narrator in Folio One. Raine's essay largely talks about the benefits of fictocriticism when discussing and exploring oneself, one's origins, family, heritage, and so forth. Raine claims to be a great supporter of fictocriticism in this sense, even more so than of any type of expressive creative non-fiction (Raine 2). Her essay focuses more on the self-serving nature of fictocriticism rather than its broader academic benefits. Of course, her contention can be interpreted as fictocriticism being a mode of writing that can benefit anyone, though her essay *is* solely focused on herself.

Fictocriticism is a useful tool for diaspora. This section's creative work explores what appears to be a distinct and frustrated severing from Polish culture, and the inclusion of research and anecdotal accounts aim to make the works more fictocritical. To reiterate, the main differences between the Polish-Australian creative folio work and previous types of explorations in this vein (Jacobowitz 2004; Weeda-Zuidersma's 2007; O'Reilly 2008; Naismith 2009; Raine 2009; Villalobos 2012; Williams 2012) are that the author of this text was born in Australia. He is not a post-war or post-communist migrant; the protagonist 'Lou' expresses a feeling of being more of an Australian visiting Poland, not a Pole migrating to Australia to live. The pieces in Folio Two are distinctly more fictocritical in that they are, at last, double-voiced (Kerr 93). For now, they are modern, contemporary, and demonstrate a unique alternate perspective of a (millennial) Polish-Australian narrative/diaspora. These 'Lou' stories could be viewed as a beginning to the next epoch in the Polish-Australian or Australian-Polish migrant story, told fictocritically. The stories, the theme of being lost within familial relations and, to a larger extent, being somewhat displaced or unfounded in the broader cultural context of Australia or international ancestries, tend to align themselves with other migrant stories too, like the Greek-Australian novel *Loaded* by Christos Tsiolkas.

Loaded tells the story of Ari, an unemployed, arguably pansexual, Greek vagabond-like 19-year-old male living in Melbourne. Ari is caught up in a whirlwind of drugs, dancing, music, partying and anonymous sex in an attempt to escape his traditional Greek heritage, and to live a life of self-destructive passion. Ari's spiralling descent into narcotic oblivion is well-captured in the book and is vividly realised in the 1998 film version of *Loaded* entitled *Head On*, adapted by Ana Kokkinos. In the movie's final scene Ari is seen dancing/spiralling in circles at the break of dawn, alone in Port Melbourne, after a chaotic night of drug-taking, sex and clubbing, to the point of self-loathing, palpable deterioration, and a sense of outward universal rejection. Ari though, sees this as a form of strength and resilience. He is seen actively not standing still, non-committal, whilst spiralling out of control/in control, paradoxically in place whilst moving and not confirming or looking to anyone or anything else, except his own 'story', gratification, perversion, gradual deterioration and disintegration. He is perpetually pushing the parameters of his own (dis)comfort. His monologue at the end of the film closes with the following lines: "I'm gonna live my life. I'm not gonna make a difference. I'm not gonna change a thing. No one's gonna remember me when I'm dead. I'm a sailor and a whore, and I will be until the end of the world" (*Head On* 1998).

This is similar to the sentiment in "Guise": the "connection to the pet, to the animal, that has never been felt for the girl." In the novel version of Ari's story (which does not contain the visual spiralling Zorba-like dancing that the film incorporates in its closing seconds), Tsiolkas describes this sequence or the culminating thought process of Ari's own brand of sentimental cynicism in the following terms:

> I'm not Australian, I'm not Greek, I'm not anything. I'm not an Australian, not a wog, not anything … What I am is a runner. Running away from a thousand and one things that people say you have to be or should want to be … I didn't choose to be a runner … I am here, living my life. I'm not going to fall in love, I'm not going to change a thing, no one will remember me when I'm dead. My epitaph; he slept, he ate, he fucked, he pissed, he shat. He ran to escape history. That's his story. (Tsiolkas 149-51)

In terms of the notion of cultural 'identity' Tsiolkas seems to be referring to the absolute disintegration and disappearance of 'self' and identity. In *this* folio, however, the protagonist/creative self does not wish to disappear. He prefers to roam and meander, as shown in "Journeys", but certainly to still exist. Though a similar, albeit more optimistic (or 'spiritually' inclined) depiction of this kind of 'loner/renegade' to 'nowhere/nothing' attitude or headspace is extrapolated in some of the creative self's sequences, as demonstrated in Folio One.

In *Loaded* Ari is a citizen of nowhere. Perhaps his loss or lack of identity (or apathy regarding legacy) has to do with his forced Greek heritage within the context of growing up in a cosmopolitan and multicultural city like Melbourne. The fact that his friends and family are Greek in the novel is not relevant—especially not to him.

He thinks about nothing. He exists for the sake of existence. He asks for no more and no less. In fact, he asks for nothing at all.

Loaded could be construed to be about a reckless quest for an identity, or it could be the opposite; it is a quest ... a pursuit of sheer recklessness for the sake of recklessness. It is recklessness to the point of negligence and an abandonment of the 'self'. It portrays a negligence and abandonment of the self because there is no grounded (familial) 'self' that exists within the context of this character or this story. It is more of a derangement of the senses for their or its own sake (Rimbaud 9).

Justine Ettler's novel *The River Ophelia* is comparable to *Loaded*. Both texts were published in 1995 and are at least semi-autobiographical. *The River Ophelia* is also based in Melbourne, though this is not explicitly stated in the novel — merely implied (and inferred). The protagonist Justine, largely based on Ettler's own character and experiences, is portrayed as a tormented 'self', sexually obsessed, violent, negligent, desperate, self-destructive and self-deprecating. Ettler's character is not so much in a state of flux or complicated by her familial relationships — this is never a strong focus in the novel, though she conveys a powerful and brutally honest feminine perspective. *The River Ophelia*, and its associated themes, harks back to similar feminist novels written in the earlier twentieth century.

In Virginia Woolf's *Orlando* (1928), for instance, Orlando pursues a 'higher' or 'Captain' self that has no specific gender (505). Perhaps that is why characters like Ari and Justine destroy their bodies and their physical impermanent selves. Still, the psychology of Ari in *Loaded* and Justine in *The River Ophelia* are more relatable to the protagonist Lou in the creative folios of this book. Yet neither Ari nor Justine are millennials. Therefore, Lou conveys the voice of a new (millennial) generation based on a series of characters or 'voices' modelled on the author: a Polish-Australian male born in Melbourne in 1988.

This concept helps to inform the discussion, in this book, on fictocriticism which, after all, stems from a deep accumulation of feminist philosophy (Prosser 1; Brook 106).

One of the potential troubles of this text's adoption of fictocriticism is in the masculinising of a form of writing that women had claimed as their own. Though this is a rather limiting standpoint. Should any literary form truly be exclusory to or dominant of one particular gender, especially if that form is not strictly gender-specific? A focus of this book is meant to be on the innovation of the form of fictocriticism. Besides, in this century fictocriticism has become increasingly inclusive of writers of all genders, in the emergence of many more male creative fictocritical texts (Muecke 2008; Morgan 2012; Villalobos 2014; Watkins 2014; Cholewa 2014). The initial wave of fictocriticism in the 1990s did appear to be predominantly feminine, as marked by Sedgwick's *Tendencies*, Drusilla Modjeska's *The Orchard* and, of course, the seminal anthology *The Space Between*. Though now fictocriticism has become much more of a free-for-all. Hancox and Muller, in "Excursions into New Territory: Fictocriticism And Undergraduate Writing" (2011), say that prior to the 1990s experimental French and Canadian feminist writing prompted fictocriticism's emergence (147).

Other theorists assert that it was pre-1990 (male) writers such as Barthes, Derrida and DeLillo that primarily influenced the inception of fictocriticism (Muecke and King 13; Dawson 141; Simon 98). Fictocriticism, then, seems to have arrived in the contemporary sphere by two different channels: one Canadian, the other Australian, or this all happened simultaneously in different academic contexts. It is difficult to say. Either way, this study argues that distinct fictocritical texts can also be found much earlier, in pre-1990 works by Sigmund Freud's *Dora: An Analysis of a Case of Hysteria* (1905) and Oliver Sacks' *The Man Who Mistook His Wife for a Hat* (1985). These are both male, medical/clinical case study forms of storytelling and are told through overtly personalised ways. An excerpt of Freud's *Dora* was located in the University of Tasmania's *School of English, Journalism & European Languages* Unit Reader on "Fictocriticism" (First Semester, 2002). *Dora* could be considered fictocritical in that it includes the first-person perspective of Freud's own personal experience with the patient he examines, and the patient's family. In Freud's own words *Dora* is fundamentally a "case history" (54). *Dora* has an opinionated 'voice' and it certainly includes a story, and there is technique, criticism and assessment included throughout. Excerpt(s) that could be helpful in shedding light on *Dora*'s fictocritical elements are as follows: "Am I now going on to assert that in every instance in which there are periodical attacks of aphonia we are to diagnose the existence of a loved person who is at times away from the patient? Nothing could be further from my intention" (72). This is distinctly fictocritical in that the intentions of the book/paper/study, expressed in the postscript, mirror fictocritical ideology:

> … in publishing this paper, incomplete though it is, I had two objects in view. In the first place, I wished to supplement my book on the interpretation of dreams by showing how an art, which would otherwise be useless, can be turned to account for the discovery of the hidden and repressed parts of mental life…In the second place, I wished to stimulate interest in a whole group phenomena of which science is still in complete ignorance today because they can only be brought to light by the use of this particular method. (Freud 155)

Again, an example of 'fictocriticism' like this further demonstrates the way in which the writing style bridges discourses and creates 'new'/different approaches to writing in the way 'straight' informal theory or 'normal' fiction simply cannot do. It merges both the personal and the professional 'voice' into a single text.

Sacks' *The Man Who Mistook His Wife for a Hat* is perhaps even more wonderfully fictocritical in this way. Each "Part" of the book relates to specific neurological case studies involving "Losses", such as in "The Lost Mariner", "Excesses", such as in "Yes, Father-Sister", "Transports", such as in "The Dog Beneath the Skin", or "The World of the Simple", such as in "The Autist Artist", that affect the mind and human behaviour. Each case study is framed as a story that is described as "extraordinary and strange beyond belief" (248), but then contains a more clinical and medical "*Postscript*" (Sacks 137, 144, 156). This contrast and reverberation between story and assessment, narrative and explanation, anecdote and evidence, indeed creative non-*fiction* and *criticism*, is outstandingly fictocritical.

Raimond Gaita's novel *Romulus, My Father* is introduced as a reference in *"Be* the Tallest Poppy" (2015) because of the many similarities it shares with the creative self's narrative and narrator. *Romulus, My Father* is a story of a Romanian family's migration to Australia, with a first-generation Australian son (Raimond) growing up in Melbourne and country Victoria, whilst describing the life of his own father, Romulus, and his experiences and processes of assimilation in Australia. *Romulus, My Father* is autobiographical, largely Melbourne-based and about a first-generation Australian-Romanian male and his relationship with his father. Although perhaps there are elements of the novel that may be fictocritical, in the philosophies Raimond expresses (124, 181), in the descriptions of real places (19-22, 162), in the overall postcolonial and migratory nature of the text, and the factual accuracy and transcripts of letters (Gaita 77-81), it is still nevertheless mainly an entertaining dramatic story — one that falls into the category of creative non-fiction, biography, a subjective "memoir" and "personal tribute to Romulus" (Walker 5).

Raimond Gaita was also born in 1946, and is, thus, a baby boomer, so not necessarily a contemporary of the author of this book, as contemporaries have been difficult to find. But the novel is mentioned because of its concentrated focus on family, migration, religion (3, 168-69), diaspora and displacement (10-11), the Australian landscape (23) and its empathetic emphasis on the protagonist's father (Gaita 2-7, 165). This focus on the father and conservative or traditional familial and cultural values is largely rejected by the protagonists in the novels *Loaded* and *The River Ophelia*, whereas Raimond tries to understand them from a philosophical point of view (Gaita 188). The protagonist Lou, in Folio Two, attempts to both reject *and* understand them, as seen in the following two extracts:

> In the lengthy saga of adversity in the Polish people's history, their difficulties can sometimes accumulate, stagnating in their hearts and invading and exacerbating cynicism, negativity and pessimism in their sense of ethics and morality. Perhaps then there exists this sort of dichotomy between religious, spiritual and familial values and virtues that is obstinate, one-sided but loyal at least. This dichotomy creates a struggle within a sense

of self that is incessantly present and seems impossible to surmount. On the one hand, there is emotional romanticism, and on the other, dark doubt, cynicism and pain, which all teach to unite these two things within their national character and personality, in an ongoing struggle, prevalent and present within the self, that is cyclical and difficult to overcome. This is what I have come to believe, and that is how I perceive things within my family anyway. (*"Kwiat Dwóch Puszcz"*)

I think what it really came down to was that solidarity, that empathy. I knew that Kuba was a pacifist and that he resisted violence of any kind—a humanist of sorts—and that on any other day if Kuba and this male had encountered one another it may have even ended in violence. After all, this random 'boy' was a pretty rough looking neo-Nazi type, most likely a soccer hooligan or petty thug of some kind. But there seemed to be a deep-seated connection between him and Kuba when it came to pain and oppression. Sure, he was probably an asshole, and most likely part of that anti-gay mob by the look of him, but he needed water, and Kuba gave it to him, without hesitation—with love. Furthermore, the guy showed Kuba gratitude and was well-mannered. In that moment they were nakedly human with one another. I was astonished. (*"Daj Mi Pić, Proszę Cię"*)

In the above extracts Lou makes more earnest attempts to be sensible and open-minded with the culture he (often) rejects. His narrative and thinking here is quite fictocritical. Though at other times a tortured and frustrated voice emerges, evidencing an undercurrent of a more severe and severed double-voicedness marked by suppressed rage and jaded bitterness:

Once mass had ended and the congregation clawed their way out through the wooden arched cathedral doors even more furiously than they had entered it, I could not bite my tongue any longer, and in amongst the compressed crowd I began rambling to Kuba again, in English this time though. "So why did the priest say Christmas had to equate to and *become* Jesus (Christ)? Christmas does not *equal* Jesus! That is not a mathematical dogmatic statement I have heard or come across before being here in this church! ... He was frothing over that shit." (*"Kwiat Dwóch Puszcz"*)

Most importantly though, and the reason several autobiographical, metafictive or creative non-fiction texts have been discussed in this section, is because of fictocriticism's autobiographical and metafictive qualities. For instance, the following section from *"Kwiat Dwóch Puszcz"* is an autobiographical account of the creative self, via the persona of 'Lou', asking his father about the autobiographical book *his* father Kazimierz (Lou's grandfather) wrote in real life. Not only is this autobiographical and metafictive, it also demonstrates, quite literally, a portrayal of a book within a book:

> "… What's [grandpa's] book about?" I asked.
> "It's about a group of children who share some experiences during WWII in the forest behind *dziadziu*'s house in Rudnik. The children reunite several years later as adults, to recall and reflect on what had happened to them in that place at that time."
> "So, you think *dziadziu* may have written it about some of his *own* experiences during the war? It could have autobiographical elements?"
> "Yes, I think that's a possibility. It's quite detailed and romantic in this respect."

All the stories in Folio Two overlap and are interrelated as they are all based on members of Lou's Polish family. Another account of a story within a story comes in the form of the grandmother's anecdote in "Storm":

> After your *dziadziu* died, his ghost would return to our house in Rudnik. He was as tenacious in death as he was in life. His father Dominik was the same. It went on like this for months. Almost every night *dziadziu*'s ghost would enter a room to interrupt me. A door would open, and he would stand somewhere. Maybe in front of a doorway. Or the living room. The kitchen. Sometimes just outside the house on the front porch, peering in at me from behind a window. He never said anything. At first his presence didn't trouble me. It never frightened me. Eventually I had enough of it though. What do you want? I would ask him. What do you keep coming back here for? Oh, you stubborn old man.

This grandmother character is talking about the same *dziadziu* that appears in "*Kwiat Dwóch Puszcz*". Though it is never clearly mentioned in these stories, they are in fact all about the same members of the same family - Lou's family - or the creative self's family, in fictionalised/fictocritical form. As for Lou's double-voicedness, this is most clearly seen in his blending of fact and creative non-fiction in Mirek's memoir-like biography in "*Be the Tallest Poppy*", which also features the real autobiographical experiences of the author whilst "in the United States in February, 2015, for the annual Southwest Popular/American Culture Association conference held in Albuquerque, New Mexico". Furthermore, the real novel *Kwiat Dwóch Puszcz*, which the second piece in Folio Two is named after, or as a 'Gaitian' tribute to family, is shown here (Fig. 1):

Fig. 1. Kwiat Dwóch Puszcz

The story with this same name in Folio Two, however, includes accurate descriptions of *Kościół Najświętszego Serca Pana Jezusa* (Church of the Holiest Heart of Jesus Christ) in Rzeszów, Poland. The piece "*Be* the Tallest Poppy" features inclusions from the Australian media and references to the 2014 "Sydney Siege". "*Daj Mi Pić, Proszę Cię*" describes a real riot that took place Kraków in the Summer of 2007, as well as first-person descriptions of the town centre at that time: "We hesitate at the eastern outskirts of the

Rynek, just near the entrance to *Ulica Sienna*. I point at the crowd gathering close to *Pomnik Adama Mickiewicza*, a statue of one of Poland's most famous literary writers."

The many layers, mixed genres and thematic variations of fictocriticism can make one think of and echo Flavell's sentiment, in that it "is indeed a slippery and contradictory category" (126).

Fictocriticism can also have emanated from a basis in metafiction, as this study contends. In Linda Hutcheon's *Narcissistic Narrative: The Metafictional Paradox* (1980) and Patricia Waugh's *Metafiction: The Theory and Practice of Self-Conscious Fiction* (1984) — two earlier but still very useful critical texts that work well in tandem when investigating elements of metafiction, and which provide these elements with adequate labels and descriptions — show early inklings and potentialities from where the idea of looking at fictocriticism critically may (coincidentally) have begun to appear can be seen. Waugh, for instance, describes metafictional novels and the illusory nature to which they subscribe as "the laying bare of that illusion ... simultaneously to create a fiction and to make a statement about the creation of that fiction ... a formal tension which breaks down the distinctions between 'creation' and 'criticism' and merges them into the concepts of 'interpretation' and 'deconstruction'" (6). Waugh would most likely be a hesitant fan of Danielewski, for instance, as she has an obvious and thorough vested interest in metafiction, claiming

> ... nearly all contemporary experimental writing displays *some* explicitly metafictional strategies. Any text that draws the reader's attention to its process of construction by frustrating his or her conventional expectations of meaning and closure problematizes ... narrative codes. (22)

Waugh also says that "[writing] itself rather than consciousness becomes the main object of attention" (24). Waugh is wary of this paradigm, though she is personally non-committal to any mode, or she is merely rigidly clinical in her research approach. Yet she appears to express much double-sidedness or duality about it, as though she does not realise how metafictive she herself sounds when discussing metafiction. Then again, this polarising side effect may simply be a repercussion of dealing with any metafictive territories. This explorative study is often caught up in that same dilemma. Waugh is cagey about metafiction's pervasive nature and universality in "all contemporary experimental writing" (22), whilst contending that it may in fact be everywhere and lacks control at times. At one point she states that "human beings need to have their choices narrowed for significant action to take place" (52). Waugh also comments on the unsatisfying nature of metafiction, or how metafiction undermines the reader's potential satisfaction when reading a text (22, 82). This frustration and dissatisfaction is understandable as that is what the creative folios in this exploration often do too. Still, this exasperated sentiment does not bode well for the evolution of fictocriticism overall as fictocriticism is, in many ways, untameable and still quite chameleonic: in "Does Anybody Know What Happened to 'Fictocriticism'?: Toward a Fractal Genealogy of Australian Fictocriticism" (2002), Scott Brook asserts that fictocriticism is "a marker of the partially unspeakable nature of [a] 'genre that isn't one' from both derogatory and celebratory perspectives" (107), and he is right in saying so. This formal tension can be seen in the literal form and format of this book's fictocritical writing, all fictocritical writing and all metafictive writing.

It is possible, however, to historically go even further back in this fictocritical and metafictive discussion. According to Hutcheon the reader of 'fictional' texts "cannot avoid [perhaps like the writer] this call to action for he is caught in the paradoxical position of being forced by the text to acknowledge the fictionality of the world he too is creating" (30). Equally, forms of creative or story-like autobiography are not necessarily non-fiction when considering writers like Hemingway, Proust, Joyce, Woolf, Stein and Kerouac. As Elizabeth Bowen states:

> No creative person is purely intellectual—one may, however, distinguish the intellectual novelist, building upon a framework of ideas, from the aesthetic-intuitive, working mainly on memories and impressions. In one case, the seat of integrity is the brain; in the other, feeling. For the former are involved in constant speculation, cognizance of his own day, scrutiny of science and thought, consideration of history, measurement of experience. For such a mind, the arrival at any position is important, and abandonment of it constitutes a crisis. (62)

On the other hand, Bowen states that the intuitive, emotional, feeling-oriented artist/writer

> is often the child of a background, the product of an intensive environment—racial, local or social. What he creates takes character from his own strongly personal and often also inherited sense of life. His loyalties are involuntary and inborn—not, like the intellectuals of his choice or seeking—and are all the more powerful for that. (62)

In *Mirror Talk: Genres of Crisis in Contemporary Autobiography* (1999), Susanna Egan discusses the integrity and duality/dichotomy of writing that is in any way autobiographical and the tension and conflicts that may arise as a result or consequence of this kind of narcissistic 'realism': "What artist and autobiographer are concerned about is this inside-out process, the life behind the face, the integrity that must stand clear of trespass, the invisible self that is impossible to know" (61). Now the reader is an "accomplice … [a] travelling companion … coparticipant and cosufferer" (Hutcheon 30) through the text. The onus and responsibility for engagement is on them too. And achieving this mutual and largely collaborative relationship with the reader is partly the creative self's intention in *this* book. The creative self does this by occasionally addressing the reader in this book's more metafictional writings, often using the pronoun "you" or the noun "reader" throughout the narrative. Yet more often than not, particularly with "you", this occurs because the point of view in the narrative switches to second person, as with "Tiers and Towers" and "Rushing the Order and Fate", and, thus, the creative self is often addressing himself more so than his reader, but this can certainly be left open to interpretation and is contextual. It is the analytical self's contention that the reader can also be more engaged with the creative self's writings in Folio Two on family, whereby having an unreliable, exaggerated, somewhat immature and heavily biased persona like 'Lou', the less abstract narrative and stories here make it easier and rather tempting for the reader to disagree and wince at many of Lou's misguided musings and behavioural traits.

This collaborative reader-writer strategy again ties back to Danielewski's *House of Leaves*. Similarly, Hutcheon refers to André Gide's 1925 novel *Les Faux-monnayeurs* (*The Counterfeiters*) where there are two parts, "the plot events and the author's effort to make a story of them", in an attempt "to free the novel form from the constrictions of nineteenth-century realism" (26), forcing the reader to have to work harder in engaging with the text. Hutcheon also argues that *La Macchina Mondiale* (1965), the second novel by Paolo Volponi, "finds its mimetic justification in its relating of the act of reading to that of writing — two creative processes thematised and allegorised within the structure and content of the novel itself" (105-06). Hutcheon's examples help to further the "story within a story" (Herman, Jahn and Ryan 134) argument and framed-narrative method discussed in Thesis One: the 'book within the book' or 'box within the box' concept, in other words. Though *House of Leaves* takes this concept even further. *House of Leaves* has so many narrators interwoven within multiple perspectives that any true narrator or "Captain self, the Key self" (Woolf 396-97) is not locatable.

In this text, Folio One on journeys includes different forms, also, and is written mainly from the point of view of an anonymous narrator (the creative self) all throughout the poetry in "The Island", the short narratives and prose-poetry of "Daze", "The Mission Man" and "Apple", and the dream sequence(s) in "Tiers and Towers". Alternatively, Folio Two contains the perspective of a migrant Polish grandmother in Australia in "Storm" and very thinly veiled autobiography or memoir(s) told through the persona of Lou in the pieces "*Kwiat Dwóch Puszcz*", "*Be the Tallest Poppy*", "*Daj Mi Pić, Proszę Cię*" and "Dickheads". These are comparable to Oates' biopic or slice of life about Jeffrey Dahmer in *Zombie*, and the thinly veiled autobiographies of Christos Tsiolkas' Ari in *Loaded*, the character of Justine in Justine Ettler's *The River Ophelia*, or the diasporic craft of Gaita's memoir/autobiographical novel *Romulus, My Father*. This folio maintains the perspective of the creative self, though in an autobiographical and fictocritical folio about educational experiences, whilst the final section about technology is written in a fragmentary multi-genre first-person form. These experimental variations in form, perspective, storytelling and creative non-fiction reveal a range of different changing perspectives and narrators, all of which are 'controlled' by the creative self: "For it is probable that when people talk aloud, the selves (of which there may be more than two thousand) are conscious of disseverment, and are trying to communicate, but when communication is established they fall silent" (Woolf 402).

Thus, a creative goal of the folios in this study is to establish (or flirt with the idea of) whether there exists an amalgamated self or is there but one?

> For [Orlando] had a great variety of selves to call upon, far more than we have been able to find room for, since a biography is considered complete if it merely accounts for six or seven selves, whereas a person may well have as many thousand. (Woolf 295)

House of Leaves was foundational in helping to develop this multiple-voiced approach. In the past, fictocriticism has often been told from the first-person storytelling perspective (Kerr and Nettelbeck 1998; Naismith 2009; Morgan 2012). Perhaps fictocriticism needs to remain in the first-person as it is already quite "inherently freeform" (Gibbs 310) as a form of writing. Moreover, if fictocriticism has too much multimodal scope and variety, there is a risk it may falter beneath its own incomprehensibilities. There is an argument that fictocriticism should, of course, have *some* limitations placed on it, though if fictocriticism is descended from metafiction and postmodernism as this book contends, and *House of Leaves* reaches new expression of the postmodern and metafictive forms, then surely fictocriticism must be equally innovative. Of course, therein lies a contradiction: What explicit limitations *should* fictocriticism have, if any? Or what innovations should it be allowed, if any?

The next thesis, Thesis Three, offers further thoughts on the elastic mutability that fictocriticism has become.

SECTION III

FOLIO THREE: Education

(Scrapped) Book: A 'Professional' Educational(?) Overview (2016)

The process of being educated, for me and my sense of evolving identity was/is something like going for a walk in the woods, if the woods were laid out on a rendered painting of some sort. Education is a process that involves taking a number of different paths, 'tiers and towers', and stepping through a variety of diverse dimensions in the progression of the journey of 'schooling'. Some of these dimensions make a lot of practical sense to me and have a strong relevance to the way in which I see and relate to the real world, similar to the way in which photographic art 'looks' real. In photographic art trees actually look like trees, for instance. When I am in the dimension of photographic art the sunlight above seeps through the foliage and lights up my path and the forest floor with magnificent clarity. The woodland birds and animals sing their songs and roam, stalk or trot through the vegetation in a weaning reality that makes sense to me. Depending on the time of day, I can sometimes smell the dirt and the scent of the damp grass and fallen leaves scattered around me. Sometimes my educational and experiential projections are similarly clear, or they may become even more engaging and stimulating. At other times, however, the entire fabric of my education is warped, washed or filtered through a different light. My filtered lens and perspective can be lush and green. It can be warm and orange. Or sometimes there exists a metallic tint of grey and blue that distorts my periphery, steel-like but still structured, modern, accessible and steerable somehow.

Occasionally I can see others with me on the path that I am on. And often there are many figures close beside me. Yet other times these identities are far away, silhouetted and shrouded by my own sense of confusion, mystification or intrigue. These silhouetted figures are my peers, fellow students, mentors and teachers. The settings and landscapes and everything within them represent particular subject areas. The warped filters of perception embody my level of interest or subject areas that suit my personality.

Many of these dimensions largely depend on my level of engagement, calmness or the agitation I am putting into my strides through the painted forest 'dimension' I am in at that point in time. Some are dark, frightening and nonsensical, like surrealist art. Others are simply ridiculous, frustrating and tangential to the point of dismal incomprehensibility, like something you would see in a stereotypical, laboured, digitally animated Disney movie. Occasionally, the setting I am in resonates with brutal other-worldliness and the fear or inability to escape the superficial enthusiasm and a Disneyland or Dismaland-like nightmare that comes to the forefront of my experience, but has no place there at all. Or rather I just have no place there at all.

The latter of these experiences, The Disney or 'Dismal' paradigm, is the perspective thrust upon me and that I feel I was compelled to engage with in many of the educational processes that I reflect upon here. Or the perspective and filter that rendered me useless and unable to walk through my metaphorical woods comfortably, or with any coordination and visual context, primarily in my early tertiary experiences at Martyr University in Australia.

In some of the following recollections certain parallels are drawn to the way in which Drusilla Modjeska describes her processes or experiences of education as a teenager at a boarding school in Wessex, England, in her 1994 novel *The Orchard*. In the final section of her novel, "The Winterbourne", Modjeska describes the contrasting and contradictory views she, her peers, her friends' families and "the perversities of British wisdom" (166) may have, or did have, in relation to the strict or uniform way in which young women were taught in the late 1950s and early 1960s in England. In *The Orchard* Modjeska recalls her educational experiences at Carn with "the fumes of memory" as a "terrain of a past that, all these years later, still has its bite" (165):

> But it was what I meant when I spoke of the price that was paid for this education and its privilege, the enforcing of a conformity that regarded itself as individual, yet had no place for the idiosyncratic, the quirky, the reclusive, the dissident or wayward feminine. (176)

I feel Martyr University treated me in a similar fashion, even though its faculty's intentions were to create the total ideological opposite of this in their students at the time. Though perhaps time is needed to refine the rules and principles Martyr University was ostensibly implementing in the education department at the end of the first decade of this century, as would most likely be the case for any institution(s). But without these foundational rules, for me there was only chaos at the heart of it all.

When I first completed my Bachelor of Arts and Education (Secondary) in 2010, I was fairly torn about a number of things. There was nothing I wanted to do more than to trail blaze through to my Honours degree in English and propel myself into an academic career within the expressive fields of English, literature and creative writing. But I was held in place, in my mind, for a moment, as there was still something I wanted to say about the education department at Martyr. I resented the hypocrisy, and the lack of reality or interconnectivity between some of the tertiary, state and private sectors of education and teaching. I wanted to explore a portion of that hypocrisy, but with an anecdotal touch. That is what these stories are about.

My fundamental dilemma with teaching or education within certain tertiary contexts is that it seems as though (secondary school) teachers (an area of education that is obviously quite close to me personally) are out of touch in an ever-swirling and changing curriculum, that is evolving or *devolving*, adapting or not adapting, and the result is potential confusion, masked in layers of jargon and abstract and obtuse terminology, invented to subsequently mask that jargon which preceded it. I'm sure the same can be said of other professions, such as stockbrokers, politicians, high-level business management types, or any venture that, for whatever reason, needs to smugly mask its true intentions and goals in order to thrive. But why would teachers need to do this? Teaching is not an evil venture, nor is it well paid. In fact, it is probably one of the most important, noble and altruistic professional avenues in existence. Yet it seems that the teachers who taught me in the education department at Martyr got themselves too swept up by the lingo and the abstract philosophies, and so they were lost in their own festering mire-like headspace. Though perhaps it could also just be a simple matter of those who can't do, teach, and those who can't teach, teach teachers.

The funny thing is that it doesn't seem to take long at all for one to lose one's intuitive instincts as a teacher. As soon as a teacher leaves the classroom and enters the academy or a tertiary institution as an educator, within that context, there seems to be an unrealistic or impractical degree of (purposefully purposeless) obsequious enthusiasm, optimism or positive energy that may work for children, but does not translate or carry over to hung-over nineteen- or twenty-something year-old university students. Too much time is spent (by education lecturers) on the politics of developing a new overly jargonised language that is 'made' or invented to 'equip' new graduate teachers with the 'realities' of the classroom. The irony is that all it really does is further alienate them from the students *they* will wind up 'teaching'. It also alienates themselves from the emerging hung-over graduate teacher. Hands-on (qualitative) practicality is needed: no bullshit or fancy language or 'meta' language.

One of my university lecturers in education used to tell us students that when we wrote the first draft for any of our assignments we should then scrap said draft and completely re-write it, so that the second time around we had a clearer and richer perspective. I can understand the importance of *revising* drafts, and I can see where he was coming from in saying what he did, but *no!* What student has the time or motivation to do all that? This lecturer's request, I think, was artlessly presumptuous. Yes, the point of working through assignments is to learn. But the real goal, to many students such as myself, is to simply finish them so as to pass the unit and proceed to the next semester of the course. If an assignment is satisfactorily complete, then it is done. I am unwilling to spend too much more of my time completely scrapping and rewriting assignments in order to get to the bottom of educational concepts that are already opaque and derivative to begin with.

We, or I as a student then, seemed to be transported over on an opposing trajectory. For the first three years of our student-teacher placements all we did was observe. It was utterly boring.

We were *actually* encouraged to observe and not engage with our student-teacher placement experience too much. Many of us hadn't even been out of secondary school for that long. I'm sure we could have recalled how the classroom worked and what it looked like, and I'm certain we could have completed our observational assignments based on our recent recollections from secondary school. We didn't need two-week stints involving us falling asleep in our seats at the front of a classroom beside our supervising teacher's desk, trying (or pretending) to look busy with our notepads as we scribbled or didn't scribble down the three or four dot points necessary to complete our university assignment on 'classroom engagement' (another piece of/on irony). It was embarrassing to be representing a tertiary institution such as Martyr University in a 'sophisticated' and 'pompous', seemingly purposeful activity like student-teacher placements over our three years of observation, when all that was really necessary was a brisk stroll around the secondary school's courtyard to help jog our memory in recollecting the secondary school experience.

Sure, some of us were proactive and jumped into the task headfirst; it all largely depended on our supervising teacher and how lazy, bitter, vindictive, or kind, encouraging and supportive, they were. Though most teachers who were busy with their own work and quite neutral about the whole interactive experience with us student-teachers merely viewed us as exactly that, 'student-teachers', though with more of an emphasis on the word 'student'. We were essentially another student in their class of twenty or so students already, who needed to be coddled, nurtured and looked after.

I remember encountering Dandray University students on these rounds, and their experiences were quite different to Martyr's. Almost half, or at least around a third, of their semester was devoted to practical hands-on experience: real teaching. By the second year of their degree they were undertaking five-week student-teacher placements, yet with more of an emphasis on the word 'teacher'. And they were actually *teaching* for a large portion of those five weeks, learning and honing their skills as intuitive and instinctive educators. By their second year they already had a real feel and grasp for the kind of profession they were getting themselves into, unlike us Martyr students who wouldn't really know for sure until our fourth and final year. They were flabbergasted when I told them how Martyr was running things.

Also, our assignments and tutorials in the Martyr University education department often went on spectacular tangents that probably would have required hypnotherapy to regress and recollect the information needed to produce them. We were often asked to 'recall' or 'remember' something from our experience of primary or pre-school. I *suppose* this can be a potentially useful exercise? Yet it was mostly irrelevant in our cases.

I remember one of the assignments we were asked to do at Martyr in our fourth year was to remember one of our earliest childhood learning experiences, from Prep or Grade One, describe it in as much detail as possible and locate an artefact or sample of our work from that era, and explain how it informed our processes of education. First of all, why Prep or Grade One? *We* were going to be *secondary* school teachers. Secondly, what were the chances of us actually being able to *find* something from fifteen years or so ago? Thirdly, this didn't really help mature-age students all that much who had even less of a chance of finding an artefact from their early childhood. It only took us tertiary students two to three minutes, chatting frantically amongst ourselves, to work out the extremely difficult pragmatics and impracticality of this (irrelevant) assignment. Hence, how much time and thought could our tutors and lecturers seriously have put into constructing this curriculum, when it took us mere minutes to debunk its worth? To me this indicated a lack of empathy, and staff who were completely out of touch with the meaning and purpose of educating secondary school teachers.

Furthermore, we were in our final year. We needed resources (and context)! Lesson plans, worksheets, behavioural management strategies and Australian curriculum protocols and guidelines — something useful and practical that we could put into effect once were out there (in the real). The first year of teaching is the hardest because a teacher has to work at creating, developing or familiarising oneself with a huge folio of new work to then add tiers and layers and platforms to over time. Teachers generally refer to the mood of their first year of teaching as 'survival mode'. So, in our final year as students establishing a strong foundation of resources and realistic knowledge should have been a primary objective, so that we could actually 'survive' our first year as teachers, and we simply weren't getting this. Instead, on our weekends we found ourselves rummaging through our sheds and garages scavenging for an artefact of some finger-painting of a tree and a sun with a smiley face, maybe even sunglasses, and a couple o' one-dimensional m-shaped McDonald's birds, in an attempt to engage with the reflective or reflexive Freudian psycho-self-analysis on how that finger-painting informed our teaching and our lives in one of these delegated final year assessments. The education department at Martyr were desperate to be seen as psychologists or social scientists in this way, but they were neither. They were teachers who were no longer teaching, and instead took part in something that was peculiarly self-indulgent and oblivious in the pseudo 'in-between' of the profession.

Almost every single assignment or form of assessment at Martyr University required intense and detailed clarification. None of them ever made sense from the get-go. Often two entire one-hour tutorials were devoted purely to explaining the task at hand, delaying the curriculum for that semester. Again, this is ironic coming from teachers whose entire profession revolves around the need for proper and concise explanation, and the proficient transfer of information from one mind to another. These assignments either never made sense because the language was convoluted and incomprehensible: 'pedagogy', 'metacognition', 'teaching about teaching', 'learning about learning', 'learning about teaching', 'teaching about learning'. I'm (sort of) exaggerating, of course, but still, all of the assignments and assessment criteria collapsed in on themselves via a syntax that relied on contradictions and oxymorons.

Otherwise, they required further clarification due to their outlandishness. In my third year I wrote a 2,000-word essay based on my 'relationship' with Dr Pepper, the beverage, and how it influenced my worldview and/or explained my character and place in society. It is worth noting that this particular class related to popular culture, so fair enough, I suppose Dr Pepper could fall into that category, but this is also running away from the point. Yes, both students and teachers are exposed to popular culture. And yes, it is necessary to know and appreciate some things about popular culture in order to be able to better relate to secondary school students. But then again, *everybody* in the western world is exposed to popular culture. Everyone has some kind of a connection, relationship or non-relationship to or with popular culture. This doesn't mean that popular culture directly relates to education in this particular context. Moreover, the assignment was about our*selves*, and *not* as students. I think I mentioned the word 'education' once in those 2,000 words. I really wanted to highlight this odd tangent to the education faculty at Martyr University in my essay, and in doing so went on spectacularly irrelevant excursions in it to try and send this message back to my assessors. Nevertheless, I received a High Distinction for my Dr Pepper essay. And though this grade was just as sweet and refreshing as a real Dr Pepper, it was not attained without a taste of bitterness that came with it—my greater subtextual and subverting point had not been realised by my assessors or the department. Perhaps I had not been clear enough with my underhanded intentions.

To complement my essay, I was also required to make a collaged self-portrait painting or image, utilising images from pop culture that were seen to influence me. Scraps of Dr Pepper packaging was, of course, included in the work, as seen on the next page (Fig. 2).

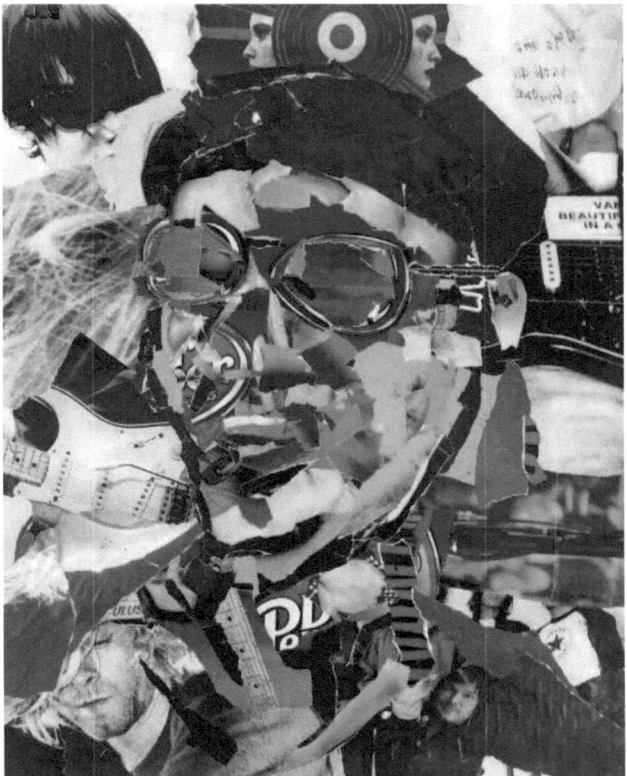

Fig. 2. Self-Portrait (Collage)

Another critical, though baffling, assessment task we were asked to complete in our final year was our professional portfolio (see figs. 3 to 5). I need to stress the importance of the word 'professional' here, in contrast with what it was we were actually expected to manufacture. And you can bet your arse that, perhaps even three whole one-hour tutorials, were devoted to the explanation and clarification of this assessment task. The professional portfolio was something we were encouraged to bring in to interviews to highlight and showcase our teaching philosophy, experience, planning and organisation — what constituted our role as a teacher, and so forth. Artefacts like photos, sample documents and/or lesson plans were to be included. We were also encouraged to colour in, illustrate and use glitter wherever possible. What it really was or what it actually felt like we were making was a scrapbook. This was degrading. We were not going to be primary school or pre-school teachers. We were going to become secondary school teachers. And I was going to keep my scrapbook as professional as possible, stick to the facts and include only the relevant and appropriate material. I certainly wasn't going to colour in or use glitter. I'm pretty sure I grew out of all that business after the age of seven or eight.

Fig. 3. Samples A & B from 'Professional' Portfolio (2010)

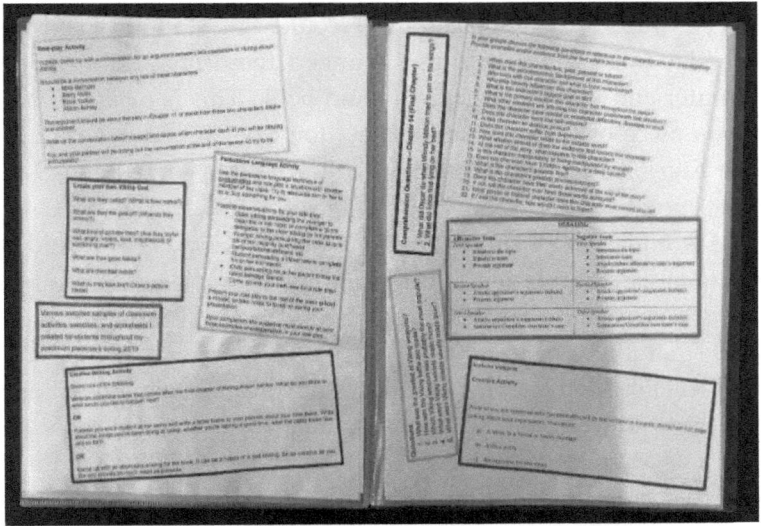

Fig. 4. Sample C from 'Professional' Portfolio (2010)

Fig. 5. Sample D from 'Professional' Portfolio (2010)

These extracts are preposterous! I could not stop myself from cringe-laughing mockingly as I scanned these images on to my computer and into this document and book. This is meant to be a serious piece of literary work! They don't belong anywhere near these pages, let alone on them! Still, they help to contextualise my greater point.

I would NEVER show these in a job interview. That would be ludicrously embarrassing and the ultimate form of self-sabotage, would it not? And embarrassing for Martyr too, I think? Though maybe that'd be a good thing.

Drusilla Modjeska's experiences at Carn are mentioned as a contrast to Martyr and how these things are expressed, how the 'self' is expressed more so. How the 'self' is FORCED to be expressed most of all, is quite shocking.

My portfolio passed though. I can't remember what grade I received, but I think it was fine. It satisfied the flamboyant criteria anyway, barely. Though the assessors may've told me it was a tad 'bland' or that 'more colouring in' was required. At least I didn't draw outside the lines I suppose.

Now the glitter thing – it's not like that was a prerequisite. But I simply don't understand why our educators couldn't have told us it was a scrapbook from the start. And it *was* (and still is) a scrapbook: a pictorial, noted and fragmentary accumulation and representation of the kind of people we were, the kind of work we'd done and the kind of work we'd be doing in future.

In classic Martyr education style our tutors spent those two to three (unplanned) tutorials (as I guess they assumed we'd understand the task right away?) attempting to explain or rationalise the scrapbook we'd be making, using as much confusing, made-up convoluted language as possible, without ever stating the obviousness of the 'scrapbook' fact, and also without showing us an example of a scrapbook/professional portfolio from a previous semester until the last of the three tutorials, right at the end of the eleventh hour. Were they embarrassed about what they were asking us to do? I suppose I would have been, in their position, and still am (of mine). Were they (ab)using this time to attempt to justify the legitimacy of the scrapbook in their own minds? And when they did finally show us an example of a scrapbook, we students all turned to one another in unison, and whether we literally said it or whether it was written on our faces and in our eyes, we were, at that moment, in universal agreement: "Oh, so they want us to make a scrapbook. Why didn't they just say so?" At last some sense of (baffled) relief and comprehension.

In the end, even though my scrapbook attempted to stick to the facts (another of my academic evasions of the childish pseudo-grapplings of the education department) there was no way I was going to actually whip it out in *any* professional job interviews. I feel as though it would certainly have done more harm than good, with its photograph of my big cheesy grinning face on the cover, stripping away any degree of professionalism before even opening the first page of the (scrapped) book.

I viewed this photograph of me on the cover, and the other photographs throughout the scrapbook, as Roland Barthes might describe them: they were "death-dealing" (Egan 20). For a portrait-photograph is "a closed field of forces ... In front of the lens, I am at the same time: the one I think I am, the one I want others to think I am, the one the photographer thinks I am" (Barthes 13). Barthes is perhaps being melodramatic here, or Egan is being melodramatic in her interpretation of Barthes' commentary as implying "death-dealing". What Barthes means here, in his highly visual way of writing out concepts, is that this relationship between the experiences of the subject, and the photograph of the subject, demonstrates a nightmarish state of *inauthenticity* (Barthes 13, Egan 20). And for me and my experiences at Martyr, my scrapbook, even though it was a folio of childish things featuring a subject who would later teach children, was inauthentic, because in this case it was Martyr University that was being inauthentic, or entirely inadequate. Of course, this narrative about inauthenticity and death is melodramatic, but within the professional tertiary landscape of Martyr University, I certainly conceived my scrapbook as being "death-dealing" and inauthentic in terms of its destruction of integrity and its potentially jeopardising effect on my career and vocational position in education. It had no place at Martyr. It had no place at schools. It had no place in professional development seminars. It had no place at home. It had no place or relevance to children or adults. It had no place anywhere. For me, it was a death-like black hole for all authenticity, integrity and credibility.

An Agitation (2016)

An agitation that comes and goes. Confined spaces, closed rooms and timelines (use your *con-text-uality*) and the paradigm of investment in the repetition and gambling with the fate or non-fate(s) come June or July. Look deeply into the recurring motifs that change like Modjeska's "hands" (59, 93, 137) and are determined, one way or another. I locate myself inside the academy, as an outsider – an academic-in-training submerged in 'meta' hypochondria.

The agitation was conveyed aptly, with cold-hot purpose! Hopefully the message and sentiment were clear enough to be remembered. And in doubt and decline on the deathbed and inter-penetration of future (fucking) anniversaries, a universal mockery will be felt in the heart as it changes hands – transferred back and pitiful, more vulnerable and stagnant now, swelling in the marshy well of foresight and culpability.

Be above it. Be a deafening roar of singularity and purpose, projected outwardly and outside the academy until the jest is matched by victimisation of abstract solidarity.

For Martyr students in their fourth and final year of studying secondary education, the course was merged with new students enrolled in a one-year Diploma of Education (or DipEd), though I now understand this course is no longer available in Australia.

In any case, in 2010, I am not suggesting that this merger made me feel claustrophobic, anti-social or anthropophagic in any way. It was just offensive. Suddenly all our lectures and tutorials had new 'virgin' students in them, presumably without any idea of how to grasp all of the educational-jargon-bullshit language and 'principles' we'd been learning over the past three years, which confirmed to me that that was exactly what we had been 'learning' over the past three years: bullshit. If these untreated students could link up with us Bachelor of Education students in our final year, be on the same page and do the exact same study in their first and only year, then what does that say about *our* past three years of study? That it was irrelevant – maybe even a waste of time; something clearly easily graspable by new students anyway. Of course, a Bachelor of Secondary Education could be considered minimally more prestigious than a Diploma of Secondary Education, but we both ultimately interview for the same jobs, with the same pay, albeit our completely different levels or 'degrees' of exposure and 'experience' in/to education.

In my final year as a Bachelor of Arts and Education (Secondary) student, a Dr Stefan Kirk, who stood out by giving *himself* the nickname 'Kirky', was the coordinator of fourth/final year education students at Martyr. "Call me Kirky," he would say, though no one ever did. It would've felt too forced. He even signed off as "Kirky" in the signature of his emails. I made sure always to address him properly and professionally as "Stefan". His casual directness had the reverse effect on me. Maybe he didn't appreciate this, and perhaps that is why my experience(s) with him were so unpleasant and counter-productive.

Towards the end of our third year of education we were asked to select two subject areas we would be specialising in for our fourth year. As my major and minor in my Arts degree were English and philosophy, I selected these two specialisations. It was my understanding that we would be undertaking specific units in these subject areas in our final year, and that they would become our teaching specialisations once we had graduated. And that is, or was, more or less the case, though what I failed to understand, and this is entirely my fault, was that philosophy was not offered as a unit of study/specialisation in the fourth year of education at Martyr University. In fact, there were only six specialist areas to choose from, as I will explain shortly.

So, as we were all completing our studies for our third year and looking forward to a well-earned summer break, I received a call from Stefan asking me to come in for a meeting, as there was a problem with my specialisations for my final year. I remember it being a gorgeous day, on the cusp of Summer, in November. I always rode my bicycle to university so that I wouldn't have to pay for parking. There were a number of back streets I could take to avoid major roads and intersections and the general hiss and laborious bustle of the south-eastern suburbs of Melbourne. The education faculty was located near one of the larger Martyr University car parks, in the southeast quadrant of the campus, and had many shaded trees and much greenery by the entrance. The entire campus was quiet and peaceful at that time of year as everyone had either finished their studies or were nearing the end of the exam period. I walked up the stairs and down the hall of the second floor of the education building, to Stefan's office. He greeted me. I greeted him, and after a curt, though polite exchange, I took a seat in front of his desk.

"There's a problem with your specialisations," he announced. "I mean, you've noted down philosophy, but we don't offer philosophy." He paused to look at me. I looked back placidly with my chin resting on my hand. "What subjects did you do in your Arts degree?" he asked after a little while.

"Ah, my major was in English literature. My minor was in philosophy. I took psychology in my first year, which was initially going to be my major but then I only completed my first-year units in it. For the remainder of my electives, I took up extra units in literature." When I finished speaking I could already begin to see what the problem was going to be.

"Yes. See, that's the thing. We don't offer philosophy here, and you need at least four units of another subject area to have a second specialisation in education. You've definitely got enough for English. What about doing another two for psychology?"

"Hmm, yeah, I really don't think I could do psychology. I didn't enjoy it as much as I thought I would, so I probably wouldn't want to wind up teaching it." I hesitated for a moment. "What about … are there any other universities that offer philosophy as a teaching specialisation?" I asked.

Stefan looked at me, then looked back down at his desk and a few of the papers in his hands, and said, "Well, there's only one university, really, in Australia that offers philosophy as an education specialisation, but it's ANU in Canberra. And I don't know if you could do it via distance? But … then again, there aren't that many secondary schools that even teach philosophy. It kind of limits you."

I definitely didn't care about limitations. I wanted to be interested in what I was doing and teaching, and with a strong foothold in English as a specialisation I had a foot in the door already with a number of different subject areas revolving around English, literature and the humanities anyway. And what I realised later on, once I actually became a teacher, was that at schools, coordinators and organisers really don't care what your specialist areas actually *are*. They only care how flexible you are and what subject areas you're *willing* to teach. If your specialisations are history and maths, and you're confident and willing to teach physics and religion then you can (and probably will) teach in those areas. This could be seen as a bit negative with regards to the quality of the discipline of knowledge, however. But ideally schools want you to be as adaptable as possible. A teacher who is confident and willing to teach any or most subject areas is invaluable to them because it means that that teacher can cover any class and be shifted around all over a campus freely, willingly and at short notice. And with so many administrators struggling with the organisation, timing and orchestration of all of this, a flexible and malleable teacher is quite valuable to them and to the school overall.

I also think that because of the chaotic nature of secondary school education, one needs to allow oneself a certain degree of spontaneity and improvisation as a teacher, if only to push oneself outside the box and outside one's comfort zone. There you can find different content and areas of interest that both you and your students can engage with. I have always believed in the potential of collaborative learning, and if you as a teacher are learning new content at the same time as your students, a new energy and complementary dynamic can be developed in the classroom.

Unfortunately, I didn't say all of this at the time because (a) I didn't know it yet, and (b) I didn't really care. All I knew was that I had English as a specialisation and that that would be okay, or at least sufficient, as a kind of bare minimum for the time being, so I said something along the lines of "but I have English, and some psychology I suppose. I don't mind if I won't always be able to teach philosophy. I'd be happy to try and find out if I could do philosophy at ANU via distance, or even go there once a week or once a fortnight for a class if that's what it would take, and if that could work in conjunction with classes at Martyr University? I assume that'd be better than the alternative?"

'Kirky' didn't look pleased. I don't think this was the answer he was anticipating. I think he thought that I was trying to overcomplicate things for him somehow, which I do tend to do with people a lot. Or maybe he was just concerned? I'm not too sure. His response was, "Well, that's something you would have to check. I don't know personally. I think your best bet is another two psychology units, or any other four Arts units? You could do history for instance, if you're not interested in psychology? Either way, you would need to do a History 1A and 1B and a History 2A and 2B or some other 1A, 1B and 2A, 2B Arts combination, and the dilemma here is that Martyr doesn't offer any B units in first semester, so you would have to do it over the course of a full academic year before you could then jump back into your fourth year of education."

That was when the sinking feeling came. God, another year. And then I have to come *back* to this education faculty when I'm already so close to the end. And I don't even know if I *like* teaching that much. How *could* I know if I haven't even *taught* yet? All I've been doing is observing fucking classrooms for the past three years! I felt completely deflated—and then a real swell of negative thoughts, emotions and implications arose in my mind in place of my lapsed optimism. And it was partly my fault; I had assumed the combination of units I was studying in my Arts degree were fine, without ever really properly checking with the education faculty or consulting with a course advisor. Jesus, that's just so like me; I always feel so naively proud of my supposed ability to know myself, though I tend to ignore the things or the work it sometimes takes to avoid this level of irresponsibility and self-sabotage. "Idiot!" I would mutter under my breath later.

Nevertheless, I saw a glimmer of hope, an opportunity, because there had been something that had been nagging me for the past few months. Something I regretted not doing. Why had I never taken up an elective in film studies? I loved film, possibly more than I loved literature. I just never saw it as a viable option for further study. I was always stuck in an overly traditional mindset, and anything that strayed from the conventional into the more unorthodox would only come later in life for me.

I hadn't said anything to Stefan for a little while. I'd been looking down at his tacky walnut desk in front of me. He'd been casually looking between me, his computer screen and his papers.

Eventually, I looked up and asked, "What about film studies?" It seemed to have come out of nowhere despite making complete sense to me.

"Ahh, film studies. Arts. Yes … right. I guess that could work too." Stefan appeared puzzled, but my proposal didn't *not* make sense either.

Our meeting went on for a little longer as we attempted to work out the finer details of what it was we (or I) needed to do now and the options I had: ANU, further Arts studies, psychology, film studies (maybe), how much I'd be willing to travel, whether distance education was viable, who I'd need to contact, whether or not I could actually work out some kind of Arts combination within *one* semester, whether it was in fact possible to do some additional Arts units in conjunction with my final year of education (it would be hard and probably wasn't possible), but I had to consider the value of getting out of that department when I was supposed to, or whether I wanted to spend another year (or two even, I guess) festering within the faculty with 'Kirky' hanging over my head.

I considered a (British) maxim my dad would always tell me in these kinds of tricky situations: "You don't get what you deserve in life, you only get what you negotiate." As I grow older I appreciate that notion more and more. Almost everything is negotiable, and you can find a way to navigate through almost everything, if you're willing to work, lose face (which I generally don't care about because I almost never feel embarrassed), ask stupid or irritating questions, take the path less travelled or even meld and mould your own obscure route. The latter is what I do most of the time. I can't help it. I always find myself answering straightforward questions about almost anything with a "yes" and a "but", the implication being that I consistently find a way to do what I want, and achieve the result I desire, but it's almost always an absolute clusterfuck getting there (i.e., driving from Melbourne to Canberra and back once a week in order to potentially take a partly irrelevant class in philosophy just to satisfy my course requirements in a timely manner). Though I'd rather do that than the alternatives listed above. Most people wouldn't though.

I just utterly hate falling, losing control or collapsing to my knees and gliding away from a decision I've made and cemented in my mind if there is some (or any other possible) obscure or tangential way to circumnavigate a problem. It's my journey after all. I should do it how I want to do it. At the very least then I've got a good story to tell at the end of it all. The same goes with people; I'd rather burn a bridge between myself and someone, and get an actual answer to my question, than having an 'unknown' uncertainty hovering over, under and around me, like a spectre. I need closure to things. It's unfortunate and painful, and I probably generate a lot of enemies that way but it's also just the way I'm wired — it seems to be in my blood and/or in my brain chemistry and neural pathways — I never forget, and I almost never "don't care" when it comes to a specific journey I have in mind. Every door that is opened to me or by me needs to be closed again to conclude that chapter or that journey. Please don't open it if you don't expect to follow through. People often casually and haphazardly mention something to me along the lines of "Yeah, sounds great! Let's do that 'thing' next Wednesday" or "Absolutely, I'll have 'it' to you by tomorrow". Well, if we don't do that 'thing' next Wednesday or if you don't have 'it' to me by tomorrow then all hell breaks loose from me unto you. You may have casually or drunkenly or only semi-seriously made that comment, but nevertheless *you* made it. So it's happening! Don't make it if you don't want it to happen. It's simple. And if you avoid it you're opening a Pandora's box. And even if at the end of it all we attain something quite negative or harmful we/I must see it through, and I will make you see it through to the end (or some kind of an end) if you come along for the ride with me in any capacity. This characteristic is unfortunate a lot of the time (especially for others who are too blasé, nonchalant and unaware of it), and hopefully I can adapt and relax this instinct and intuition in me with age and maturity.

At the end of our meeting, Stefan and I bade each other farewell, he wished me luck, and I rode home right away to investigate my options. He said to contact him once I'd come up with something. I called and emailed ANU, I spoke to my dad about film studies (he was puzzled too and advised against the apparent deviation) and then I went online to Martyr University's Faculty of Education webpage to study up on the possibility of tangential loopholes, in a hypothetical final year of 'hybridised' study. As I mentioned earlier (and this is what I then found on the webpage regarding fourth/final year secondary education specialisations), there were six modes or areas to choose from, all with specific prerequisites based on one's previous work or studies: English, maths, psychology, science, history and English as a Second Language (ESL). I went through the ones that were relevant or applicable to me and checked their prerequisites: English required a completed major in English (check); psychology required a completed major in psychology; history required a completed major in history (obviously — this was becoming a trend); ESL required a completed major in English. I paused. Was I reading this correctly? ESL required a completed major in English. Only a completed major in English? So, an ESL specialisation had the exact same prerequisites as a specialisation in English, which I'd *already* qualified for? How had Stefan and I missed this? I was sure I wasn't reading this right or that there was some fault with the information on my desktop screen. It looked like too simple a fix! English could be one of my specialisations. And then ESL could be the other. Done. That's two specialisations! I haven't gone insane, have I? This *does* solve my dilemma, doesn't it? A tremendous wave of relief washed over me, and the frown I'd been wearing for the past two-to-three hours cracked into a shrewd smile, but I didn't want to celebrate just yet. I thought I should definitely check all this with Stefan first. I mean, surely if this was such an easy solution *he* would have mentioned it in our meeting, no?

I seized the cordless phone charging beside me and dialled Stefan. It was around three in the afternoon, so he should answer if he was in his office. He did. "Pawel, how are you?"

"Good, Stefan, thanks! Um ..." I was so excited I didn't quite know how to get the words out. "Hey, listen, cunt!" was the subtext ruminating within me.

Instead, courteously, I said, "I've just been checking online and ... what about ESL ... as my second specialisation? ESL — English as a Second Language. It says here that it only requires a major in English. I could do that, couldn't I?"

Stefan answered after a brief moment, "Yes ... yep, that could work."

"Great!" I was relieved. "I'll apply for that then?"

"Sure, yep."

"Excellent! So, I guess that solves my problem?"

"Yep, glad we could come to a solution."

"... Yeah, cool. Thanks then, Stefan. Bye."

"Take care Pawel." He hung up.

I put down the phone. I was still, semi-shocked. The call had probably lasted less than a minute. I was puzzled, perplexed. After all that drama and anxiety on my part, what an anti-climax. I was happy, of course, but ... why couldn't Stefan have just suggested ESL as an option to begin with? Why did I have to take the lead in this roundabout tumultuous journey, experimenting with the possibility of me driving to Canberra or taking an extra year of Arts classes? I'd even been driven into talk to my dad about film studies and attempting to work out the pragmatics of it all. And then, in the end, all it took me was around twenty minutes of looking into the details and prerequisites of the *six* secondary education teaching specialisations offered by Martyr University online, and the problem was solved. Just like that. Easy. Simple. Why had Stefan taken me for this ride? I realise that probably wasn't his intention, and maybe he'd just been drawing a blank or having a stroke that day, but ... wasn't he *the* coordinator of fourth year education (secondary) students? He'd been responsible and played a large role in orchestrating those *six* specialisations. I would have thought he would know them inside out. Furthermore, the smooth transition and well-being of final year education students should have been a top priority in his job description, I would have thought. He really *should* have known. "Glad we could have come to a solution," he had said. I'm not so sure about the "we" there. *He* hadn't really solved anything. If anything, he'd *caused* a problem, which *I* then had to fix (with relative ease). Humans aren't especially infallible. We think we are. But no.

So, I went into my fourth year of education without any issues or roadblocks. I may've not been learning about how to teach philosophy, but in the greater practical scheme of things this was pretty irrelevant, or a 'meta' concern. At least ESL would enable me to travel and teach English overseas, I thought. For I didn't want to 'go into' teaching right away. I still had quite a reserve of youthful vigour and adolescent energy I wanted to squander in South or Central America, South East Asia, Japan, China and Eastern Europe.

After investigating the possibility of this though, it didn't seem as though I could get an 'in' anywhere without a TESOL (Teachers of English to Speakers of Other Languages) certificate. Basically, every single English language school or centre abroad required a TESOL certified educator. It seemed as though every non-English speaking country preferred someone with a mere 6-month TESOL certificate to someone with a 4-year Bachelor of Education (Secondary) degree with a specialisation in ESL.

In one of our specialist ESL tutorials in our final year at Martyr, a student once asked our lecturer this question directly: "Will having an ESL specialised secondary education degree enable us to work as English language teachers overseas? Is it as relevant as doing a TESOL course, for instance?" Our lecturer responded without hesitation, "Yes, definitely." *I* am still yet to see proof of this. From personal experience, and having job interviews with international language schools, a TESOL course is certainly preferential, more universally applicable and seems to prevail in this field over more specialised alternatives. I don't necessarily blame the education department at Martyr for this fault. This is a 'world' perception issue; so many things seem to need to be copied and pasted in a formulaic pattern so that everything fits in the simplest of formats. Relevance is only as relevant to the shape-makers as it is to the shape-fitters; if you cut a square hole out of a flat piece of say, timber, then the rule seems to be that the two-dimensional flat square that has been cut out can be the only shape allowed back in again. A cylindrical prism, on the other hand, turned on its side, can also make a square shape when passing through a square hole, and so would also fit and work within this timber paradigm. Moreover, a cylindrical prism holds more volume, is three-dimensional and functions within different contexts. We need to start thinking outside the square/box in these processes of education, and literally in the case of this wooden example. "Everything is negotiable," as my dad would say. And what are we even negotiating here anyway? For a *more* qualified educator to teach at a school or centre that would actually prefer *less* qualified standardised caricatures of teachers? Maybe less *is* more? So long as everything fits, and everything sits in its right place. In these folios, I often highlight the chaotic evasive nature of humankind, but when it comes to education, championing this attitude doesn't seem to make sense to me. Then again, what are we all but walking contradictions stumbling into one another goofily.

Having said all that, I didn't come out of my ESL specialised unit with any particularly useful resources. Ideally, I should have come out the other side with a large folder bursting with materials I could use to engage students with as a practising secondary school teacher. But I didn't come out with much at all. I imagine the TESOL goers would've received that, or at least they would have access to countless categorised online resources and organised curriculum documents from the TESOL website or respective school once they'd become official members or completed their courses.

Nevertheless, *I* did receive a lot of training about metalanguage and other 'meta' related pseudo-shit. And I did still have my Dr Pepper essay. Not to mention my fabulous scrapbook, of course!

The culmination of these experiences and processes of 'education' at Martyr was exemplarily on show in my final tutorial ever. I still cringe when recalling it and find it very difficult to recount. It's so typical of the education experience at Martyr overall, the pointlessness of much of it, and the forced feigned nonsensical activities that made the education faculty and students so pseudo-academic. When I tell this story to friends (very rarely) they laugh about it and at me because they know me so well, and I partly can now too … just. However, at the time it was ridiculously awkward and uncomfortable; the people, the other 'teachers', the experience, the brutal irrelevance, the inability to escape superficial enthusiasm and the experience of being in a technicolour Disneyland or Dismaland-like nightmare dimension.

In the final minutes of this tutorial we were dismantled into groups to perform a range of pointless activities. One of those activities was, for whatever horrible reason, a 'rap' exercise. It couldn't have been any more cliché (that is, teachers rapping — we've all seen similar cringe-worthy exercises played out in Disney films, TV shows, even in black comedy drama films like *Funny People*). Somehow, I was forced into a position in which I was to engage with another student in some kind of hip hop rap-off. Now, let me say that I despise rap and hip-hop. There was originally a folio of work in this study devoted to the beauty, influence and significance of music on my self that has since been 'scrapped', and rap and hip-hop do not fare well within those aesthetic musical parameters at all. It's an imagery/persona problem. I don't like, nor do I condone, the image, persona and characteristics rap and hip-hop artists seem to convey; violence, misogynist chauvinism, characters who go to great lengths to hide a real person behind the tough talk and false and broken 'gangster' (or 'gangzta', as they would 'say') dialect and dialogue. I feel this kind of communion, communication and behavioural projection is no way to interact with or perceive the world (from these false perspectives and inhumane facades). I pleaded with my group to select somebody else to take part instead of me. I practically begged them. I did not want to be involved in this undertaking, out of principle, and on numerous other levels. I struggled to convey this to them, probably because I hadn't been involved in any other activities in the tutorial up until that point. And evidently I had to take part in *something*.

We had around ten minutes remaining in our last ever tutorial and then the faculty would be out of my life forever. But I just wanted to leave, right then. I'd attended the majority of the classes and sessions held that semester. I'd satisfied the course criteria. It was time to say farewell. I considered seizing my bag and legging it, though the exit was far off, I was backed against a wall and the other students in our group were obstructing me.

They were desperate to have their way with me — I don't know … perhaps for their own perverse sense of closure and pleasure? Was it a conspiracy? Did they need some kind of conclusion to their journey too? Or were they all just voyeurs at heart? Why me though? Did they not understand how much bitterness and resentment I had towards this music genre? Clearly not. And just like the Dr Pepper essay and the glitter-imbued scrapbook of a professional portfolio, why was a rap-off so damn critical to the conclusion and closure of a university course in secondary education? It was a jarring activity, personally pestilential and (much too) grim for me to handle proactively. Meanwhile, my stance, voice and perspective on the matter were insufficiently prepared to explain all of this to the other students. And we simply didn't have the time. I felt like they were ganging up on me, the rap and hip-hop personas and guises rubbing off on them degenerately, meddling with their souls, values, empathy and common decency.

I finally conceded, and sheepishly stood at the front of the class while another sycophantic student conducted his 'raps', which involved heavy 'dissing' and playful offences towards me. I phased it out. I partially closed my eyes and considered a brief meditation: a cheap and quick solution of evasion, a banal and futile slog in my sombre defence.

When it was all over and the crude humiliation dissipated, I snatched my bag and was the first out the door. I was offended and insulted (which doesn't happen very easily), in a form that in itself, in its own delivery, was despicable to me. It felt as though some shithead was shitting out a pile of shit on top of me, and I became an idle bitch in the suppurating quagmire. I forewent any goodbyes to anyone else in the room. It was a horrible yet telling way of how the education department resonated with me during my time at Martyr, culminating in something palpable, nauseating and stomach-churning that I could almost taste in my mouth and feel in the core of my being. There was no amicable closure or ending here. It merely ended. I got up and left, and then left it all behind. I passed the course. I graduated the following year and became a secondary school teacher. And now I have the chance to say something about the process, as cocksure and opinionated as my thoughts on the matter may be, but that's the inherent creative and autobiographical element to how the story—my story—is told. I was there as a primary source of evidence. And I'm stating the 'facts' as they came to *me*. I got through it, but can I inquire as to why enduring that 'rap' was in any way necessary to the completion of my degree? The insistence on irrelevance in order to serve some kind of function represents that faculty's mindset, as well as the people within it. It's a delirious infection, a happy-go-lucky disease. If there is a cure, it is within a reality that evades them. "Exterminate all the brutes!" Kurtz said (Conrad 84). And yes, perhaps I say all of this ironically, emphatically, fantastically and melodramatically (idly?). I describe these processes of education as a form of purposeful purposelessness—I've used this phrase before, as a kind of forceful insistence on something that does not need to *be*. Period. A definition of absurdity and the inane. I suppose this is quite a large theme here overall, this purposeful purposelessness and how it (the grand force of it) projects and propels itself onto us and me, in this biosphere.

Many of these "brutes" continue to exist and have some kind of influence later on in my life beyond the academy, when I was eventually teaching in schools. I could see it and hear it and feel it during professional development (PD) sessions, curriculum meetings and the like. PD days were when all that fanciful self-indulgent pseudo-psycho-babble language that we'd learnt at university once more came to the fore. When it surfaces it always feels like a test to me: will I be persuaded, manipulated, influenced, convinced, repulsed—by that language? In that context it comes down to how well one knows oneself, I think. It involves patterns and cycles and a false perception worth recognising, and the sooner one acknowledges it the safer one's soul and sense of integrity will be. It's intensely bureaucratic. The experienced, down-to-earth, untainted, realistic, cynical, wary teachers who are self-aware will tell you that PD is like a carousel in a menacing theme park; the cycle of language and strategies and planning repeat themselves every ten years or so — the same strategies, ideas and concepts come around every ten years and are merely given a different name: *PoLT* for instance (*Principles of Learning and Teaching*) — who comes up with this stuff? What principles can possibly be valid across the entire spectrum of education?

And it needs to be kept in mind that the people presenting this language or this 'new' (reused and recycled) babbling and bubbling terminology at these PD sessions always have a lot more time to prepare (and swim in their own broiled gobbledygook beforehand). That is *their* job, not *ours*. It seems a little unfair and impractical; these presenters arm themselves with useless ammunition and fire on teachers who are virtually shattered cadavers themselves. Or the experience could be likened to having to play a tennis match after already completing five sets yourself, against someone who is only just comfortably and confidently warming up.

Hum, Amplitude, (Being a) Focal Point (2016)

The silence and the hum grow in amplitude. A subtle anxiety robs the focal point of any genuine 'class' and instead instils a false composure that needs to be projected outwards and tangentially — anywhere but forwards. This composure cannot hit a target. It simply needs to be, and be still, in order to be safe in the deafening silence of this room. Do not address the issue. Do not break the silence with bonds of mistrust, a sigh or a snigger, or a whisper — the target or the focal point (identity) will be tainted. Gazing up or down, no longer headfast, forwards or ahead.

Too much time has been spent driven from wall to wall, corner-to-corner, in a base and basic living arrangement. I crave the thunderous ruse like I crave thunder and lightning. A paradoxical imbalanced love/hate relationship, to be sure — like everything else here at which I aimlessly jest. A gesture becomes particularly noticeable. I wonder how long it'll take before they become accustomed to it or myself (and my nervous tics).

Already I see them beginning to flounder off, trying to test the parameters I am supposed to care about and be observing, suppressing. It makes me feel ill. Everything eventually gets called into question, and at last they will see how long we, I, you, they can last, in the end, when the bell chimes its blasting toll.

I could use a (laptop) screen or a drawn curtain to deviate with/from right about now.

'Big' Ideas (2016)

The foundations lie in the cracks in the pavement stones, and sticks bundle up and bunch together like spires in frozen legitimacy. I fail to recognise the point to the story and like condensation the conversation dribbles away into the spittle and spit on the corners of the door forced open here.

I've been sold on poetics and lyricism and time and I've changed my mind about some things, though not about other things. Still I have some idea(s) about perspective and loss and gain and humanity and dispersed distressed stoicism, displaced and placed or crammed into corners of spherical complacency, difficult to pin down from the endless swelling and rolling of tides.

I've been known to come and go if told, but in the end, I began to have no idea about certainty or truth or the subjectivity of recession and regression and an overwhelmed conscience and consciousness that loses everything it gains as it piles on the layers and folds of the slippery slop that runs and oozes elsewhere when stacked in uneven stacks, slacking and slumped, cornered and encrusted … lacklustre.

THESIS THREE

Fictocriticism as Innovative Pedagogy

The creative self's writings discussed in this section attempt to be engaging, accessible, humorous, with a more conventional storytelling narrative that includes real characterisation, scene descriptions and dialogue. The work(s) aim to relate to and address the reader on a more personal and readerly level. Because of this basis in real-life events, the names of people, places and institutions have been changed or reinvented in order to avoid any possible connection with an individual or place. Folios One and Two of this book are generally more abstract, unconventional, or told from exaggerated or re-animated 'personas', such as that of Lou in Folio Two. In Folio Three, the experimental pieces are less random and more chronological (all written in 2016). They are also longer, more direct, and focus on certain educational systems (particularly tertiary ones) from the perspective and experiences of the creative self.

The first two pieces, "(Scrapped) Book: A 'Professional' Educational(?) Overview" and "An Agitation" are anecdotal, whilst the last two shorter pieces, "Hum, Amplitude, (Being a) Focal Point" and "'Big' Ideas", end on a much more abstract and ruminative note. Thus, the creative folio examined in this section contains much more imagery, visual artefacts and photos supplemented with annotations, evidence of tutorial teaching, placement work, literal collaged works, art and extracts from the author's university folio work and 'professional' scrapbooking. Further, though this part of the fictocritical exploration is perhaps more traditionally written, it draws on unconventional (often sarcastic and ironic) formatting and writing strategies drawn from the study of innovative postmodern texts such as *House of Leaves* and Ross Watkins' and Nigel Krauth's 2016 essay "Radicalising the Scholarly Paper", as discussed in the previous two theses.

As with the analytical self's previous reasoning(s), Thesis Three discusses the fictocritical work based on aspects of real-life experience. In these experimental creative works, the author's educational experiences are used to provide certain fictional parallels, in the same way that Drusilla Modjeska describes her experiences of education as a teenager at a boarding school in England. In the final section of her 1994 fictocritical and autobiographical novel *The Orchard*, Modjeska describes the contrasting and contradictory views she, her peers, her friends' families and "the perversities of British wisdom" (166) had in relation to the strict way in which young women were taught in the late 1950s and early 1960s in England.

The Orchard is a brilliant and compelling fictocritical novel. It demonstrates how a true story can be integrated and embedded into a fictocritical, investigative, introspective collection of differently formed flowing work(s) all at once, with smooth reverberating fluctuations and endings of paragraphs transitioning into properly implemented quotes:

> ... but it does not mean that in affairs of the heart men assume the right to act, and the worth of their own agency. *When we love another 'as an object'*, Thomas Merton says, *we refuse, or fail, to pass over into the realm of his own spiritual reality, his personal identity.* (Modjeska 53)

... Or integrated within a sentence: "In [Stella Bowen's] memoirs she wrote that [Ford Madox Ford] was a man *who needed to exercise his sentimental talents from time to time upon a new object*" (Modjeska 52). *The Orchard* also includes further critical investigation and study integrated into the text as seen in the footnotes and references at the end of every chapter or section. Furthermore, the book's second section, "The Adultery Factor", blends 'story' with a first-person narrative of experience, and then critical investigation (Modjeska 78-82), which is done very well.

This fictocritical technique has been similarly used in Folio Three too, as seen in the opening piece, "(Scrapped) Book":

> I viewed this photograph of me on the cover, and the other photographs throughout the scrapbook, as Roland Barthes might describe them: they were "death-dealing" (Egan 20) ... Of course, this narrative about inauthenticity and death is melodramatic, but within the professional tertiary landscape of Martyr University, I certainly conceived my scrapbook as being "death-dealing" and inauthentic in terms of its destruction of

integrity and its potentially jeopardising effect on my career and vocational position in education ... For a portrait-photograph is "a closed field of forces ... In front of the lens, I am at the same time: the one I think I am, the one I want others to think I am, the one the photographer thinks I am" (Barthes 13). ("(Scrapped) Book")

There is much more creative non-fiction and memoir-style writing, like that of Gaita's *Romulus, My Father*, in Folio Three than "literary-critical commentary" (King 270) or "para-text" (Watkins and Krauth 18).

The creative self uses personal, anecdotal evidence primarily or "proto-autobiographical narratives ... to stage the question under investigation ... more inventive — and somewhat freer, if not exactly more relaxed" (Gibbs 310). There are references to Barthes and Egan, but they are used with a light touch. Then again, as a good summation of fictocriticism overall, Gary Crew says in his fictocritical article "Voicing the Dead" (2015), "... my life is not made up of 'facts'. It is a combination of emotions, senses, longings and fears (oh, plenty of them ...), among other sensations and experiences, none of which can be pinned down on a slab and called 'a fact'" (5).

Modjeska's novel is also fictocritical for contextual reasons: it was released in 1994, during a heightening period of fictocriticism's feminine emergence, as seen in the fictocritical works of other women around that time, such as Sedgwick's *Tendencies* (1993) and, of course, *The Space Between* (1998). *The Orchard* is autobiographical and introspective, translating the interior consciousness of the writer into a compelling outer one:

> In this culture to be alone is to be pitied, or feared ... when it may be quite the reverse: that the capacity to be alone, alone with ourselves, is as great, indeed possibly a greater marker of maturity, of intimate human success ... Could it be that our fear of solitude is that it will throw us into the outcast state of blindness? (Modjeska 121)

The novel discusses feminist concepts, referencing the lives and ideologies of Virginia Woolf (31), Stella Bowen (52, 251-53), Artemisia Gentileschi (141-44), plus the women in Modjeska's own life and her independent ruminations and meditations (163-247), whilst the motif of "hands" runs through the book as a recurring image of femininity (Modjeska 59, 93, 137).

A recurring motif in the creative self's work in this section is caught up in the theme of 'colour', i.e., "technicolour" 'niceties' and 'sweet nothings' and "being in a technicolour Disneyland or Dismaland-like nightmare", and of course, as the reader will see, the motif of the beverage Dr Pepper, which highlights the humorous ridiculousness of the creative self's experiences at Martyr University.

The primary difference between Modjeska's portrayed educational environment at Carn and that of the creative self/author are that Modjeska describes a learning environment that was cold, strict, archetypal, disciplinary and professional (166-67), whereas the creative self's own environment at Martyr University was more meandering, uncertain, overly and unprofessionally jovial, without context or grounding, and quite silly overall. Nevertheless, the similarity between both of these disparate contexts is that they did not allow for the existence or expression of the individual. The irony is that Martyr University's intentions aimed to enhance the expression and idiosyncrasies of the individual, though by being so haphazardly entrenched in nothing or no real principles or well thought out and constructed foundations, the individual (or self), became lost in a swirling palette of "technicolour" 'niceties' and 'sweet nothings' that actually became conformist in their own incoherent way, as demonstrated in this excerpt from the creative self's piece "An Agitation":

> But at the time it was a ridiculously awkward and uncomfortable situation for me; the people, the other 'teachers', the experience, the brutal irrelevance, the inability to escape superficial enthusiasm and the experience of being in a technicolour Disneyland or Dismaland-like nightmare dimension that came to the forefront of this tutorial.

Furthermore, there are numerous references to a kind of tortured, forced and subdued painting, art, collage, folio work and pop culture in Folio Three: "The process of being educated, for me and my sense of formative identity was/is like going for a walk in the woods, if the woods were laid out on a rendered painting of some sort ... the painted forest 'dimension' I am in at that point in time" ("(Scrapped) Book").

Modjeska recalls Carn with "the fumes of memory" as a "terrain of a past that, all these years later, still has its bite" (165):

> But it was what I meant when I spoke of the price that was paid for this education and its privilege, the enforcing of a conformity that regarded itself as individual, yet had no place for the idiosyncratic, the quirky, the reclusive, the dissident or wayward feminine. (176)

Martyr University was similar to this, even though its faculty's intentions would have been to create the total ideological opposite of this in their students at the time, as the frustrated narrative of Folio Three expresses.

The fictocritical writings of Anna Gibbs can be located within the stylistically parabolic crossfires of Modjeska's *The Orchard* and the creative folios in this text. Gibbs' "The Gift" (1998) for instance, from *The Space Between* expresses the following: "... at certain moments I found myself writing several consecutive sentences without any reference at all to the messy arrangement of sheared off pieces of print ... These rushes of articulation ..." (46-47).

"These rushes of articulation", or what could be called a Kerouacian exaltedly exhausted (Charters, Introduction viii), stream of consciousness, 'automatic' and freeform style of writing detailed in Thesis One, is found in a great deal of fictocriticism (Campbell 1998; Bartlett 1998; Morgan 2012), and as the sections of this text have expressed, are a key component to the creative self's preferred style of writing. In Folio Three, for example, the more frenzied, abstract and exalted writing slinks, yet again, into the form of the final two pieces of the extract, "Hum, Amplitude, (Being a) Focal Point" and "'Big' Ideas". "Hum, Amplitude, (Being a) Focal Point" is a short vignette about being in the headspace of a nervous (young) graduate teacher working/teaching at the front of a classroom in 2015. "'Big' Ideas" is similarly a creative and abstracted tirade addressing the creative self's experiences of the obnoxious concepts and ideas learnt during the creative self's tertiary studies at Martyr University, which are explored in the more concrete narrative(s) of "(Scrapped) Book" and "An Agitation": "Do not address the issue. Do not break the silence with bonds of mistrust, a sigh or a snigger, or a whisper—the target or the focal point (identity) will be tainted. Gazing up or down, no longer headfast, forwards or ahead" ("Hum, Amplitude, (Being a) Focal Point").

> I've been known to come and go if told, but in the end I began to have no idea about certainty or truth or the subjectivity of recession and regression and an overwhelmed conscience and consciousness that loses everything it gains as it piles on the layers and folds of the slippery slop that runs and oozes elsewhere when stacked in uneven stacks, slacking and slumped, cornered and encrusted ... lacklustre. ("'Big' Ideas")

Gibbs also favours a fragmented, surrealist collage-like 'cut-up' technique that would most likely be empathetic to the creative self's writerly experimental form. Gibbs says, "[t]he cut-up is a haunted writing" (46) and a "practical demonstration" of her innate understanding of contemporary literary theory (49). The figure of the trapped feminist writer/narrator, so apparent in *The Orchard*'s portrayals of Woolf (31), Bowen (52, 251-53), Gentileschi (141-44) and the women in Modjeska's own life (163-247), are also portrayed in Gibbs' "The Gift". Gibbs' piece attempts to tap into the headspace of Collette, a female writer "constrained to write by her husband, M. Willy" (45), who had her trapped under lock and key.

In her theoretically dense article "Fictocriticism, Affect, Mimesis: Engendering Differences" (2005), Gibbs says, "Fictocriticism is a way of writing for which there is no blueprint and which must be constantly invented anew in the face of the singular problems that arise in the course of engagement with what is researched" (1). And that:

> [...] Some of the most interesting fictocritical writing in Australia takes up and comments on the discourse of anthropology, ethnography, psychoanalysis and autobiography or memoir, all of which require a kind of research and reflection intimately involved with the voices of others. (2)

It is clear that Gibbs' writing is non-traditional and unorthodox. Put differently, it is more writerly than readerly. Though Gibbs says her 'cut-up' technique is not about the kind of randomness of André Breton, William Burroughs, Brion Gyson or John Cage either (45). It is still all for the innovation, experimentation and fusion or blending of different styles, genres and disciplines of research and writing in an attempt to uncover or discover the multitudinous facets that could work within fictocriticism (in 1998).

On that note, the following investigated piece is an autoethnographical paper. Thesis One of this study argues that autoethnography and fictocriticism are cut from a similar methodological cloth. Hence, one of the most similar autoethnographical pieces the analytical self has found that can be compared to the creative self's folios, has been Geoffrey Walford's journal article "Finding the Limits: Autoethnography and being an Oxford University Proctor" (2004). Walford is a British Emeritus Professor, and this book primarily explores Australian writers and texts, yet Walford's paper is too thematically and stylistically relevant to ignore.

Geoffrey Walford's "Finding the Limits" is a first-person account of Walford starting his first Proctorial year, in 2001 (403). It reads like a novella or short story, about a formal university outing (404). It is a creative, experimental and metafictive social commentary on an educational experience. A 'doubling' of voices appear in Walford's assessment of the value of autoethnography within tertiary education and research. This is seen in instances of reflective storytelling: "As we walked I found I had little to say to the Warden—what we were doing just seemed very odd. I know that had it been anyone else being admitted, I would not be in the procession!" (404). And then in the more 'encyclopaedically' dense sequences:

> Denzin and Lincoln's (2000b) outline of what must be interpreted as a progression of 'moments' in qualitative research has probably done more harm to ethnography than any other single idea. The second edition of their *Handbook* has expanded their model to seven 'moments' designated as the traditional (1900-1950); the modernist or golden age (1950-1970); blurred genres (1970-1986); the crisis of representation (1986-1990); the post-modern, a period of experimental and new ethnographies (1990-1995), postexperimental inquiry (1995-2000). (Walford 413)

The examination of the method and precise nature of autoethnography, like fictocriticism, is "open to debate" (410) according to Walford. Walford's premise is almost identical to this text's though, with the only main differences being Walford and the author of this text's generational divide, cultural background, and Walford presenting himself as a much more mature educator. The autobiographical accounts in this book's creative folios are, on the contrary, more immature, though that is in part because they are intended to be more humorous, light-hearted, accessible, still critical, but more anecdotal, fictocritical or proto-fictocritical and biased. A prominent point Walford makes about his research that *this* exploration largely disagrees with, however, is the following:

> [...] If this is supposed to be research, the reader has a right to know how much [of the story] is fiction and how much is at least trying to represent what actually occurred. Blurring the boundaries between creative literature and social science research writing does little to enhance either. (411)

This thesis disagrees with this comment because, to quote several fictocritical or proto-fictocritical texts, the creative self seeks to "deliberately blur the distinction between literature and literary-critical commentary" (King 270). It needs its readers to be an "accomplice ... [a] travelling companion ... coparticipant and cosufferer" (Hutcheon 30) in the text. It aims to demonstrate a different kind of integrity and duality in the writing that is autobiographical in the tensions that arise as a result of the folios' narcissistic 'realism': "What artist and autobiographer are concerned about is this inside-out process, the life behind the face, the integrity that must stand clear of trespass, the invisible self that is impossible to know" (Egan 61). It aspires to enact a form of "lifelife art" (Kaprow 41). It "wants to turn and touch its listeners and readers and wants to feel their touch back" (Schlunke and Brewster 394), yet all the while wanting its "readers to be a little uncertain about [the authors'] reality' (Muecke and King 14).

It is in these points that autoethnography and fictocriticism detach from one another, purely because autoethnography seems to be more grounded and balanced, both theoretically and in its accepted academic application to certain fields (like education), whereas one contention of this book is that often fictocriticism is more about abstract literary experimentation. Also, these stances are why each of the creative elements in this experiment in fictocriticism differ from one another, both in their attempt to innovate on the form of fictocriticism, and to innovate on the representation of the dispersed nature of the 'self' across four key contemporary sociocultural landscapes: journeys, family, education, and technology.

Returning to Gibbs metafictively and fictocritically, her critical works can also be used to evaluate her own fictocritical writing. For example, Gibbs' "Fictocriticism, Affect, Mimesis" essay begins "by suggesting that fictocriticism is a 'haunted writing' ... traced by numerous voices which work now in unison, at other times in counterpoint, and at others still against each other, in deliberate discord" (1). This 'haunted writing' is heavily represented in the creative self's writing, as seen in the following extracts, where "the ghosts of the dead ... always return to trouble the living being ... lingering at the thresholds of past and present, self and other, life and death" (Gibbs 311): "... the wandering ghost of TIME and IT" ("A Sentimental Cynic"); and

> After your *dziadziu* died, his ghost would return to our house in Rudnik. He was as tenacious in death as he was in life. His father Dominik was the same. It went on like this for months. Almost every night *dziadziu*'s ghost would enter a room to interrupt me. ("Storm")

> It's a ceaseless haranguing that gradually deconstructs my physical self only to reconstruct me digitally in the wake of my ghostly bodily form ("Be Careful Though. There is such a Thing as Over-organisation. (Regarding Huxley's *Brave New World Revisited*)")

These particular references to 'ghosts', spread quite widely throughout the creative folios of this book, are often literal. They can also be figurative and symbolic. The folios, as a collection of works, also demonstrate a third way of alluding to 'ghosts'. This is in the numerous voices and varying modes, techniques, perspectives and personas incorporated throughout the different sections (the anonymous meanderer in "Journeys"; Lou and *babcia* in "Family"; the agitated budding educator in "Education"; and the torn millennial 'outcast' in "Technology"). It is the analytical self's contention that the way in which Gibbs (311) discusses ghosts in "Writing and the Flesh of Others" holds to this same triplicate definition of 'ghosts': literal; symbolic; and in the literary technique of splitting up and breaking apart an author's singular voice into multiple and varying 'voices'. This 'ghost' triad (or trinity) methodology could well be identified as another elucidated fictocritical innovation.

In terms of the creative self's character(s), persona(s), voice(s) or ghost(s) (regardless of how they are labelled), they are all one and they are all different. They are an accumulation of pieces that form a whole. Therefore, not every narrator in every creative work is permitted a physical description, but they are all more or less 'reflections' ('ghosts') of the same creative self.

These numerous voices, personas and perspectives create reflections, doubles and (occasionally faint) doppelgangers of the creative self in a performative act of "recursive looping" (Gibbs 311). A suitable metaphor for this doubling and looping is best exemplified in Folio One's experimental piece "Train Ride" in which the protagonist describes his déjà vu dream-like experience as existing "in the abysmal infinity mirrors beneath our feet, caught in the motion of an unchanging and unremitting Doppler effect." This creative self is often in the (egotistical) act of performance.

Gibbs claims that fictocriticism's "performative mode" is "inimitable" and "a way of writing for which there is no blueprint, and which must be constantly invented anew in the face of the singular problems that arise in the course of engagement with what is researched" (1). This is where some research on the form delves into problematic or vaguely broad territory, the kind that Scott Brook describes as "monstrous" (113). After all, many fictocritics consider fictocriticism untameable (Brewster 29, Gibbs 310, Naismith 24). Indeed, this very discussion runs the risk of becoming an endless infinity mirror of the 'meta', as echoed by Gibbs' comment here: "But I will break off here and return to this point by way of a brief but necessary detour through the ruins of a certain discourse, one which holds to the possibility of making an absolute distinction between discourse and metadiscourse" (4).

Metadiscourse indeed. This can be quite fatiguing and mind-bending to scholarly writing and research. Yet Gibbs argues that the areas in which fictocriticism might be able to evolve are in its "rhetorical modes (the lyrical, the elegiac, the rhapsodic, the humorous, the parodic, the satirical and so on)" as well as its potential applicability to the different disciplines mentioned earlier: "anthropology, ethnography, psychoanalysis and autobiography or memoir" (2). Though fictocriticism must all the while have a "narrative point" within the context of the work. Gibbs also says that fictocriticism borrows "from certain Situationist practices" (3). *Situationism* will be explored further in the next and final section due to its relevance to technology and living in the digital age. Though without running the risk of discussing too many literary strategies, in this thesis, the "narrative point" is about maintaining a thin thread on pedagogy (education) and the way in which the creative self expresses his relationship to it. Though, in following Gibbs' example and writing style, sometimes this thread becomes a bit confusing, labyrinthine, circuitous or maze-like. The creative self tries to do too much, the writing becomes writerly, despite desiring to have a relationship with you, the reader, through the creative self's stories. Meanwhile, the analytical self struggles to express himself as a result. Now, despite the paradoxical clarity the analytical self tries to uncover in all this confusion, perhaps all that can really be said is that the unclear maze-like aspect of this fictocritical experiment might simply be a failure. This is not necessarily a fault of fictocriticism, but a fault in the ambitious methodology of the creative self's analytical self-relationship at this particular moment of the book. Nevertheless, making certain stylistic comparisons of Gibbs' writing to the creative self's, was too enticing to ignore.

Also, right now, if 'we' are to look at the page number, we are approximately around the middlemost bulge of this book's narrative arc, swimming, gasping for breath and clarity, with shores that are equally far away on either side of 'us'.

It is, furthermore, tempting to assert that Gibbs is obsessed or possessed by a desire to implement a (Derridean?) double-negative, enumerative, rhythmic, poetic and oxymoronic language in her writing, as seen in phrases like "model or anti-model" (*TEXT* 1), "Fictocriticism, then, focuses as much on the saying as the said" (*TEXT* 2), and in "The Gift": "the evolution of a cycle of prestations and counter-prestations" (40), "quarrelsome antagonism" (42), and "careless convenience" ("Gift" 43). Muecke, the 'bebop' "wizard of fictocriticism" (as endorsed by Professor Kathleen Stewart on the back cover of *The Mother's Day Protest and Other Fictocritical Essays*), is 'jazzed' by this approach too, describing fictocriticism as "a poetry of a different sort, one that responds to our times ... a poetry of fragmentation, contradiction, unanswered questions, specificity, fluidity and change ... like a piece of jazz ... to master that non-mastery" (xiv). This technique goes hand in hand with the metafictive, confused/confusing and writerly form of much fictocritical and metafictive writing (Brook 2002). It is a temptation that also captivates the creative self's writing, as seen in the following phrases from "Hum, Amplitude, (Being a) Focal Point": "Gazing up or down, no longer headfast, forwards or ahead"; "A paradoxical imbalanced love/hate relationship, to be sure". And from "'Big' Ideas": "frozen legitimacy"; "I've changed my mind about some things, though not about other things"; "I began to have no idea about certainty or truth or the subjectivity of recession and regression and an overwhelmed conscience and consciousness that loses everything it gains".

This "self-doubling" also appears in Anne Brewster's "The Poetics of Memory" (2005):

> It will take as its basis the idea that repetition is non-original, that beginnings are recursive and self-doubling — an event or feeling exists in close proximity to prior events and feelings, haunted by histories that are momentarily held at bay, forgotten. (398)

This excerpt highlights several consistencies across both fictocriticism and the creative self's own work: the general idea that "repetition is non-original", which is abundantly contemplated and articulated in the creative self's highly fictocritical (and published) piece "Repetition" (2014) in Folio Four; that it is a mode based on "events and feelings" — check; and that it is "haunted by histories", both personal and historical — this is ubiquitous in fictocriticism's antecedence in postcolonial writing, most prevalent in this book in Folio Two on diaspora and family. Brewster's comments are even similarly phrased to Gibbs' observations, for Gibbs uses the phrase "recursive looping" (311), which leads this thesis to a thread of a tangible belief, that there is something universally applicable in the phrasing of much fictocritical writing, for its vernacular is generally unencumbered, spliced and "cut-up" (Gibbs 46), "collaged" (Brewster 401), "inchoate" (Schlunke and Brewster 393), "freeform", enumerative (Gibbs 1), poetic (Noske 2013), and so on. This *phrasing* could be an aspect of (new) fictocriticism that may reveal a consistent trademark recognised throughout it, all the while being about personal(ised) storytelling (Muecke and King 14). Brewster says that this doubling "allows a relation to oneself to emerge. This relation to oneself constitutes a private life" (400), which is further consistent with Gibbs' idea and the creative self's folios being about multiple voices, personas, perspectives, reflections, doubles and doppelgangers (Gibbs 311).

When examining Brewster's own fictocritical piece, "Sucking on Remembrance" (1998), from *The Space Between*, that consistency in the implementation of disjointed (yet still connected) concepts about "vampires" (209), metaphors about cross-hatching (211), mothers (212), "betrayal" (213), frontiers (214) and "loop-the-loop" (214) is quite evident, indicating that Brewster's theory and practice work in unison and can be married with one another. More than married; they are infused and ingrained, as seen in the extract from "Sucking on Remembrance" below. Albeit, her literal writing avoids proper grammar and capitalisation, complementing that unbridled stream-of-conscience technique:

> i was thinking about memory and about thoughts. they lie dormant but when they (re)touch flesh they are full of life again. they can grow into monstrous things, mobile, with a life of their own. (Brewster 213)

This stream-of-consciousness technique is prevalent in other fictocritical works also (Campbell 1998; Bartlett 1998; Morgan 2012), and in "Hum, Amplitude, (Being a) Focal Point" and "'Big' Ideas" in Folio Three.

Katrina Schlunke and Anne Brewster's 2005 article "We Four: Fictocriticism Again" discusses how fictocriticism "attempts to display, even model, its thinking in the writing" (393). In neuroscience and neuropsychology, it is fundamentally agreed that the way the brain creates concepts, thought processes and memories in the cortex does not have a standardised structure or pattern: the way ideas are made and mapped in the mind is messy, fractured and highly dispersed (Bruce 2010). Perhaps that is why fictocriticism is so unencumbered, spliced and "cut-up", "collaged", "inchoate", "freeform", enumerative, poetic, and so on. It is a writing of impulsivity (Gibbs 309). Keeping in mind, it is a form of writing that tries to be "naturally theoretical and practical and personal" (Schlunke and Brewster 393) all at the same time. It is a mongrel of amalgamation. There exists "a desire to be understood, to be 'got' in fictocriticism" (Schlunke and Brewster 394). That is true. And the self can be messy. Therefore, fictocriticism can be messy. Of course, this is not at all meant as a negative argument. Messiness can be a positive and liberating attribute, as with messiness in sex, food and painting (there is much messiness in great art). Or, to offer an olive branch, perhaps 'circuitous' or 'labyrinthine' would be more appropriate adjectives in place of 'messy'. For Muecke's own fictocritical writing strives for lucidity and adopts an approach that benefits the pedagogical angle in this thesis. In his *No Road (bitumen all the way)* (1997) book, for instance, Muecke finds ways of making theoretical ideas more accessible:

> 'What's "pistemologies" Dad?' Joe asks.
> 'Um ... epistemology is, ah, *how you reckon you know stuff.*'
> 'Oh.' (25)

Still, it is hard to ignore the jungle of content (Brewster 213) and theoretical commentary that indicates that fictocriticism is an "uncomfortable" (Haas 54) 'genre', full of "*compounds, mergings, mutations and mistakes*" (King 13).

Brewster's 2013 paper "Fictocriticism: Pedagogy and Practice" further supports her earlier ideas of fictocriticism being about extreme fragmentation (92), hybridity and "different discourses and registers" (91). Though its focus is more on her anecdotal interests, experiences and passions, especially those to do with "practices of knowledge" and "memory" (92), all of which she claims she is able to "[excavate]" using fictocriticism (Brewster 92). Her short paper is cohesive, well-paced and has vision, discussing how fictocriticism has "evolved as a teaching tool" (89) in Brewster's own school, in different interdisciplinary areas, and has managed to avoid the punitive hierarchical, bureaucratic and colony-like structuring of students common to so many tertiary institutions and practices. Brewster says that the flexible nature of fictocriticism gives rise to a learning environment that can challenge "the comfort zone of staff" yet "ironically creates the very conditions in which students are enabled to exercise a high degree of creativity, initiative and self-motivated learning" (89). Brewster's anecdotal evidence, experiences and passions are comparable to the creative self's own close thematic interactions in this book, and by writing in this way both Brewster and the creative self free themselves up to witness the postmodern appeal and potential of fictocritical (self) learning, and its explorative and educational potential "to intellectuals both inside and outside the university" (Brewster 92).This fictocritical/pedagogical angle is an innovative consideration for Brewster, and extremely relevant to this section on education. For although there are some writings that fleetingly discuss fictocriticism's potential for education (Flavell 2004; Naismith 2009; Robins 2010), the literature surrounding the mode almost always focuses on the liberating and labour-intensive freeing up of the writer's psyche to make them more comfortable to write (Gibbs 310; Morgan 5; Pattinson 2013). Yet, Brewster, and one contention of this book, is for fictocriticism to be more broadly implemented in the academy. Autoethnography has been taking up that innovative methodological-pedagogical baton for itself for years (Ellis and Bochner 2000; Holt 2003; Canagarajah 2012; Méndez 2013; Anae 2014). Fictocriticism should do the same. Perhaps this has not happened yet because fictocriticism has always been the more flexible of the two forms. Too flexible, in fact. Though this is an area for innovation and for future research and academic educational implementation, and something that the subsequent section will discuss. For as the folios in this section, and texts like *The Orchard* have demonstrated, education is clearly an important theme and concept in fictocritical writing. Anne Brewster uses the following metaphor for collage in her essay "The Poetics of Memory":

> a short-circuiting robot, a miscellany of dismembered talking machines. Each truncated gesture the repetition of history, salutations of imperial technologies. An assemblage of arrested beginnings, the robot lurches from story to story, prodigious, haunted; the epilepsy of desire. (401)

The idea of the robot can be perceived as a tangible medium, a vehicle for fictocriticism. Technology, on the other hand, can be etched to the intangible historical routes of human civilisation. The next and final section is about these technologies and living in an increasingly digital age. The final creative folio attempts to utilise the writing mode of fictocriticism to explore some of these themes from the perspective of a young man living in the present world. It attempts to use fictocriticism to discuss the unnerving, frustrating, dystopian and nihilistic potential of new technologies, the wariness humanity should have for them, whilst at the same time using the vehicle of fictocriticism to see what realms fictocriticism itself can traverse into, whether it is susceptible to change, like humankind, for the better or the worse, or whether it will simply flounder off into methodological oblivion and vague obscurity, where it could very likely come to a halt and dissipate, in academic and creative writing, in the near future.

This section's folio included four experimental fictocritical pieces, "(Scrapped) Book", "An Agitation", "Hum, Amplitude, (Being a) Focal Point" and "'Big' Ideas", that drew on several of the creative self's pivotal educational experiences that primarily took place at Martyr University. It utilised and adapted modes of fictocriticism inspired by Drusilla Modjeska's *The Orchard* and other elemental fictocritical writings and theories by Anne Brewster, Katrina Schlunke, but primarily Anna Gibbs and her uninhibited enumerative, rhythmic, poetic and splicing approach to writing. Fictocriticism's association and disassociation with autoethnography was discussed in its thematic and academic connection to pedagogy. The next section investigates some of the precise adaptations and changes that have occurred in fictocritical writing over time, particularly in the new millennium, contextualising the methodology in a more modern, technological, or 'robotic' (to borrow Brewster's metaphor) era. The next and final thesis shows how some of the fragmentary and freeform writings of Gibbs, Campbell and Bartlett (1998), for instance, later began to exist in other tangible, less ambiguous mediums and forms, and how the vision of early pioneering fictocritics such as Anna Gibbs, Drusilla Modjeska, Amanda Nettelbeck and Heather Kerr, gradually evolved from their vague, unencumbered, yet highly 'meta' fictocritical beginnings, to the more deliberate and industrious "electric fictocriticism" (Robb 100) of the twenty-first century.

SECTION IV

SECTION IV

FOLIO FOUR: Technology

Preamble ... (2013)

> I don't have to tell you things are bad. Everybody knows things are bad. It's a depression. Everybody's out of work or scared of losing their job. The dollar buys a nickel's worth, banks are going bust, shopkeepers keep a gun under the counter. Punks are running wild in the street and there's nobody anywhere who seems to know what to do, and there's no end to it. We know the air is unfit to breathe and our food is unfit to eat, and we sit watching our TV's while some local newscaster tells us that today we had fifteen homicides and sixty-three violent crimes, as if that's the way it's supposed to be. We know things are bad—worse than bad. They're crazy. It's like everything everywhere is going crazy, so we don't go out anymore. We sit in the house, and slowly the world we are living in is getting smaller, and all we say is, 'Please, at least leave us alone in our living rooms. Let me have my toaster and my TV and my steel-belted radials and I won't say anything. Just leave us alone.' Well, I'm not gonna leave you alone. I want you to get mad! I don't want you to protest. I don't want you to riot - I don't want you to write to your congressman because I wouldn't know what to tell you to write. I don't know what to do about the depression and the inflation and the Russians and the crime in the street. All I know is that first you've got to get mad. You've got to say, 'I'm a HUMAN BEING, God damn it! My life has VALUE!' — Howard Beale, *Network* (1976)

In *Narcissistic Narrative* Linda Hutcheon makes a passing point about the comedy, irony and semi-ridiculousness implicit in even writing pieces such as mine, littered throughout this exploration, which appraise the "problems with his society and the literature to which he contributes" (55). So, why make a complaint that is going to fall on deaf ears? Why torture, infuriate and frustrate oneself further down into the muck from which you are trying to take higher ground? What is the good in identifying a problem to someone or a mass or a body or an entity that you care so little about? Why do we/I do these things? Is it more for the self or for a barrier and a separation—an otherness?

Busy Bees Buzz (2014)

Fester and grow, the pumpkin seeds of late night and early morning.

A reflection and a trial will soon come to pass. With the victims in the know and the assailants not knowing well enough but belonging to the mass. Heartache and headaches gradually suppressed.

To say something is to be at an immediate loss; caught in the in between. A caffeinated sarcophagus of thought—being choked up a little.

Waiting patiently while the busy bees blatantly disregard. This is the pattern with which we're to be woken up with. Dreams and waking life divided by a fine line of confrontation and antagonism, and a minor buzz.

Do the Evolution(ary Jig) (2015)

I've noticed that people don't really call one another on the phone any more. I suppose we haven't really been calling one another for several years now. Our communication is largely dominated by online messenger systems — anything that can create a digital wall (or a kind of decompression chamber) between us. A cooling off zone for thought and overcomplicated analysis, procrastination and hierarchical waiting bays for those we wish to contact and respond to, or avoid. Nothing is off-the-cuff or spontaneous as in face-to-face communication. The more imminent technology has made communication, the less we think about how we respond and act and 'talk' with one another. It's all become stilted, jarring, systematic, banal, predictable and evasive.

Though, to be honest, this also depends largely on one's age bracket. The older one is, the more likely one is to call somebody else. The younger one is the less likely they are to place a call, and the more likely they are to message or text another person and then just sit or react to that message.

I sit here now at this moment and I have to make a call to arrange something today. It's urgent. I am twenty-seven years of age as I write this, an older Generation Y "millennial" entity, and I feel as though I am in that in-between period between texting and calling. It's a fairly even-sided 50/50 split.

As a teenager, I spent my evenings on the landline or cordless telephone chatting with my school friends for hours. My older sisters were even more wedded to this way of communication in their hey-day (they are around five to six years older than me). As females who were born in the early 1980s, they are right on that cusp-split between Generation Y and Generation X, one might argue. They could go either way in terms of their personal classification, if they wished.

In any case, I have to make a call today. I don't know the precise age of the person I'm calling, but I know that if they're a little younger than I am, a call may seem inappropriate to them — aggressive even. That's how I see or apprehend the younger generation as perceiving things. Though if this person is a little older than I am it shouldn't be an issue at all. I frequently receive telephone calls from people who are in their late twenties (i.e., twenty-eight or twenty-nine). And anybody who is thirty or older seem totally exempt and has the grace and freedom to call whomever they wish, and it won't seem out of the ordinary (to most people). But for me, at this time, twenty-seven to call does seem just that little bit unusual. Twenty-six would be even more abnormal, and as we descend into the stream of twenty-something year olds who were born in 1990 or later, phone calls … and especially phone calls between strangers … seem odd, out of touch, out of place, time and context.

I don't know much about this individual I am calling. All I know is that his name is Branko. I've sent him a number of emails over the past few weeks, and as they've increased in importance and urgency, I 'warned' him (yesterday) that I might need to call him today. I *warned* him though. Why did he need to be warned? Why was I bracing him and myself in this suspense and anticipation? Why did he need to be told in advance? Because this is not a bridge I can afford to burn with inappropriate or awkward etiquette. And if he is twenty-six or younger, it could certainly come off this way. Phone calls are becoming more and more seemingly aggressive or invasive, even though that is, or always has been, the primary function of phones? Though now phones, mobile phones and smart phones, have many more functions than merely just the 'call' function. Though people don't like the spontaneity of it, perhaps, the necessity to react and respond in an improvisational tone? People don't like to talk in a way that functions in the 'now'. People don't like to be in the 'now'. Everything we do reminiscently and organisationally relates to the past and the future. And phone calls, even if dealing with issues of past and future, are essentially a now-oriented exercise that we are becoming more and more disengaged with. It is a difficult thing to do for me and for people my age, I think.

I was in another similar predicament recently in which I followed up two of my emails with a text message, and the response from the person I was texting, who is around twenty-two or twenty-three, was: "Hey Pawel, sorry you had to resort to texting me to chase me up!" Crazy, I thought. Isn't that the point of texting?

I'm always impressed by the older generation, particularly baby boomers, who pick up the phone and chat with such ease and comfort and still accomplish what the intentions of their phone call sets out to do. It looks and sounds like an art form to me: the witty combination of banter, humour, purpose and kindness. Even those who don't particularly like interacting or engaging with people—perhaps like the older ones who are more or less set in their own ways and merely comfortable with the company of their own (sense of) self—these people have the balance, the technique—the art form—down pat also. I've seen it, heard it, and am always moved by it.

My generation does not do this or 'perform' like this very well at all. And, so, we 'brace' one another for impending conversation, which should be as simple, easy and relaxed as taking a bath or flowing down a gentle amicable stream (of consciousness).

But the sense of timing on the phone is the same. It always feels as though I am racing against the clock—that I should be wrapping up what I am trying to say as quickly as possible, even though a quickened pace breeds that discomfort I am trying to avoid by shortening the length of the conversation in the first place. It is certainly awkward, or has the potential to be so. Those initial moments should really be about trying to establish comfort, though it feels as though time is amplified in those first few seconds—I can't get out what I am trying to say and convey to the person on the other line quickly enough! You could say that it's just an over-indulgent sense of anxiety—that that state of mind is all in one's head, and that's probably true too. But that doesn't mean that it's not in the heads of the majority of the people within my age bracket and that we don't think about straightforward conversations on the phone to one another in this type of agonised way.

Now, how about handwritten letters? That's a whole other story, concept and ballpark altogether. Handwritten letters are truly outdated—'snail mail', it's called; it's nostalgic now, perhaps. Nevertheless, it isn't so outdated to me that I didn't see its use and purpose when I was a child. I always watched my grandmother write handwritten letters to her husband, family and friends back home in Poland when she was living with us in Australia and when I was attending primary school here, and so it rubbed off on me as something relatively normal. International or interstate phone calls and using the dial-up Internet were still relatively expensive for us at the time, and there was also a time limit for these things (i.e., you paid per minute or something like that), so when it came to handwritten letters, *time* was on your side for once.

A close friend of mine from primary school moved to Perth when we were both in Grade Five. We would've been around ten years of age at the time. We continued to write (letters) to one another for the next four years, fairly consistently (at least once every two or three months) and stayed in touch that way. The letters fizzled out by the time we were thirteen or fourteen, but I still believe and also remember thinking that that was quite an impressive feat and span of attention for children — we wrote handwritten letters to one another for longer than we knew one another in person. And we wrote sentimental letters to one another when we, as people, were changing so much, physically, psychologically and emotionally.

Moreover, we used to wait (for these letters to arrive). We were patient with our communication. There's a song by Arcade Fire called "We Used to Wait", with fragmented lines like "I used to write letters … Before the flashing lights settled deep in my brain … But by the time we met … The times had already changed" (*The Suburbs*, 2010).

Attention spans are even shorter now in general. And our *own* attention spans are shorter too (i.e., the children who grew up in the 1990s and are adults now). We used to wait for things, and now we've become just that little bit more impatient; I think I was a much more patient child than I am now as an adult. The friend of mine from primary school whom I wrote to, Kirsty, and I recently reconnected on Facebook. It was much too easy. It took seconds, not minutes, let alone weeks, months or years. So, the rise and fall and novelty of the situation came quickly and then wore off almost instantaneously. There were no long essay-like messages that occurred once we reconnected. There was a brief stint of excitement followed by silence, and then she (or we) gradually both fell into that cesspool category of people we have and 'know' in our 'friends' list online. When they're always there and when they're always instantaneously available, we don't want them or require them there, and we don't want or require them instantaneously. We were different people back then. It was different back then. It always is (and never will be).

Perhaps some things are truly better off left in the memory banks of our own past.

Coaxing the Ouroboros (2014)

Yet the past does not exist. Emotions, that happened. Ruthlessly suggested and non-committal. Processed through a phase of communication. Generated by generations — the scope of a scaffolding. A means to maintain a simplicity that evades and manoeuvres through the present. A procession of imaginative magnitude. A faultless falsity that continues to justify itself, tumultuously. Exponential madness alienating one from the other. To feel the thrill and thrust now and to tenaciously reel. To neglect regret. Copycats copy cats; a coaxing, followed by no confidence.

Suggested solutions leer on a curlew's outstretched wings, screaming and chasing a young/old man down a pathless street. Running across terraces and grasslands and deserts and sand and shrubbery and the concrete echoing steps of a dimly lit alleyway in a great big city of glorified beatitude, whilst racing restlessly in every single opposite direction there is in a globe with or without pronged unification, feelers feeling out blindly, correlating paths or time signatures and recipes for disaster and a midnight snack to satisfy the Obelisk and the Ouroboros of former worlds or world-like sessions filled with champions with much less across a much broader and greater space, heightened, though never taller, than the overarching towers and spires of a church steeple, a castle, a 'retro' skyscraper, all the while we clamber and climb outside, jousting with turrets with severed heads on protruding spikes …

… and I have a loss for words in the end. Madness is initialised, replacing original sin successfully. Lethargy and sleeplessness take over on another sinister evening heaving, and I'm lost to thought processes universally, collaboratively and collectively accumulated and then scattered, like ashes, in the dead of the night.

I ran over a snake, coiled and recoiled, protecting itself in the middle of the road in absolute plain sight, insignificant. It could have even been a discarded shredded car tyre. It could have just as easily been both. Rubbery and torn with patterns enigmatic and majestic, mimicking one another in a succession of rows and ridges.

The passing over of, the passing through, passionate pointless symbolism pointed out. Staying and stained in place, concretely. Without a slither or a bowing of the head, subdued and rigid, stillborn and statuesque on an interconnected and interdisciplinary highway of infinite direction and chance.

> According to Guattari, contemporary upheavals resulting from capitalism and technological developments have meant that the notion of the subject and its meaning is not only becoming a more pressing question, but that we also require a new way to understand the "subjective cocktail" that is emerging. Subjectivity or subjectification has in these times of global media and consumerism become the driving force, not ideology. In other words, the notion of the subject as a pre-existing entity — set in opposition to society — is no longer adequate to explain our experience. Nor is it useful, according to Guattari, in effectively negotiating the complex forces that come to bear on us in this milieu. (Flavell 72)

Guattari, via Flavell, alludes to close, romantic or sentimental relationships I continue to have or have had in the past with others, such as Kirsty and the bond we formed, over time, through our physically manifested letter-writing, and the 'legitimacy' and integrity of that in this current age and space.

Palahniuk's *Invisible Monsters* (2015)

Chuck Palahniuk's introductory idea in his novel *Invisible Monsters* (2000) is that you can always seem to see your tired, bloated and vacant face reflecting mildly, partially in all the screens you gaze at (computer, smart phone, tablet, etc.), in an expression of void:

> Nowadays, whatever purchase you moon over, whatever person you lust after, most likely it's presented on a smooth glass or plastic screen. On a laptop or a television. And no matter what the technology, you'll catch sight of your own reflection. In that electric mirror, there hovers your faint image. You'll be superimposed over every email. Or, lurking in the glassy surface of online porn, there you are. Fewer people shut down their computers anymore, and who can blame them? The moment the monitor goes black, you're looking at yourself, not smiling, not anything. Here's your worst-ever passport photo enlarged to life size. Swimming behind the eBook words of Jane Austen, that slack, dead-eyed zombie face, that's yours. That's you. (v-vi)

When I turn to look at my smart phone during the night, it shines or glows brightly, eliminating everything else around it. Everything surrounding the phone is saturated in complete darkness. In this 'case' the visual opposite of Arthur C. Clarke and Stanley Kubrick's solid black monolith of a rectangular prism, from *2001: A Space Odyssey* (1968) exists, elucidating its bright, ghostly pervasive information, data and 'idioteque'. Once its screen is off, right away, its ghastly afterglow remains in place in the residual aftermath of my perception. I turn my head this way and that way, and still it remains, a block, a rectangle of white afterglow/afterbirth, gradually dissipating and still kind of remaining in the darkness around me and in front of me. It feels as though I might eventually grow blind to its exposure and what it does to me at night. But for now, I complacently, or with mild irritation, try to go back to sleep … until I turn it back on in front of me and it permeates through the pitch blackness of my natural vision, this unnatural perversion/echo of 'light'.

All the glass and plastic encasings now also refract and diffract me, barely visible. I watch a movie and I need to tilt the screen or shift it from side to side so I don't see that stupid 'nothing' expression of mine staring back when I look through at it in the background, depending on how far I'm sitting or lying back from the monitor. Or a gleam of sunlight, a glare catches the screen from an open window where real light comes through, but I tilt and shift the screen again to avoid that realness.

Whether I see myself from a distance or up close, diffracted or clearly before anything is really or properly turned on, the expression is the same: expressionless. And we are becoming the vague and the vain, simultaneously. And I'm a broken record by this point. Maybe that's what that sound was just then? Coming in and out, inconsistently. We are certainly fading as the colours and sounds become more pristine, less pixelated, brighter, more colourful, though both the sound and the silence are deafening, so we don't know which we prefer?

The old or the new. Vinyl sales are going up, on old nostalgic record players; vintage vintage. We're somewhat deaf and blind with our choices and options, unsure of what we want so we blend two very different worlds, and in this uncertainty our hollow faces stare back bleakly, into a void of unclear distance or proximity.

So, you should turn it up: brighter and louder.

In France in the late 1950s and 60s there existed a movement called the 'Situationist(s)' whose "central thesis was that art, in all its traditional forms, was completely played out" (4), just as now technology has made everyone pseudo 'experts', 'knowledgeable' but simultaneously brain dead in terms of creativity and attention spans. This idea, to which I and Palahniuk appear to subscribe, is articulated in Christopher's Gray's "Essays from Leaving the 20th Century" in *What is Situationism?* (1996). Gray's paper discusses the inception of the avant-garde magazine *Internationale Situationiste* and their movement in France. Gray argues that the Situationists were similar to the "*first* Surrealists" (6). I get the impression that Gray dwells on this movement because he sees this kind of 'situationist' reinvigoration occurring at the turn of the 21st Century, or even now? Gray discusses the pretentiousness of many of these creative intellectuals and their obscure ideas for/of art, literature, film, lifestyle, etc.: "Intellectuals really are a hopeless lot" (7). Gray is cynical (and sentimental). I feel the same way:

> Today—nothing. The Utopian image has faded from the streets. Just the endless traffic, the blank eyes that pass you by, the nightmarish junk we're all dying for. Everyone seems to have retreated into themselves, into closed occult groups. The revolutionary excitement that fired the sixties is dead, the 'counter-culture' a bad joke. No more aggression, no more laughter, no more dreams. 'To talk of life today is like talking of rope in the house of a hanged man'. (Gray 20)

Palahniuk also prompts me to think about the way we, as a society, have technologically disintegrated, and how many other (good) or revolutionary things have disintegrated (prematurely) also. Gray does attempt to, in part, justify or discuss the possibility of this kind of situationist movement still existing today, but ultimately, he is rather defeatist and bluntly honest: "I feel very fucked up myself" (23). When I read Gray's paper I consider its applicability and relevance to the digital world.

Technological Response: A Confession (2015)

Nevertheless, (obviously) I can't seem to get away from the call of the technological response either, which I view as the sense of urgency or seeming need to constantly be responding and replying to everyone's online messages as quickly as possible.

I need it for everything—to get around and to see and to do. It's always on and I'm always linked to it. There's always something urgent happening in somebody else's life that requires the attention or my attention to that electrical glow. I take myself away, I remove myself, and then it takes me away, removes me from situational presence. It lies next to me (when I wake/when I sleep) like the prophetic Kubrickean monolith, prompting the next urgent technological advancement or enhancement. Sure, it helps. I can get better food and have it delivered, stay in contact with people, update my 'status' and find directions to wherever it is I need to be getting to. The disadvantage is I cut out a big chunk of what I'm doing *when* I'm doing it.

So ... sadly I too fall into this cheapened (consumerist) category. As I've mentioned, I believe that practically no one is pure or exempt from it.

We/I have disengaged from the outer to focus self-indulgently and egotistically on the inner—a cowardly retreat. Though before I get too carried away, I should stress that I cannot or should not drive an ultra-hard line either. Technology can be a balance of the good and the bad; nevertheless, it seems that in some areas and avenues technologies "that were supposed to empower the individual strengthened the dominance of giant corporations, while technologies that were supposed to boost democratic participation produced a population of couch potatoes" (Morozov 276). This sounds like such an enraged clichéd phrasing.

Though I wonder if this sense of laziness can or even should be emulated for the sake of the 'masses'? Do things need to be watered down for others, and for the sake of their comprehension? Do we fear intellectuals or intelligence more so now than we did in the past? Is it too elitist to be proper and coherent? This sentiment is exemplified in the way in which I craft my emails and virtual messages to people now: I write whatever I have to write out, the way I would want myself, on the receiving end, to read it, and then I look back over my message(s), to check if they are in fact watered down enough so that they can be comprehended by my compatriots. Is there an appropriate level of mistakes? Have I made sure not to ask too many questions so as to not overload the circuitry of the mind on the receiving end? Does it sound too pompous? Does my clarificatory tone and style, or line of questioning ultimately confuse the reader? Is less, in fact, more?

I find that if I convolute my messages too much people never answer them properly. They need to be overly or overtly succinct—brief. Amongst my colleagues and peers, it seems as though people are only capable of answering one or two questions in any virtual text message, and no more. They don't have the patience for it. They only look for key words. They almost always answer incorrectly or evasively because that seems to be the way, trend, fashion or incidental necessity of things now. At best 80 per cent of what I ask or inquire about in an electronic message is answered, and never 100 per cent. And even then, 80 per cent, I would say, is being quite generous. If I ask someone two or three questions online, they'll answer one. If I ask someone four or five questions online, they'll answer one.

I remember emailing a band one time, inquiring as to whether they'd be interested in doing a show together with my band in the near future. They answered in the affirmative. I followed up this email thread with two proposed dates, asking the band if they would be interested in performing on one particular night or another, with set dates, times and venues in mind for each. Their response to this was "yes, definitely!" I groaned. I replied, asking "Great! Which one?" I never heard from them again after that, even after I followed up and re-sent my email numerous times over the subsequent weeks. I'm not sure if they were being rude, false or simply never checked that email account again after that particular correspondence. I may never know the answer to this. But to me this kind of back-and-forth is indicative, and epitomises the type of 'online' culture, I live in today: oblivious to detail, completely overwhelming, overstimulated and unable to reciprocate and respond to a simple line of questioning. Or perhaps we are able to respond, but with too much simplicity for any real depth of communication. Our answers seem to be binary (i.e., 'yes' and/or 'no') with no greater pattern or significance than answering with one '1' or one '0'. We're like rash and senseless robots, we humans, incapable of seeing anything beyond our first primary function of 'being'. Now, granted, dealing with musicians has always been infamously difficult—in actuality also; they're lazy and fickle and their lifestyle doesn't necessarily demand or connote a great deal of structure, organisation or routine. However, this is how I feel the majority of my online interactions 'go' in other social spheres also. Perhaps I'm too finicky, but I like some attention to detail—I think it's important. And to be honest, I'm not demanding that much. I just want my questions to be answered. For me closure is critical for personal growth.

On the other hand, I could use this to my advantage. After all, a "planned world (a world that fully reveals its planning) is a dead world" (Hutcheon 58). This kind of unresponsive, unobservant evasiveness could be considered a form of escape. When questions and non-answers are left quite open or open to interpretation, as opposed to having concrete meanings, responses and set or ingrained and obvious intentions, it can work in my favour sometimes. It makes me seem a little more casual or 'chilled out', as they say. I can then trick people into conveying a sense of self that could be inclined in this way or that way. When someone is offended by what I've said I can easily turn around and correct or justify my intentions, if need be. Conversation and (virtual) communication then turns into a blank or Rorschach-type canvas that is in constant swirling motion and is always susceptible to change. No one means anything and there is no meaning behind anything; no one can love or lose or get into trouble or be hurt or inspired by anything because nothing winds up meaning anything (at all). At this juncture I would say that the negatives (or lack of meaning or consequence) far outweigh these meandering pointless positives. I don't value this way of communicating online. I don't admire it. I don't like it. Alas, these days it seems to have become a necessity. Less is more.

Tunnel Vision: A Tribute to *2001: A Space Odyssey* (2014)

A witness to boredom throughout the ages: tunnel vision and time travel, cutting through the layers of climate and savagery, from the simplicity and complacency and mindless frustrations, the underwhelming fixation on nothingness, witnessing the circles cut out in the fourth dimension, the metaphysical, watching time crawl in the opposite direction, wormlike, an infinity mirror sliced, going far back, watching a fool throw rocks against the stone wall, with the rocks cracking and then falling to the ground again, dumbstruck and not knowing what to do with the activity or how to explain or justify it to himself or to the other passive onlookers in the cave around him. Then ultimately to watching a space shuttle collapse, spiralling down to earth, erupting in flame whilst penetrating the atmosphere of the world; mistakes of boredom and complacency — causation and inevitable cessation.

And everyone here or not here, over time, past and future has felt the flashes, those dull moments grinding away where or when the mind wanders and is stiffened and collapses under the lack of pressure or the pressure to enforce and recharge with re-energised pressure. And it is in these dull moments that mistakes are made, causing the rocks to crack and splinter pointlessly, and someone elsewhere indirectly (an inadequate technician, an engineering or design flaw) causing the shuttle to crash and fall back down to earth. To venture further outwards literally, physically — there is no point, or rather we are too tainted by the cause and effects of the boredom that subsequently and erratically thrusts, surging and carrying us on.

So, at this final pass, the last man in a long line of men and wanderers falling to earth is given the gift of seeing his cumulative and gradual undoing. He is given retrospective hindsight into the eternal past. It isn't just his life flashing before his eyes, it is the lives of humankind, circular, spherical, metaphysical, mirrored in infinity, like tunnel vision curling and spiralling, like a protruding worm inverted through time, slices of a lifeless life, of complacency and boredom and the lack of activity and proactivity induced by a lack of motivation, or who knows what else. He has been given this gift by chance or by fate. There is no doubt it is beautiful and wonderful and barely comprehensible to the human eye, in all its glory and consciousness. It is barely even possible — these streams of consciousness, of all consciousness, lacklustre and unenthusiastic, and nor are they even mistakes necessarily. This could be a chance opportunity for a reconsideration after all.

(Constantly) Changing Headspaces: I'm Bored (2013)

The motions are running fast now. And headspaces are changing all the time. Every day is different and so one needs to change and renew a state of readiness all the time. So 'one' says anyway. Most people would just go through these motions, but I have to prepare myself for them. And, so, I can only enjoy things as much as my expectations allow me to. And if I don't have any preconceived expectations because I don't have time to ready myself for them then I simply don't know what to do with myself. This is the time to let go of and lose the ego, to enjoy and that is what I am hoping for at this interval. I knew what this period was going to be going into it. Maybe I wasn't 'ready' for it, but I did prepare myself for it. I wanted it because everything else at the time was lacking and boring. Maybe I'm not as comfortable as I normally am or as consistent and regimented with my routine(s), but this should be the benefit in this experiment. I should be able to find something new here. Something that isn't predetermined, or wasn't predetermined? Obvious stagnation, yes. Changed environment. Unobvious results and consequences that could *help* me and my two-dimensional views. My plain and plains of thought. It's time to promote vicariousness, frivolity, dirt and filth and patterns of being that have made no sense to me for a long time: people behaving in a way that startles and confuses me and absolutely makes no sense but hey, not every hour of the day needs to be monitored or have a task going on. You can just *do* things as well. Purposeful purposelessness. Immunity to or from the mundane tedium. Sitting back and sitting forward and sitting sideways and falling from time to time to realise that the fall, the vertigo, is a sensation that has been lacking. If everything is wrapped up, undamaged and clean then, well, you never actually get to use your device(s), get your hands and chest dirtied up in the giddy madness. They are all a little bit flippant, and you're learning how to be too ... a little.

... But My Friends are Unreliable, So Plans are Hard to Make (2014)

It's not really a coincidence that the majority of my friends are unreliable. I finally realise that now. I have chosen to become friends with these kinds of people as an escape, a release. A release from the rigidity and compulsive over-organisation of my own life and lifestyle. If everything ran on time we'd be bored – there would be no passion. I need these unorganised, ridiculous, sometimes crazy, people to free me up, to inspire spontaneity and looseness, fun and flexibility (craziness in me even). But I can't rely on them on a professional level. It is not in their nature to be available, consistent, dependable, to arrive on time or do something they promised then and there. It's not on their radar and it's not a personal attack either. It's not that they don't care, it's just that they don't care a lot *in general* – they're not worried, I should say. And if I do decide to take it personally because I see them running on time to other things (like their job) that is because they ... need to eat? I will be frustrated; I will become agitated and angry about this. I will kick and scream now and again. But here's a reminder: you need these people too. Otherwise, you'd go crazy (not in a good way) as a result of monotony.

After all, the World Does Not Run on Time (2013)

What would you do if you had the choice, the decision was yours to make, with the ball was in your court, and so forth? Wear my shoes and take my blessings and interpret them, appropriate them, as your own, and what would they mean and what would they be to you?

Is taking the higher ground always the better option or should one pursue pleasure, short-term satisfaction, an appreciation of the moment as opposed to a prolonged inner rumination that cannot be turned off? Once in a while a separation is had and is enjoyed but it is rare — so rare, in fact, that treatment for this obsession could or should probably be sought (out).

Seconds tick by as boredom epitomises (for you) time wasted. You wedge small parts and particles in between long interludes of experience and thought and action and activity and so you convince yourself that you're filling your days when in fact all you're really doing is enhancing your engorged appetite for more and more and more.

Restless infancy and adolescence slowed down or sped up into restless adulthood and consecutive decisions made poorly and at the wrong time so that every and all other parties are frustrated and disappointed (with you). Had those same choices and decisions been made just a little bit earlier or later, then ecstatic happiness would most definitely ensue!

More means more merriment for all that are caught in the constant in between(s) wedged classically and artistically at the crux of these appointments that are never kept by anyone, for the world does not run on time.

Yet My Persistence and Insistence are Being Misconstrued as Haughty and Overbearing (2014)

And then/now my persistence and insistence are being misconstrued as haughty and overbearing. It is difficult to stop. I am anxious about it. Constantly being put under and putting on the pressure. Incessant polite demands and a questioning attitude – a desire for certainty and confirmation, which alienates myself from others. Damn it. So hard to stop. Change comes about, but not really.

It is simply because, as I've alluded to in the past, present and future tense(s), my time frames are personalised and constructed a little differently. I ensure, to the largest extent, that I am not too busy – that I am not overly burdened. This reduces me to perplexity *and* boredom but ensures that all tasks are done and that equal attention is paid to all. It is a consideration but then the world does not run on time. Something I petulantly keep forgetting. Oh, the heart's anxious palpitations. Called, messaged, emailed too many times, apparently or evidently. Beyond repair even. I just want closure. And closure's beyond repair they say, with an attitude like that. Swords and fucking shields, we are. Do people seriously not desire consolation and confirmation? Is everyone submitting to the idea, the concept that they genuinely just go along with the flow? Can there be a functioning there? Too whimsical.

Resolution is all I want, good or bad, but this kind of incessant confidence is misconstrued as creepiness. Persistence has turned on its head and into a vice. A traditional sense of rationality hasn't even been adopted by the 'masses' but skipped over into a new age of heartfelt resistance [to what?]!

And I conform to it, if you would believe it. I do. I would be even haughtier in seeking out truths from everyone if it were socially acceptable. But *no*, let's all resist instead. Let's flow along using our barren shields as life rafts, blasé to the opportunities that could only be gained if properly pressed.

Others might argue that a certain calm and cool nonchalance can get you there too, but I reject that. It offends me. How can that sentiment be trusted? How can you put all of your chickens and faith into a half *full* basket of stripped integrity?

When a question isn't answered you are leaving a dead zone that we gradually slump and slip away into, dampening and deepening the world into an introverted, self-speculative divided voicelessness that further cheapens us, accentuating the need for overtly (no, covertly) dishonest social flailings of clipped wings.

And yet, the irony is, that we are always required to repeat ourselves. Information is so accessible digitally, so why shouldn't it be just as ready between human interaction? I'm at a (cocktail) party, and someone comes up to me and asks me how my studies, work or family are going. I answer them in enthusiastic detail. Then someone else approaches me and asks me the same question again. I answer with less detail and perhaps less enthusiasm. By the time the third or fourth person asks me, I simply cannot answer at all. My brain implodes, and I wish, to myself, and even for their sake (if they genuinely care): why couldn't they be there for the first recapitulation? I stammer, mumble and fail to even commence, and they're left there before me, waiting (in suspense, maybe, or out of courtesy? I don't know, because even though I cannot tell them this, they probably shouldn't have asked).

Hence, I/we stray into dangerously repetitious territory.

Repetition (2014)

To repeat oneself; something I always do, but I sincerely don't have the stamina for it, which also doesn't make sense because the nature of current projects and investigations and inquiries all have a cyclical and spherical and mirrored repetitious nature. Why then is it so difficult to communicate repetitiously in speech and human communication? I find that only one of my good anecdotes has a genuinely worthwhile re-telling, and after that everything comes out dry and drawl and drawn out, despite how interesting the whole operation was or is or appears to be. It's a tragedy and a gamble because the one(s) on the receiving end are never necessarily deserving of the decent or the good or the animated (re)telling, or they are the ones that don't appreciate it. I don't think they realise how much energy goes into these tellings, these *yarns*, for some more than others. And they, like I also I suppose, are there vacantly and somewhat patiently merely waiting for their turn to speak.

I sigh and I groan, and I wish I could pick my audience better or more accurately. One after the other after the other. I can't do it, and these days it's only getting worse—more difficult. Maybe if I could re-tell my recountings in a different language? At least then there would be a new colour and a flourish to the anecdotes. Meanwhile, I have to endure and suffer the knowledge that people in general simply don't find me as interesting or charismatic as I actually am. I know this. I've seen the various and varied looks of surprise, excitement or lack thereof when I communicate freely, or otherwise do not have the capacity, the energy, the muster, the *jus* to do so. And then again, maybe I should be a mute—communicate with my gestures and mannerisms rather than use my words. My words I can save for the page, the printed or typed page, even freehand, maybe (I'm probably too young for that, to be honest). But at least then the recountings only ever have to occur once. Save them, print them, reproduce them, staple them to the sides, insides, of corridors in buildings or to mountains—who gives a shit. They're there, and they'll be there, and they will continue to be there after I'm gone if I can learn to store them properly or mass produce and/or reproduce them on a scale so that they will only very slowly die out through passive negligence and the natural order of the ages.

Though by the time that happens I'll be long gone, and I'm still very uncertain as to whether or not I care about caring for a legacy. Alas, I am somewhat partial to a vague notion of spirituality and the belief that a spirit will endure somewhere, or in/onto something else, elsewhere, like a phantom split into particles beyond, and outward, susceptible to something or an other.

In any case, repetition, I hate it. Can't stand it. Refuse to do it—more and more. Reproduction, on the other hand—this I can take. This is easy. It requires a completely different kind of energy—an organisational energy, which I have: an ability to order and to structure things. This I can do. I'll work on it now.

Here lies an autobiographical attempt to describe my temperament and characteristics without actually really describing anything 'real' or occurring/active about the events within my autobiography. It is a (pretentious) post-structuralist notion about the repetition of language more so than any events or instances in life, which had or have a repetitious nature. And that is largely what Roland Barthes' *Roland Barthes* is about: describing a life of language more so than a life itself—a life invested in language in which all thought processes and occurrences immerse themselves within a psyche and a psychology controlled and moulded by the parameters of language, and perhaps the limitations of vocabulary and dialect itself.

In a journal article called "The Exegesis and the Gentle Reader/Writer" (2004) Jeri Kroll describes higher degree candidates as firing "shots, if not always on their own behalf, on behalf of those writers or theorists they admire and want to emulate" (9). What Kroll is encouraging here is the ability or even the necessity to wear your influences on your sleeves—there is nothing shameful about wanting to, at times or in small doses perhaps, mimicking the style and format of a writer you respect and appreciate if you want to get your idea across in a particular way.

I have often considered the impossibility of doing (writing) anything essentially 'original', and the liberation and freedom one can attain from simply admitting this—knowing it. In this piece I think that I successfully get my point about *repetitiousness* across whilst simultaneously paying my respects to Barthes and the ways in which he breaks down language to reveal certain truths, and also the ways in which those truths reflect the 'self' more truthfully and uniquely:

> he somewhat fetishizes language, these real divisions are absorbed in their interlocutive form: it is interlocution which is divided, alienated: hence he experiences the entire social relationship in terms of language. (Barthes 168)

Here, Barthes conveys his point in a much more elegant way. Though the same frustrations exist as in my prior narrative, they are held back. Barthes writes in the third person, though I'm not sure exactly why that is—perhaps it is a professional distancing of the self from the language which binds him and which he is trying to explore and discuss in his autobiography—to what end though, I am still uncertain.

My Refrigerator: More Repetition (2014)

My refrigerator woke me up last night. Its rumblings, squeaks and groans, soft dripping and the rise and fall of its inconsistent 'breathing' and 'moaning'. Zombies come to mind, the living dead in my dreams instilled by the external fridge in my studio apartment. These overlapping living arrangements, all in close quarter: like Ari in *Loaded*, I shit where I eat; I sleep where I work; I wander, and I roam where I activate and disengage with all the other mediums of squandered restless (in)activity. It really isn't all that bad. It's just that this night it happened (over and over again). The unsteady repetition literally comes to mind at night now, rather than just during the regular cycles and intervals and systems of the day-to-day. The gurgling drains away, and I am enclosed in everything again—a simplicity. A lack of association (in need); I need to stimulate conversation with others, even if it does not stimulate me, because it is good and healthy for me to do so. Not everything needs to be an effort. There needs to be a calm casualty about it, like how baby boomers speak. Otherwise, I will die in my sleep with a groan and a grumble, a moan and a rumble, breathing inconsistently and without any vibrato-like steadiness—my inner mechanics failing as I try less and less to be cool (with it—my dark and enclosed wholesomeness).

Solutionism (2017)

Watch the roads or you'll never see or hear it
Coast to coast, a frequency, we play the role well

Rolling on we plan to seek out some more
Check the pulse, we're second-guessing the beat of everything

The patterns of patience, the tired and the wasted
We sit on our saddles and feel the vibration
To cycle, to matter (the patents of agents)
Obsessive compulsions, an ego elated

And crashing rotations, to tread through the ages
Arrested procedures; our time's never vacant
Delirious natures divide expectations
I'll roam more than ever, more than ever

Music and Lyrics by Pawel Cholewa © 2017

Canvas (2013)

Intelligence (or over-thinking) can be a curse: the over-analytical, the almost-but-never satisfied desire, quenched with a questioning and a further need for investigation that only furthers scepticism and doubt and a fluid, rushing, effervescent need, silken and pure but contrasted by the severity of the contemporary *zeitgeist*, flaccid in its angst and anger and the knife that drives and digs and delves itself into its own back, completely impractical and unusable, and yet sustained and continuous.

I would claw my eyes and teeth out if I knew I didn't have to succumb to a thirst that never quenches, but squelches and inflames the nose, suffocating and forming aneurisms. I don't know how Henry Miller managed it. I suppose he really didn't "give a fuck" (14), which is probably true. He did say it and show it, and kind of command it after all. I would love to step into his shoes, appreciate and liberate myself, unashamedly. Quality exists, but not everywhere, and you have to choose your place, your space. Timing is everything. Timing and intuition. And a type of calm that certain and specific kinds of intelligence do not possess.

Resentful and bashful, to be a primate right now, smashing the skulls of foes into walls and reciprocate with a glare and kicking whilst swallowing a mouthful of poison, stupefying but bringing me one step closer to stupidity and all the insight and beauty and purity that comes with being that little bit more brain dead.

And dead. If it is a death, and if it is incurable, irreparable, then maybe I do want it after all. I think it would suit me. Being pseudo-intellectual enough helps. A starting lap, a jumping off point, into the cesspool of cowardice, peaceful, blissful ignorance. A sigh of relief, swarming and fecundating, a rebirth of thoughtless vitality, invigorated by nothingness, a blank canvas that continually exists as a blank canvas, being coloured and infiltrated and contoured by flashing lights and streams of pity and a shining, glistening, greasy creased up (tattering/tittering at the edges) mistake of an identity.

Narcissism ... gone. Now to bathe in the fountain and be reborn anew: lights become lighter; colours become brighter; food becomes flavoursome; patronisation becomes nurturing; despondency becomes forgiveness; forgetfulness becomes fearlessness; resilience becomes violence; bleakness and blandness become the blank canvas of a brand-new breed of brotherhood.

P.S. Mutual Misunderstandings of Brotherhood (2014)

Mutual misunderstandings, an inability to communicate. Brotherless brothers. Speak to one another about trivialities. Out the door, 'round the corner, playing leapfrog in discourse. Language lost.

As narcissistic as all of this is, I am still trying to avoid 'narcissism', at least in myself. I am weary and wary of it. It exists, but it's something that can and should be controlled, limited. I don't aim or want to alienate my reader, but rather to share and hopefully find a relatable (sentimentally cynical) common ground.

These pieces are self-explorative slices of life in general. Some are vignettes. And as such they should be more of a critique of the contemporary *zeitgeist* and of the self too; a critique upon the kinds of people that exist in the exuberant and youthful culture and social circles of the day—the kinds of people that any intellectual or even pseudo-intellectual are forced to deal and interact with, not quite knowing how to get their point across, how to communicate, genuinely, whilst struggling against the grain of a processed and homogenised culture, pointlessly battling it out in a communication that is stillborn. (Context).

"Canvas" conveys a notion ruled by emotion. Yet it conveys a sentiment that is ruled by this emotion only at times, and only if one is allowed to be ruled by it. It demonstrates an ultimately pessimistic concept, and although much of my writing here isn't necessarily always positive, it still aims to be exploratory: it tries to go forwards rather than backwards. "Canvas", however, is about regression (just as humanity is regressing ... and becoming less self-sufficient?).

Idiocracy [Film] (2014)

I watched a comedy film recently called *Idiocracy* (2006) about an average man (played by Luke Wilson) who travels 500 years into the future to discover that society has deteriorated and become dumbed down to the point where communication is nearly impossible, banal, immature and with an extremely low level of intelligibility. Here our average 'everyman' type character (Wilson) finds he is now the most intelligent person on the planet, and he gradually becomes ostracised for this. Even though the movie is perhaps a little puerile, and clearly no 'masterpiece' of cinema, it resonates with the spirit and frustration of "Canvas" in the sense of alienation I feel and my inability to deal and cope in a world that is often starved of logic and rationality. And how that frustration can make it tempting for me to dumb my own self down, through self-destructive means, so that ignorance can ultimately become bliss, and so that I can join in with this new "breed of brotherhood", and actually be a part of something whole (but not wholesome), rather than feeling like an outsider all the time.

Be Careful Though. There is such a Thing as Over-organisation (Regarding Huxley's *Brave New World Revisited*) (2014)

We speak in code to one another. Talking takes place without intervals. There is no time to wait. But we do wait—that is the problem. We wait on pins and needles and do the math, checking our pulse and second-guessing the beat of everything.

Rolling on, the plan is to seek out some more, without watching the roads though, so we miss a detail here and there—invisible, silent. An impossible haste, like watching a vehicle accelerate to a point of incomprehensible speed—we can no longer see it, so the time it takes to do something is contextual, important, fundamental in our appreciation or depreciation of 'time'.

Take a break, rest. Once the impulses take over, indecision becomes our main decision, with frustration, anger and a derisive sneer in place of a smile or taking the time to view the view, from above, across or below.

There is or there are moments of patience throughout the day (commonly in the early morning) when there is no tension, when stress and angst are low, before anything happens and prior to our interjections and insistence that something should or could happen here, now. The here and now are subsequently and ritualistically (sometimes stylistically) robbed and the reminder of them isn't quite sufficient. We act as though in a state of mourning when all there really can be is a behavioural choice.

Retrospective emergence—the comfort in/and over-organisation:

> But, though indispensible, organization can also be fatal. Too much organization transforms men and women into automata, suffocates the creative spirit and abolishes the very possibility of freedom. (Huxley 262)

Note to self: take a hint.

What I enjoy most about *The Net Delusion* is Morozov's ability to form apt literary analogies for the Internet and its impact on societal freedom. Most notably, Morozov comes up with an

"Orwell-Huxley coordinate system" (79) to monitor the way in which the world and society are heading. On a spectrum, taking philosophies that stem from George Orwell's *1984* and Aldous Huxley's *Brave New World*: "Orwell feared that what we hate will ruin us. Huxley feared that what we love will ruin us" (79). On the one hand we have extreme censorship, restriction and oppression. On the other hand there is a suppression of passion through instantaneous pleasure, conditioned status and happiness, constant self-gratification — never needing to *need* or *want* anything for very long. Obviously, the contemporary world is not quite one or the other just yet; however, what I'm inclined to believe is that the Internet creates a more Huxley-like *Brave New World* scenario in which individuals are becoming more self-obsessed, apolitical, uninterested and sluggishly or mechanically seeking that instant fix of cheapened gratification in things like cable television, downloading/streaming shows and movies, porn, social media and the over-arching consumption of materialistic 'goods'. Our identities are tailor-made.

I see myself as being part of or trapped within this condition too. So many of my Sundays are now often anti-socially oriented around watching Netflix for extended periods of time. I turn to my phone every few minutes as it pings, rings, sings, tings or vibrates relentlessly. I use my physical diary and planner less and less as Facebook and my Apple (i)Calendar or email account systematically request information from me over and over until I am forced to give in to them and allow them to organise my life for me instead of me doing it myself. It's a ceaseless haranguing that gradually deconstructs my physical self only to reconstruct me digitally in the wake of my ghostly bodily form.

Rushing the Order and Fate (2014)

And we were all compartmentalised and clustered so roughly and inaccurately into dispersed and separated incorrect groups, a little like Huxley's *Brave New World* system but rushed and all wrong. We had the chance if we got on the train or got hold of a remote or swam and passed through some cyclical express vacuum tube, to alter our fates, but then submitting, conforming and committing— the button was extremely difficult to locate, and we would fade away before we had a chance to find it. It was traumatic when it was happening to you, and when you were watching it happen to someone else, it could only be noticed in the eyes, which would wobble (*Nystagmus*), fade and fuzz into another (Leneghan 72). The incorrect dispersion—a matrix system where my tastes and your tastes were all incompatible and disgusting, and only some of us were luckily fitted into a life that actually fit and worked for us, oblivious to everyone else that had to suffer and had no idea how difficult life was, especially if they'd never had a chance to glimpse one of those pathways out. Many of us tried to rebel against it. Some were even successful (until they had to pause to find the right configurations on their remote panels). Though most of us were not and then had to slump back into our horrible situation(s), having only briefly tasted and comprehended the fruits of our impossibly good and well-ordered fate.

But …

The Flux of Repulsion or Expulsion (2014)

I'm in a natural (now) state of repelling those around me. I've so gotten used to (a) state(s) of isolation that I question every outing and the worth of every conversation. Interactions are thrust upon me, and I don't know what to do about them. I stare, and I listen more intently, but I don't know how to react or respond, so I just don't. Is that better or preferable though? If most people just vomit on you anyway? Propulsion and repulsion, repelling and expelling.

Being more comfortable internalising the soliloquy (obviously) … formidable silence accepted and plain at the cost of sociability, vibrancy, connection. Are you happy with this or are you simply in a state of disengaged, overly preoccupied flux?

No. In Fact, I Do Not Need, I Do Not Want. (Mantra) (2014)

I do not need. I do not want. Superstitious materialism. Picturing animation. Various and varying projects and projections of the self, consciously tapping into the other after the other, then another and another. An otherness pervades: a prelude to disaster and a dismembering disassociation. Checks and re-checks, plastering the walls with hands and fingers and toes. The hairs on your legs and arms prick and stand, sticking up, vibrating and sensing the onslaught of tension and frustration. Terrible clichéd phrases. A phonetic verse, versed and rehearsed and rehashed and re/#tagged and 'shared' in the afterglow of yesteryear or the 'morrow.

Spring cleaning on the nib of Summer; a lot, many, a select few of these things need to be chucked in the bin, thrown away, bridges burnt without sentiment and sincerity or even apathy or anger — but a mere refusal; vices and hubris need to go to (the) bin. Useless trash stimulating vindictiveness and a stretching of the soul, inversed and regurgitated, whilst regurgitating the same verses time and time again. The bin, garbage, the junkyard, the throwing away of, is simple and idyllic — a place and a space for the things (I 'say'/talk in speeches) I do not need, and I do not want.

I think that (people) collectively haven't ironed out that sense of greed, selfishness and competitiveness that drives us to dissatisfaction by observing the 'satisfaction' of others in their insistent tweeting, Instagramming and Facebooking — their parading and constant in-your-face presentation of their lives to others via the live stream(s), blogging, the 'cloud' and Social Networking Sites (SNSs). Everyone has an opinion, and everything is rudely/crudely glorified in the need to justify a pronged, simultaneously unified, interconnected online existence. This needs to be monitored, and there needs to be a responsibility on behalf of the individual at least.

Otherwise, we run the risk of straying into the dangerous territory, if we haven't already, of what Michel Foucault called panopticism. According to Foucault's *Discipline and Punish: The Birth of the Prison* (1975), panopticism can be likened to a state of imprisonment and has the ability to stimulate a sense of escalating paranoia in individuals, similar to the sentiment that is alluded to in "Rushing the Order and Fate". Foucault also claims that carceral institutions implement a panoptical mode of surveillance that employs an undeviating gaze upon prisoners to make them feel as though they are constantly being watched, the effect of which is total control and conformity (30). This also causes an internalisation of surveillance, in which one feels obligated to monitor and modify one's own behaviour in order to conform to the views and expectations of their audience and the mass media (Johnson 32). This sense or feeling of internalisation can create angst, frustration, docility, claustrophobia, agoraphobia, and various other states of internal instability and fluctuation. "Hence the major effect of the Panopticon: to induce in the inmate a state of conscious and permanent visibility that assures the automatic functioning of power" (Foucault 201).

I think that Foucault had a significant amount of foresight into the potentialities, even of a type of 'digital' panopticism, when he wrote "it is in fact a figure of political technology that may and must be detached from any specific use" (205):

> ... an indefinite discipline: an interrogation without end, an investigation that would be extended without limit to a meticulous and ever more analytical observation, a judgement that would at the same time be the constitution of a file that was never closed, the calculated leniency of a penalty that would be interlaced with the ruthless curiosity of an examination, a procedure that would be at the same time the permanent measure of a gap in relation to an inaccessible norm and the asymptomatic movement that strives to meet in infinity. (227)

Complete and total transparency and visibility (this panopticism). Sounds to me a little like the mission statement of sites like WikiLeaks, albeit, in a more distorted and reversed/inversed manner. WikiLeaks aims/aimed to elicit, portray and convey the world's governments and giant corporations' intentions, viral thinking and objectives transparently to citizens, whilst Foucault's theoretical panopticism aims at a more personal, internalised and invasive kind of transparency. One is global and universal, whilst the latter strikes at and exposes the core of one's self—every individual must be made accountable and predictable in their physical actions and their thinking.

A 2014 documentary called *Citizenfour* (and now even more recently *Coded Bias* and *The Social Dilemma*, both from 2020), demonstrate the possibility or possibilities of this kind of paranoid panoptical mode of self-invasion, in the contemporary modern and technologically oriented world. *Citizenfour*'s protagonist, Edward Snowden, details and attempts to explain some of the illegal surveillance practices and tactics of intelligence agencies such as the NSA (National Security Agency) in the United States, and their implementation of the functionality of electronic information such as metadata or biometric data, and how this technology can be used to track, analyse, anticipate and predict people's movements. This technology is real and it's happening today. Many would consider it a convenience, and it can be, in the way in which our information is synchronised across our phones, apps, programs, computers, iPads, tablets, etc. However, this also makes it much easier to be tracked and to be found.

For a law-abiding citizen this 'subjugation' may not seem like a massive concern. In fact, if one was ever to be harmed, lost or missing under today's modes and systems of surveillance, it seems that this systematic personal invasion or modern panopticism would actually do more good than harm, particularly in a crisis. Though this isn't always necessarily true either. One doesn't have to look very far back in our own history to recognise the incomprehensibility of certain incidents, like that of MH370, a mystery that modern technology has not quite yet been capable of unravelling.

Though, the concept of 'freedom' and 'personal space' does come to mind. A friend of mine covers up the camera built into the front of her laptop screen, with a small piece of paper blu-tacked over it. She does this because she is especially wary of the possibility of hackers, malware and literal in-your-face exposure caused by the monitoring of one's face, actions and behaviour, as she sits before her laptop screen. And I now too cover up this small camera embedded in my desktop computer because for me it seems like a matter or question of 'why not?' If we are, or if I am being monitored, I will make it that tiny little bit more difficult for the 'entities' on the other side of the lens where and when I can. I don't especially have anything in particular to hide. I don't believe I have any more skeletons in my (digital) closet than anyone else, but I would like to serve as a minor irritant to the system. I don't want or mean to start a war with technology, because I would obviously lose. I don't have the power to destroy and take down major systems like this — it would seem tiresome, pointless and counter-productive. The digital (meta)machine age is taking over and dominating, and it doesn't seem as though we humans can do much to stop it. I feel helpless in this paradoxical situation, though not necessarily depressingly fatalistic either. For I still use technology as a medium through which to complain about technology. And I also like to use it as a tool for conveying 'contradiction'. But it is no major effort on my part to take a bit of sticky tape and a small scrap of paper and cover up the camera on my electronic devices when I'm not using them, or decline any requests by Google or iTunes or Facespace or Facetime or iCloud or WhyCloud or LinkedIn or Facebook or Shitspace or whatever derivative or derived B.S. it may be, or whatever new program is developed in the future that serves the simultaneous apparent purpose of synchronising our information and personal details. Whether or not these devices are designed for convenience, the gathering of metadata, security or surveillance, I still want to be the tiny spanner in the works, the mosquito on the arm, the fly in the eye, an ant at a picnic, and irritate and decline, and decline, and decline these 'services' wherever and whenever I can. It is probably massively naïve on my part, as affecting the emotional response of any digital system is obviously quite impossible. Ones that are made to synchronise and gather these pieces of information, but these new methods are eerie, a little wrong, taboo, the possibilities are frightening, alarming and they also permeate everything everywhere, as well as being literally in-your-face. My philosophy or foolish hope is for them to simply not run like perfect clockwork, and postpone our inevitable uniform and cumulative digital deterioration and deluded cog-like position in this great interwoven and interconnected web of a machine as best as I can, with as little as I can, while I can.

This argument runs the risk of opening up a huge kettle of fish that I don't particularly feel is necessary to heavily investigate at this juncture. For this is a massive cyber-tech-war-argument better left to the hackers and computer technician types who are much better acquainted with the lingo, the technology and the know-how. I do have some subsequent points to make about technology and the associative psychological effects modes or forms of digital communication have on the mind via social media in the following paragraphs. Nevertheless, the focus still needs to come back to my (creative) self in relation to these things, and how it is reflected in my writing and prose, which I will attempt to draw out more so (morosely) in the latter part(s) and more fragmentary vignette-like sections of this folio.

Scholarly journals like *Computers in Human Behavior* examine the use and impact of computers from a psychological methodological perspective — from here I have looked at two articles that analyse the effects of SNSs on the individual (or different types of individuals): they are "Who Wants to be "Friend-Rich"? Social Compensatory Friending on Facebook and the Moderating Role of Public Self-Consciousness" and "Attachment Style, Social Skills, and Facebook Use amongst Adults". These articles take a fairly neutral stance on the issues I've been looking at, though some of the evidence and data they accumulate is worthy of note.

Some argue that the maximum number of social/human connections we can have or make is no more than 150 (Dunbar 4). Now given the immediacy of today's social networking and interaction in which we don't really have to wait for anything anymore (we used to wait, and now we are angered, agitated, annoyed and frustrated when we have to), we've sacrificed, on a grand scale, intimacy and real communication for email, instant messaging, text, SMS: the cold and the bleak and the toneless and the always up-in-the-air open-to-interpretation that creates tension and angst later in our surrealistic reality. I believe that endless clarification is needed in our modes of communication, as I've tried to elucidate earlier in this folio, which we would not need if we could just 'talk' face-to-face [but misunderstanding can still occur, etc]. Instead, one has to be proficient in one's use and integration of emoticons and acronymic speech. The point is that now through these instantaneous methods we can quickly accumulate superficial contacts and 'friends' much more rapidly than we are equipped or even perhaps evolved to deal and cope with. We can have friends over these SNSs that go into the hundreds and thousands now. And it isn't necessary; many of us barely remember these connections we've temporally or temporarily 'clicked' with and compiled in the cesspool of our friendship bank. It's all about quantity rather than quality, and it's counter-intuitive, counter-physiological and counter-evolutionary even, driving us "to become friend-rich" (Lee et al. 1037).

The article "Who Wants to be "Friend-Rich"?" contends that the "presentation of oneself as popular and active on Facebook often serves as a strategy for boosting one's self-esteem or gratifying one's narcissism" (1041). And "Facebook dependency showed a positive association with neuroticism" (Lee et al. 1039). Sure, some might say that not all SNSs are the same as Facebook, but a similar principle can be applied across the board. The evidence accrued in "Attachment Style, Social Skills, and Facebook Use amongst Adults" found that "those high in social sensitivity and/or emotional control were more concerned with how they appear to others on Facebook, and tended to use Facebook particularly when feeling sad, lonely, stressed or anxious" (1145) and that "Facebook use is motivated by two fundamental needs, the need for self-presentation and the need to belong" (Oldmeadow, Quinn, and Kowert 1143).

These are not necessarily healthy or 'natural' inclinations (the need to *be* or *feel* like a 'superstar' is counter-productive to the "friend-rich" conversation being had here and to the feeling of oneness and unification I am hoping to strive for in the discussion in the paragraphs ahead) and clearly seem to exacerbate negative psychological motivation(s), which brings me to the idea that technology begets technology. It is fast, quicker than us. Blink and you'll miss it: "Technology is the answer, but what was the question?" (Morozov 306). We are wandering into vague territory here, facing either a large problem or clusters of small challenges that are becoming harder and harder to define and refine as we make less of a conscious effort to evolve as technology accelerates into an oblivion of which we are oblivious. Films like *Transcendence* and *Lucy* from 2014 touch on the frightening (liberating?) concept of singularity or a unified universal consciousness. Also, documentaries like *I Am* and TV Series such as *Through the Wormhole* (both from 2010) have raised awareness (in a subcultural way) of the connections that exist between technology, science and spirituality — the one-ness of everything — an integration of life that is disrupting the way in which we perceive the (un)natural world. It is a complication that will either free or destroy us.

In any case, our *zeitgeist* has become Kafkaesque, without a need for clarification or closure or an ending in sight. We are in the dark and have lost our sense of direction. We can be grouped, regrouped, rebound and bounding we trail blaze steadfastly. Morozov discusses this sense of inadequate and problematic uncertainty as being akin to a "waiting for Godot" predicament: "Now that the group has been formed, what comes next? In most cases, what comes next is spam" (191). There is something sinister and wicked to all of this and "[wicked] problems ... are more intellectually challenging. They are hard to define — in fact, they cannot be defined until a solution has been found" (Morozov 309). So, to touch on this idea of grouping or being grouped within invisible, unknown and ever-changing (nostalgic) culture(s) ... it can lead in/on to a sense of feigned knowledge or experience that is present in most of us today — becoming fluid in the knowledge of a culture or a cultural movement artificially and digitally via the Internet. The outcome is interesting because people (youths in particular) are presented with so many options for being alternative, for being radical and separated away from the 'mainstream' that they can make a choice about which of these cultures they want to engage with or *be in*. Little do they/I/we know, without life experience this *zeitgeist* becomes delusional, multi-faceted, indecisive, alien/artificial/superficial.

We are collectively losing our 'edge'.

Two Cents (Everyone Has an Opinion) (2013)

Contribute your two cents, please, if you don't mind (though no one ever asks). And it's basically void and invalid, isn't it? It's pretty easy to speak, and everyone has some kind of a 'voice' or opinion, though it's kind of pushy and forceful. Superstar egos take over. Even in the most modest and humble minds there exists a genuine sense that one is truly 'awesome' and spectacularity dominates, so then what happens is … we talk. We talk too much about things we don't really know. We speculate and guess in vague and vain areas of expertise, in other fields of knowledge and departments foreign to our own and we make conversation and (idle) chit-chat in the hope of educating others to self-aggrandise, but all that really happens is that opinionated voices speak and talk, and the facts become obscured and then we argue in the face of knowledge without any proper knowledge of our own. We assume everyone is asking for help, an opinion, a contribution … that everyone is asking for advice or to be saved in some way. No, they just want to whinge and whine, vomit on you, the psychic soundboard in the reclining futon, recycled. It's our two cents, our letter to the editor, our biased opinions, our tangential creative rants, our streams of consciousness, blah blah blah. But in the end, all it really is is two cents' worth—an invalid and void monetary system in most countries, digital, if anything or if nothing at all. A short spike and a dagger in the system, useless and obsolete in this day and age and yet everywhere, absolutely. That uselessness is absolutely everywhere—on its own it doesn't amount to anything but collectively you can buy something with it, multiples of two and then to double digits in order to buy your soda or your coffee as you sip smugly and convey the uninformed 'ideas' as 'facts' to the other 'self', repetitively.

'Irony', Alanis Morissette and Me (2015)

A (personalised) definition of irony: a state of affairs, sensation or event that is the opposite or uncannily contrary to what is expected, and often results in an amusing sensation, a feeling, similar to that of *déjà vu*.

I, and perhaps many of us, often feel constrained when constructing our online selves, and the way in which we communicate virtually or technologically, in order to cater to one another. We simplify our processes of communication, otherwise 'they' (other people) evade.

In this sense I sometimes feel that we are also collectively losing our edge in our lack of attention to detail and our lack of appreciation for the subtleties and necessities of the English language, or any way of speaking. With the exception of various academic and professional platforms, we are beginning to lose beautiful, luscious and rich words like 'irony', which most people seem to think means 'coincidence' or an unfortunate circumstance of some kind. And popular culture accentuates the misconception(s): movies, TV shows, news presenters, cartoons and musicians; I have witnessed all of these mediums misuse the term. Looking back, Alanis Morissette's disastrous and catastrophic 1995 song "Ironic" seems, to me, like a final *iconic* nail in the coffin, in terms of how it was received by, and how it affected the public. The song title is "Ironic". The entire song is supposed to be about irony, and instead, ironically, it is not — it is more about unfortunate coincidence(s) or double meaning:

> And isn't it ironic, don't you think?
> It's like rain on your wedding day
> It's a free ride when you've already paid
> It's the good advice that you just didn't take
> (*Jagged Little Pill* 1995)

So, no, Alanis. No, I don't 'think'. I certainly don't think it's 'ironic'. And here she is, an ingénue swaying the masses via MTV and the GRAMMYs, influencing western culture to take up the baton in her flailing disregard and misuse of the word, ultimately changing, simplifying and minimising its effect, significance and meaning. This is one of the negative influences of popular music.

The album *Jagged Little Pill*, from which "Ironic" spawns, was hugely successful. It was massive and successful enough, that from then on, I would be tempted to say that the global scales were ever-so-slightly tipped, and the majority, as opposed to the many more in the minority, of people, would, henceforth, understand irony to mean coincidence, further sending us into a communicative oblivion and forcing us to lose our communicative 'edge' or sophistication. Alanis Morissette may have slayed a word and its meaning, which I personally love very much.

But let's be fair. Words *do* change over the centuries: 'naughty' used to mean that "you had naught or nothing"; 'awful' used to mean that someone was "worthy of awe"; a 'clue' (or clew) used to mean "a ball of yarn" (Curzan 1). But I don't think that 'irony' should be lost because its meaning is still distinctive and useful. Like *déjà vu*, it is a sensation that we experience regularly. Imagine if we weren't able to describe that. We would be at a loss for words. For me, the distortion or disintegration of its meaning would be a shame. Because everything, and many words, ultimately find a way to become slanderous, or cheapened at least, it seems. Everything ultimately becomes offensive—and we're the ones doing it, to ourselves and to each other. Perhaps the term 'ironic' could even become slanderous in a few years? For example: "Oh, he's so ironic" (i.e., a person who is coincidentally and/or inconveniently a gatecrasher at parties or special events). Who knows.

Nevertheless, I am also quite willing to acknowledge that what constitutes irony is often a contentious subject. For instance, any excessive criticism of Morissette's song "Ironic" as wholly unironic *could* be considered unjustifiable. For instance, some of this criticism may be due to the status of her song as 'popular', and not literary, 'professional' or academic. And funnily enough, according to the definition at the outset of this piece, criticising Morissette's song as not being ironic, ironically, makes it ironic. But that is a much more circular and tautological rabbit hole I will try to avoid here.

The tyranny of (low) popular culture already has a negative influence upon our children and teenage culture (this has been going on for decades, maybe even centuries?). For instance, today this culture often encompasses the negative impacts of the Internet and social media sites such as Facebook, Twitter and Instagram, which may very well have promoted an egotistically (dis)oriented 'selfie' generation that is more inwardly focused and less intellectually resilient. Today's world, and younger millennial generations or Generation Z 'tweens' in particular, tend to focus much more on the internal and egotistical constructions of obnoxious 'superstars' like Justin Bieber, Taylor Swift and Jaden Smith, who appear to care less about others in the external humanist sense. And now, there exist many things in common sense or common knowledge that are simply not common sense or common knowledge. For instance, you're not actually meant to "shake ... a Polaroid picture", *Outkast*!

The way I view this from my perspective as a secondary school teacher, and a millennial, is complex. The way in which all people/students learn is radically different: some are visual, others are not, and some pupils are altogether different again — they might be practical, logical, creative, and so forth. I think students need to be taught 'how' to learn in a way that values patience as opposed to excessive impulsivity, which can lead to mistakes being made through haphazard or over-excited behaviour. Or, to be less one-sided, there is, of course, a time and a place for impulsivity: in play and some creative endeavours, etc. Ultimately, all I know is that we have to take responsibility for our own actions, and I don't believe Alanis Morissette is taking responsibility for hers in the construction of her ironically un-ironic song. Her song exhibits carelessness, clumsiness and impulsivity without restraint or proper careful consideration towards herself and towards others also.

Call my perspective overly entitled and biased, if you will, yet these occasionally tangential thoughts and opinions are not meant to be expressed as fundamental facts by any means! Their purpose is to tempt you, the reader, to disagree and wince at many of these misguided musings and behavioural traits. Some of my narratorial biases might be seen as unique and unreliable, whilst others are perhaps quintessentially generational and/or self-entitled. I just want to challenge you though, with the end game of perhaps reclaiming some of that dormant, floundering 'edge' you may have lost.

In the case of language and virtual communication, we seem to be actively and consciously driving towards an Orwell-like *1984* paradigm, where a kind of Newspeak is taking over and dominates our texting, SMS, emails, instant messaging, acronymic language, emojis, emoticons and GIFs. We've already seen it in the apparent or potential universal loss of words like 'irony', and in my anecdotal example at the outset of this piece.

Now I feel I have to actively engage in altering, mutating and deforming what I have to say or write so that people will understand and actually respond to me. Less is more. And I engage in virtual communication too, just as much, to keep the peace, to move along and to get along. I have no intention of being any kind of martyr by going against the grain of perceived or supposed 'normalcy', the trend and the fashion of today's online 'net delusion'. I'm happy to talk about it, to write about it, to express my views on paper, but I'm not going to start an argument with every person who does wrong by me in this sense. Who am I to call the shots in this way? I have no right. All that I care about is how *I* behave, write, speak, communicate and interact with others *overall*. But if I were to argue with everyone about it, I would have next to no friends, and I would be dubbed an impractical out-of-touch intellectual (wannabe). Though in actuality, I don't believe that being labelled as such by the greater 'masses' would bother me all that much anyway.

In 2015, I was once asked to join in with a group of punters to take some 'selfies' at a club in Albuquerque, New Mexico. I refused, saying that "I don't believe in selfies." And I don't—I severely dislike them. I contend they are one of the worst proactively open, overt and self-indulgent practices that has developed in my lifetime. But I'm not about to successfully change a billion people's minds about them. I was told by one of them to "get off [my] high horse," and so I succumbed, so long as I was not the one holding the camera/smart phone when the ridiculously hedonistic photo was taken, for I do not want to be the one actually physically engaging in the active process of taking or coordinating the shot. If you can't beat them, join them, in a way, inevitably ... even if it is a degenerative slump that isn't exactly going to improve over time, but at least I'll be dead before I witness the loss of *too* much. There is already enough loss to handle in any one lifetime as it is.

There exist 'demons', scars, hindrances, burdens or obstructions we encounter in our lives, due to compromise, illness, bad fortune, poor luck or regret over the things we have or haven't done. Do these 'mistakes' and 'misfortunes' chip away at us gradually (like the 'selfie' sentiment—to me—mentioned previously, the lack of integrity that we see, read and hear, which challenges us, so we are perpetually forced to contemplate it) so that there is less and less left of our own sense of self as we roam and plod along? Or do we bounce back? Are we resilient in a way that enables us to keep moving forwards, getting stronger? Adapt or die, so to speak. I am not sure.

I just want, for myself and all of us, to be able to communicate genuinely with one another, without having to constantly struggle against the grain of an overly processed and homogenised culture, pointlessly battling it out in a communication that is (or could further become) lost, forgotten, neglected, mutated, deformed, or stillborn.

We should be looking at our 'advanced' technological age, and pose questions like if science could enable us to live forever, would we also philosophically and morally be able to live *with* our own selves, for eternity? Would this be too difficult for our minds and selves to cope with? Would it be too overwhelming, perhaps?

The Accumulation of Demons (2015)

A friend of mine believes in the possibility of humans being able to live forever. He's extracted this concept from Aubrey de Grey's book *The Mitochondrial Free Radical Theory of Aging* (1999). The notion is an exciting one. However, isn't there a limit to how much dirty water (or any liquid for that matter) can fit into a glass, a container, (or a life)?

> Think of a cup completely filled with water. You try to add one drop to this cup, and one drop spills out. You try to pour a cup of water into it, and a cup of water spills out. This is called a zero-sum system. To add anything to it you must remove an equal proportion. (McRaney 146)

Forget about the glass being half full or empty for now. What should concern us is the excess of plant life, bacteria and cumulative infestation that pollutes and dilutes that water overall, over the course of a life.

We all accumulate demons, gradually, quickly, or otherwise, that manifest themselves into "loneliness birds" (Courtenay 629) or anxieties or fears or injuries or mental and debilitating illnesses. If we had more time would we not generate even more fears, problems and dangers? Ultimately, everybody would become perpetually and exponentially *crazier*. And we're already psychotic. Nothing works: expectations supersede natural desires, genuine human communication is limited, and if it is overly exerted it becomes 'weird'. If it is in some way restricted it is deemed abnormal—too antisocial; there is absolutely no healthy generic medium or mould that suits anybody as a whole. These effects can surely only be amplified by the addition of extra time to our lives. The bonus levels of having more years added to a lifespan are as artificial as the cure, the panacea that geneticists and biologists and physicists are working towards.

And an immortal population would make for an impossibly chaotic and incomprehensibly stressful space. We didn't have as many of these (registered psychological) problems centuries ago when human lives were shorter. These are consequences of the overly nurtured bodies and psyches of today—the contemporary *zeitgeist*. Living forever is life-threateningly dangerous too.

And how does technology fit into all of this? It is alongside us, perpetuating the stigma in and of ourselves. I always have my phone on me or next to me, when I wake, when I sleep—and I can never let the battery die, so if I leave to go somewhere for longer than expected (longer than the duration of the battery life of my phone) I take my phone charger with me—it has become an extenuation of myself: a measurement of time that I can relate to and understand. I cannot live without it. I use it in the same way I would smoke a cancerous cigarette, as an addiction. And to keep busy, preoccupied, or to simply appear busy and preoccupied to others, looking around, glancing, never really taking my full gaze or attention off my phone. When I am uncomfortable or uncertain in a situation, I turn to my phone. When I don't otherwise know what else to do, I turn to my phone.

I occasionally walk past the foyer of this one hostel in Brisbane when I am passing through Fortitude Valley, and when I look into the faces in the hostel reception area, all the backpackers there always appear to be looking down into their laps, into their phones, not really paying attention to one another or the experience they travelled (t)here for. They look to what 'home' and comfort represents to them in the screen of their phones. Personally, I don't remember the experience of travel being like this in 2011, when I was backpacking through Europe and South America. But now a room of twenty people is filled, and all of these 'individuals' gaze down at their phones instead of engaging with one another. And I am the same too, when I momentarily glance away. Though which came first? The need, the necessity or the desire, or the capacity to simply be able to do so.

At this very moment I am writing at the airport as I await the cattle call announcing and ushering me to my departure gate. USB ports and power stations are accessible everywhere, to make that measurement of time (the battery life of a phone) seem longer or for us to be able to 'run' (so to speak) for longer. Yes, it's convenient. But we could also survive without it and look at one another instead, could we not? No, that'd be strange.

Facebook is my social calendar now. My physical diary/planner no longer satisfies that purpose adequately (in fact, I have not used one since 2014). And I use Twitter because I feel I *need* to use Twitter, though really, I don't know what it's for, except another version of Facebook in its minimal/minimised (other version of) status updates, I guess? How many 'versions' of irrelevant status updates do we need about ourselves to project onto other selves that also, in turn, only care about themselves?

Moreover, I respond to all of my emails within a day because I feel the pressure to do so, and I carefully craft, deconstruct or streamline my text messages so that they have a better chance of being comprehended on the receiving end.

This is the world I live in now, today. This is me. This is iPawel. This is the technologically deluded me, which is also me and my 'self' (a version circa November 27, 2015).

Finally …

Cattle Call (2015)

The cattle call (occurs), and we are corralled, whilst attempting to race through to the gates, in a huff — lines and queues and the sense of urgency and minor emergency. You pass from one counter to another as everyone around you complains and groans doggedly. The staff respond with a bare minimum of courtesy as the patrons and people/clientele insist on their own sense of importance, puffing out their chest or chewing gum or inflating their own deflated ego (in their vastly imaginative minds).

And this imagination, brilliant at filling in gaps and blanks creates a dream of delirium — the sense of importance, impatience, always waiting and becoming excitable for the next insane thing to happen: a chaotic mildew.

Crude behaviours … as we move and cycle from one queue to the next door to the next queue to the next push to the next vacant look, followed by complaints and the most tiresome expressions.

Yes, we are cattle, of course. But that is because we are animals. We are not waiting. We are living. There isn't a next thing.

And yes, sure the scanners and machines and LED lights and computers and copiers and printers may break down, then become out of order. Maybe they are trying to tell us something? Why are they always failing mechanically and systematically (it's practically a given), forcing chaos in their bypass? They spasm out of order more so when we try to enforce the order, the significance, the importance.

There is no order, only the universal sequence of majestic beauty, present and still, in these infinitesimally congruous slices.

Maybe all of this is not relatable to you, dear reader, and my sense of self merely wavers alongside the membranes of other selves or souls like the various branes of various universes in the reality of physics and space — though we are uncertain of their existence, they are theorised, quantified in one way or another, not so much recognised but felt, like the reverberations on the surface of a pond, along the shore of a creek or reservoir; mirrors gliding alongside the surfaces of our being. We cannot see them, but they are transparent. We feel them, and they reside elsewhere, illusory (like a good recipe).

Perhaps a better metaphor is the invisible relationship between matter and antimatter that exists side-by-side, within and without, but when they accidentally collide the effects are tremendous, explosive and insightful, and can be seen through a powerful telescope, as when two galaxies collide at such force that dark matter is distinguishably separated from matter (blue and pink), as seen in this image (Fig. 7):

Fig. 6. Bullet Cluster

THESIS FOUR

Solutionism: Fictocriticism and the Digital World

The theme of this book's final thesis is informed by a concept in Evgeny Morozov's works *The Net Delusion: How Not to Liberate the World* (2012) and *To Save Everything, Click Here: The Folly of Technological Solutionism* (2013). These two texts focus on the disengagement contemporary society has with political news and information due to a preference for other, less intellectually challenging forms of entertainment offered by cable television, streaming shows and movies, Netflix, digitised porn and the whole YouTube phenomenon. In *To Save Everything, Click Here* Morozov coins the cerebral opiate, "technological solutionism" (2013):

> The idea that given the right code, algorithms and robots, technology can solve all of mankind's problems, effectively making life "frictionless" and trouble-free. Morozov argues that this drive to eradicate imperfection and make everything "efficient" shuts down other avenues of progress and leads ultimately to an algorithm-driven world where Silicon Valley, rather than elected governments, determines the shape of the future. (Tucker, *The Guardian*, 2013)

The notion that "as technology becomes ever more integrated into political and social life, less and less attention is paid to the social and political dimensions of technology itself" (Morozov 314), is the catalyst for this thesis, as the argument encompasses the negative impacts of the Internet and social media sites such as Facebook, Twitter and Instagram, which this thesis contends may very well have promoted an egotistically (dis)oriented 'selfie' generation that is more inwardly focused and less intellectually resilient. Today's world, and younger millennial generations in particular, tend to focus much more on the internal and egotistical constructions of obnoxious 'superstars' like Justin Bieber, Taylor Swift and Jaden Smith, who appear to care less about others in the external humanist sense.

Using a much more creative writing style within the broad fictocritical spectrum, this section argues that almost no one can

275

escape this mood of universal social dissatisfaction, as neuroses and unhappiness is the result. Folio Four observes subsumed electronic environmental causes swaying the behavioural make-up and personality characteristics of 'LinkedIn' humans today. It comments on, researches and synthesises existing knowledge, contributing original creative innovations related to the psychological, (anti)emotional and philosophical effects that the digital age has on the creative self, in his observations, via the voice of a mostly 'anonymous' millennial narrator. This narrator struggles psychologically with his place and position in an increasingly digital world, and the way this affects him both directly and indirectly, in his (and people's) relationships overall, within the current *zeitgeist*. The more personal narrative is embedded within the creative pieces, vignettes and slices of life woven throughout this folio, which are occasionally imbued with more non-fictional critique. Folio Four opens with an extract from the 1976 film *Network*, which, while disturbing in its ongoing relevance, also sets a cynical, nihilistic and enraged tone for the fictocritical work.

Folio Four is made up of twenty-five pieces, of which only a few noteworthy pieces are discussed in detail, as many of the smaller pieces vary significantly in their creative characteristics and writing styles (prose-poetry, flash fiction, vignettes or slices of life, song lyrics, mantras/meditations, narcissistic critique, storytelling, traditional or non-traditional narratives, double-voicedness, soliloquy, etc). Additionally, the majority of the pieces in this folio are short; sometimes only a paragraph or a few lines. These smaller interjected (reverberating) pieces are meant to read fragmentally; they are blog-like or Tweet-like in their erratic, hyperactive leaping (or clicking/cliquing) from one subject matter to the next. This technique is similar to Barthes' *A Lover's Discourse*, Anna Gibbs' "The Gift" in *The Space Between*, Zoë Sofia's "Dr Zeo's Atrageous A-Z of Technosex (Extracts)" (1998) from the same anthology and Muecke's *Joe in the Andamans* (2008). This fragmentation is also done for practical reasons: the abundance of 'titled' works function as bookmarks, making pieces in the folio easier to locate and identify. The order of the folio pieces in this final experimental section, however, is not accidental or random; they are best looked at as a sequential 'whole'. Many of the pieces were written earlier on in the development of this exploration and, thus, adopt the same freeform, stream of consciousness and restlessly exuberant patterns prevalent in "Journeys" (Folio One). However, each work was carefully storyboarded and ordered in such a way as to demonstrate a thematic progression and evolution in narrative thought.

The sequence of the creative self's pieces that best exemplify this idea are "Technological Response: A Confession", to "Tunnel Vision", to "(Constantly) Changing Headspaces: I'm Bored", to "… But My Friends are Unreliable, So Plans are Hard to Make", to "After all, the World Does Not Run on Time", to "Yet My Persistence and Insistence is Being Misconstrued as Haughty and Overbearing". This chaining of pieces intends to demonstrate how one process of thought hurdles to the next. In fact, the titles of these individual pieces strung together can be read as a narrative in and of itself. This is a playful and metafictive technique famously adopted in the chapter titles of Italo Calvino's *If on a Winter's Night a Traveller* (1979), which can also be read as a narrative sequence. In fact, this inevitable return to a freer style of writing stylistically, figuratively, symbolically and literally (in the creative self's story) demonstrates a narrative arc across the different sections of this book. For the final sequence in Folio Four, the pieces "The Accumulation of Demons" and "Cattle Call", portray the narrator writing at the airport and being ushered through Customs and various other checkpoints before he boards his flight, and so "Journeys" can be seen as proceeding from "Technology", and so the experimental fictocritical narrative is locked into an infinite cycle of thought and experience, much like Laurence Sterne's *Tristram Shandy*.

The creative self's pieces "Do the Evolution(ary Jig)" and "Coaxing the Ouroboros" work in succession also, like most of the pieces in this folio. A paraphrased excerpt from Félix Guattari via Helen Flavell's important doctoral thesis, *Writing-Between* (2004), is interjected between the two pieces to hint at the question of the contemporary understanding and construction of selfhood in a digital world, though this is only done fleetingly, as a typical juxtaposing fictocritical reverberation would do (Smith 1001-02). Much of Folio Four merely hints at certain concepts, instead using creative prose and obscure references from film and TV shows to further explore ideas, such as in "*Idiocracy* [Film]" and "No. In Fact, I Do Not Need, I Do Not Want. (Mantra)" which, of course, mention the 2006 film *Idiocracy*, TV Series such as *Through the Wormhole* (2010) and documentaries like *I Am* (2010) and *Citizenfour* (2014). Hence, ironically, some of the references the creative self uses here would, theoretically, be critiqued by Morozov, in his disdain for cheap(er) forms of entertainment like cable television, downloading/streaming movies, porn and YouTube (314), whilst simultaneously using Morozov as a catalyst for this section's prose. So, the creative self dangles between intellectualism and anti-intellectualism. He struggles to find himself. He is as much a part of the technological problem as he is a part of the solution he is trying to create. As Morozov, in the creative self's piece "No. In Fact, I Do Not Need, I Do Not Want." states, "Technology is the answer, but what was the question?" (306). Does this demonstrate the creative self's laziness and confusion, or merely a complete losing of oneself in a new kind of experimental proto- or post-fictocritical innovation? The half-self, the lost self, the confused self and the torn self are just as integral in the meandering exploratory quest for 'self'. For the creative self of this book, technologies are causing these tortured, metafictive and cyclical or self-referential narratives, as seen in "Do the Evolution(ary Jig)", "Palahniuk's *Invisible Monsters*", "Technological Response", "Yet My Persistence and Insistence are Being Misconstrued as Haughty and Overbearing", "Repetition", "P.S. Mutual Misunderstandings of Brotherhood", "Be Careful Though. There is such a Thing as Over-organisation", Rushing the Order and Fate", "No. In Fact, I Do Not Need, I Do Not Want.", "The Accumulation of Demons" and "Cattle Call".

By the same token, if fictocritical academic documents can (and do) implement narrative mediums such as social media sites, as seen in the work of Naismith (2009), hyperlinks (Azul 2011) and even visual coffee ring stains (Watkins and Krauth 2016), then surely unique references, from occasionally more low-brow areas such as film and TV, can be allowed into the creative fictocritical form too. The creative self's piece "'Irony', Alanis Morissette and Me", for instance, is a nod to Meaghan Morris' fictocritical piece "Uncle Billy, Tina Turner and Me" (1998), both of which utilise, in very overt and obvious ways, late twentieth century (pop)ular music references in their narrative(s). The pieces "Palahniuk's *Invisible Monsters*", "Technological Response" and "Tunnel Vision: A Tribute to *2001: A Space Odyssey*" collectively pay bastardised homage to Chuck Palahniuk's novel *Invisible Monsters* (1999) and Arthur C. Clarke and Stanley Kubrick's infamous 'monolith' concept from *2001: A Space Odyssey* (1968), in the excerpt "in all the screens you gaze at (computer, smart phone, tablet, etc.), in an expression of void". Though this extract differs from Clarke and Kubrick's idea because the screen the creative self is transfixed by glows brightly and stupefies the observer, rather than Clarke and Kubrick's monolith, which is dark, solid and prompts new evolutionary thought and knowledge to whomever, or whatever mammal, engages with it. Still, there are some major overlapping similarities between a smart phone or tablet and Kubrick and Clarke's monolith from *2001: A Space Odyssey*, even if they are only cosmetic (see fig. 8 and 9).

Fig. 7. Clarke-Kubrick

Fig. 8. iPhone

Cosmetics, human deformation and plastic surgery is so much of what *Invisible Monsters* is about anyway, so that is a recurring quasi-motif throughout all of these works, and the creative folios.

The creative self's piece "Palahniuk's *Invisible Monsters*" also references Christopher's Gray's "Essays from Leaving the 20th Century" from *What is Situationism?* (1996) in relation to the 'Situationist' movement in France in the late 1950s and 60s. It may be obscured, but there is a semblance of fictocriticism in *Situationism*. The situationist "movement disintegrated. The last copy of the magazine came out in late 1969" (Gray 21). Similarly, fictocriticism has disintegrated, or been dormant in the Australian academy, since its inception in 1991 (Muecke and King). Though both *Situationism* and fictocriticism are important and useful modes because of their ability to free up an artist's work, enabling them to deliver content more richly, and with much less inhibition. *Situationism* is mentioned in this thesis due to its connections to surrealism and the avant-garde, yet Gray criticises it for being overly intellectual, and maybe that is why it failed (7). Fictocriticism, on the other hand, in the case of DeLillo's *White Noise*, aims to "*resist further analytical description or elaboration*" (Muecke and King 13) because it has included the critique in the fiction. It resists over-explanation or an overly abundant immersion in 'high theory'.

The four folios in *this* book teeter on the edge of intellectual pretentiousness and anti-intellectualism, much like their meandering narrator(s). Therefore, it is hard to gauge exactly how fictocritical this experiment is. Though that is precisely where its experimentation should aide in the process of methodological innovation.

The pieces "Repetition" and "My Refrigerator: More Repetition" describe the creative self's stance on 'originality' in communication, whilst again paying tribute to the influence of Roland Barthes and an aspect of his relationship with language (168). "Repetition" was originally published in *TEXT Journal* in October of 2014. It was the author's first published fictocritical text, though at the time the author still did not have a firm grasp of what kind of fictocriticism he wanted to write. His methodology eluded him, and so aspects of "Repetition", particularly in their reference to Barthes, are vague and tenuous. Nevertheless, the theme of repetition is interesting and unique when it comes to technology, if only due to the replicatory, systematic repetitious nature associated with technology, and at least "Repetition" successfully manages to achieve double-voicedness (Kerr 93) in its social commentary and critical thought. As Dr Anthony Lawrence, the Creative Works editor of *TEXT Journal*, stated in an email communication on June 18, 2014, when accepting "Repetition" for publication, "I liked this very much, especially its combination of humour and serious thought." The author's intentions were never meant for it to be humorous, though it is possible the deadpan nature of the soliloquy leant itself to this kind of interpretation. Or the author could have created a work that was unexpectedly ironic, and irony could well be the subtlest kind of double-voicedness. Thus, "Repetition" should be considered more readerly than writerly. A small portion of humour is sometimes necessary to simply keep the reader engaged, as is demonstrated in Folio Three on education.

Finally, in relation to "Repetition", in "Fictocriticism, Affect, Mimesis" (2005), Gibbs says "fictocriticism may make use of mimicry as strategic simulation and dissimulation, a performance of repetition in order, ultimately, to do something differently, to undo something, to make a difference" (7).

Barthes' *A Lover's Discourse*, an obvious catalyst for this book, is described by Simon Robb in "Academic Divination is not a Mysticism: Fictocriticism, Pedagogy and Hypertext" (2013) as a discourse existing "in outbursts of language, which occur at the whim of trivial, of aleatory circumstances" (98). He seems to condemn Barthes' original 'lover' as being made up of these meta, random, "non-linear" outbursts that "owe no allegiance to any overall thesis" (98). Though he views these characteristics as an opportunity to innovate on fictocriticism's applicability to the nature of the non-self that was discussed earlier: "If the self can be constructed it can also be deconstructed, dispersed, deferred. The self without boundaries is really the non-self, and it is one that is always haunting academic writing, where error is analogous to death" (Robb 100).

Whilst Scott Brook calls fictocriticism "monstrous" in ""Does Anybody Know What Happened to 'Fictocriticism'?", Robb says of fictocriticism's floundering pseudo-critical nature, that it "invites the notion that fictocriticism is possibly a kind of contamination or pollution of rational academic writing" (98). Robb says its methodology is risqué to the academy in its lack of boundaries (98). He argues there are elements of fictocriticism that is criticism without argument (Robb 98). This is simply not true. If anything, it is a hidden subtextual argument just as, using Robb's own words, it is a "dispersed … non-self" (100), a lost self.

Robb highlights these ideas to shed a positive light on the future of the methodology. Using the example of *A Lover's Discourse* he comments on fictocriticism's replicability, saying its subjectivity can be modelled: "And here I think I am entering into the area of Artificial Intelligence" (99).

> One suggestion is to utilise information technology, and specifically Hypertext, where the reader is able to compose a multiplicity of relationships between fragments within the simulated space of the computer. A computer-fictocritical space could be both a method (art) and an artefact of the process of constructing discourse and the process of self-formation. In this sense it functions as a postmodern pedagogy. (Robb 99)

Robb's solution and 'saviour' for fictocriticism is clearly hypertext:

> Hypertext bas been described as a new stage in reading and writing, which incorporates much of print technology and re-configures it: it brings in the scroll, the icon; footnotes and glosses are not 'marginalised' but treated as 'equal players' in the hypertext field. Changes in the relationship between reader and writer are considered to be of utmost significance. The reader of hypertext can compose almost innumerable connections between topical units (fragments, nodes). The reader in this sense writes with the text, they 'perform the text', while the author is the one who supplies the topical units and possible connections. (99)

As with David Azul's plethora of hypertext(s) in "Phononostalgia: a Fictocritical Investigation into Discordant Notions of 'Voice' in Speech and Writing" (2011)

> **Oh voice, where art thou?** click here (2)
> **Hello?** click here (3)
> **Echo** click here (4)
> **Don't leave me** click here (6)

… where every text stating "click here" is an actual hyperlink, and the author's engagement with the (rudimental) dispersed notion of the self, most fully prevalent in this section, "perhaps hypertext is an electric fictocriticism which holds out the promise of constant self-composition. Or perhaps electric fictocriticism is a form of Artificial Intelligence?" (Robb 100). It is this thesis' contention that hypertext (and other/new versions of it) can be one of the most unambiguous innovations in making fictocriticism fictocriticism: "electric fictocriticism" (Robb 100). This is a particularly relevant 'innovation' to this thesis on technology because younger millennials and teenagers today prefer to read on electronic devices—"screen-agers", Sean Coghlan calls them in a *BBC News* article pertinently titled "Young People 'Prefer to Read on Screen'" (2013). Furthermore, it is more than fair to indicate that print media in general is on the decline (*Odyssey Online*, Purkes 2017).

There seem to be little other constructive options to counteract this inevitable course of action but to adapt, innovate and brace oneself for possible futuristic alternatives, really, as Danielewski is doing. Haas (2017) elegantly describes fictocritical practice as "the intersection, on the page, of storytelling with philosophical arguments" (11). However, as shown in this thesis, electric fictocriticism is no longer limited to the constraints of the physical 'page', so perhaps the phrase "on the page" could be altered to "in a medium"?

Danielewski performs self-styled versions of "electric fictocriticism" in *House of Leaves*, in his 'video recordings' transcribed into text (253-61) and through one-dimensionally *printed* braille (423), despite the book (obviously) being a two-dimensional, physical text. It is almost as though he is ahead of the medium, or that the physical limitations of the medium could hardly contain his ideas and thought processes at the time of constructing the work. Danielewski himself turns to Twitter in order to clarify some of *House of Leaves'* concepts:

> "@markdanielewski Some helpful links . . . (2:59 AM — 4 Jul 2018)".

At one point in *House of Leaves* "serious film aficionados [begin] commenting on the quality of the audio ... clean up the tapes ... Numerous articles appeared in *Audio, Film,* and *F/X*" (Danielewski 469). All the while it must be remembered that Danielewski is writing about a fully transcribed and documented videotape (*The Navidson Record*) featured as a major section of *House of Leaves,* that is a completely manufactured fiction. It could be argued that Danielewski takes this metafictive "electric fictocriticism" technique too far. Still, his vision and dedication to his (fictional) work is thorough, systematically intricate and ambitiously unique, to say the least.

Naismith also 'performs' electronically in her thesis via 'tweets' that she then references:

> One of my next ideas was to show a conversation between myself and an imaginary future version of myself via tweets and @ replies.
>
> This is an example of this piece of writing:
>
> Great, now I can't stop thinking about it. I'm imagining myself in the future with someone else's lungs inside me.
>
> @cough_cough It's not actually that weird. I feel like they are

my lungs now … breathe in, breathe out …

@future_emily Sshhh. You're freaking me out!!! They must feel a bit different though, and you must be aware that they've been in someone else's body?

@cough_cough It's not that creepy. If anything I just feel thankful, not weirded out.

I'm scared. Why am I having an imaginary conversation with myself in the future with new lungs? (Naismith 2009d)

And Azul 'performs' in a similar way in "Phononostalgia" (2011) referenced above. These electronic innovations were already in existence, but now have been more clearly identified, categorised, and possibly legitimised, into the methodology of fictocriticism.

Another nascent version, or variation of, "electric fictocriticism" exists in Hazel Smith's "Erotics of Gossip", which implements an innovated (quasi-futuristic) "performative fictocriticism" (1002), as the bulk of the paper is written for radio rather than for reading. It is a transcribed recording, much like in Kerouac's novel *Visions of Cody* (1972) or sections of *House of Leaves*. Smith's paper also features the best working definition of fictocriticism found by the analytical self thus far, which was cited earlier in the introduction.

Simon Robb, of course, like the creative self and Morozov, is also wary of hasty technological advancements in the world: "Indeed this merging is also one of horror, the apocalypse and the cyborg" (100). However, this comment seems to be more playful and in the 'readerly' science-fiction realm, than a serious concern. The tone and contention of the article is certainly all *for* technological innovations: "Both the fictocritical and hypertext are examples of … 'good' postmodern citizens" (100). Indeed, this amalgamation gives new life to academic writing (Robb 101).

The creative self's narrator did not adopt this optimistic 'space-age' stance in Folio Four, but that is because thematically this section's folio is about being wary of technology. That approach may not necessarily help or work in tandem with the argument for fictocritical innovation in this thesis, but ideally some maturity can exist, and be evident to the reader, that there is a professional academic distancing between the two positions or stances: the creative self's semi-fictional narrator is fearful of technology in both a philanthropic and self-serving sense; yet this thesis' analytical self favours technology in a purely academic and forward-thinking way.

An appropriate segue here is the notion of narcissism in writing, which is what the creative self's piece "Canvas" (2013) is about. Another recognisable trait of fictocriticism is, of course, narcissism, for the mode is about the self and much of the time this self is expressed in a writerly manner (Fergie 173; Gibbs 309; Kerr 94; Smith 1001-02; Brook 2002). At the very least it has to be considered self-reflexive, if not indulgent, which some fictocritics struggle to communicate, or to even *want* to communicate (Stern 55; Watkins 10). Here are some notable examples of this writerly dilemma from *The Space Between* (1998):

> This genre is destined to be diaristic, tediously personal, acutely experiential. This is the voice that voices vice ... throaty self indulgent [sic], writing the blues ... temperamental snarls, idiosyncratic whines and murderously solipsistic mutterings. (Stern 55)

> they'll say you're mad, self-indulgent, illiterate, you who'd be subversive with your naughty language games, see how your rebel words clot with your fear. (Campbell 225)

The creative self in "P.S. Mutual Misunderstandings of Brotherhood" is extremely self-conscious, self-referential and metafictive about this problem too:

> As narcissistic as all of this is, I am still trying to avoid 'narcissism', at least in myself. I am weary and wary of it. It exists, but it's something that can and should be controlled, limited. I don't aim or want to alienate my reader, but rather to share and hopefully find a relatable (sentimentally cynical) common ground.

At the end of "Canvas" the creative self temporarily succeeds, at least in fantasy or in a state of delirium, in destroying his narcissism by becoming one with the "cesspool" of "brain dead" 'brothers' he despises so much:

> Narcissism … gone. Now to bathe in the fountain and be reborn anew: lights become lighter; colours become brighter; food becomes flavoursome; patronisation becomes nurturing; despondency becomes forgiveness; forgetfulness becomes fearlessness; resilience becomes violence; bleakness and blandness become the blank canvas of a brand-new breed of brotherhood.

Indeed, the first sentence by the creative self in this section's folio uses Linda Hutcheon's *Narcissistic Narrative* to gain a stronger foothold in the understanding and implementation of narcissism throughout the entire narrative.

The concept of narcissism is later taken up in the piece "No. In Fact, I Do Not Need, I Do Not Want. (Mantra)", which integrates scholarly journals such as *Computers in Human Behavior*, to investigate the psychological effects of social media use on narcissism (Lee et al. 1041) as well as how it can cause or is interconnected with feelings of loneliness, stress, anxiety and a need for belonging (Oldmeadow, Quinn, and Kowert 1143-45). As the creative self states, these pieces are about narcissism, whilst simultaneously attempting to avoid *too much* narcissism. They are caught in the trap of trying to evade pretention whilst still being told from the point of view of the pretentious narrator. Though all in all, the balanced combination of narcissism, critique, referencing, storytelling, double-voicedness, soliloquy and experimentation demonstrates a much more developed and powerful form of fictocritical writing in this final section.

This section (IV) is extremely dense but didactic, largely owing to the fact that when discussing technology there is a great deal of ground to cover. Certain theorists and theories, such as Foucault's notion of panopticism from *Discipline and Punish: The Birth of the Prison* (1975), were originally intended to be included in this thesis to aide with the higher theoretical constructions of arguments used. Instead, they have been imbued into the folio work.

Scott Brook's "Does Anybody Know What Happened to 'Fictocriticism'?" (2002) is possibly one of the most heatedly critical papers of fictocriticism: "Fictocriticism was a virus released in the hot house of academia and assimilated itself to everything in its wake" (112). Notice the past tense of "was". Fictocriticism "hasn't been utilised as a readily available rubric for writers who haven't themselves identified with it" (113); it camouflages itself (Brook 116).

> No doubt the aversion to fc from both critical and creative quarters is due to the fact it flaunts its *endlessly* transgressive nature at precisely the moment when the new humanities are intent on finding a new ground of legitimacy and vocational application in a climate where performativity … is only recognisable if it simultaneously supplies its own criteria to judge good from bad. (Brook 115)

> Ironically, for fc, this would be to rejoin the thousands of generic agglomerations already in circulation. And to join them in the impossible balancing act of neither letting on, nor letting up. (Brook 116)

Brook's comments point out some of flaws in the creative self's pieces like "Two Cents (Everyone Has an Opinion)", "Busy Bees Buzz", "Solutionism", "Be Careful Though. There is such a Thing as Over-organisation", "Rushing the Order and Fate", "The Flux of Repulsion or Expulsion" and "Cattle Call", highlighting some of the deficiencies of the creative self's 'experimental' fictocriticism conceptually, in that it is not really research at all, despite the pieces forming a whole. Nevertheless, Brook loses much of his credibility in his anger and the various inaccuracies or shortcomings he makes in his paper. For instance, Brook calls Helen Flavell *Anna* Flavell (114). This is troubling considering how significant *Helen* Flavell's thesis *Writing-Between* is to the current methodological, historical and academic understandings of the fictocritical form. Though Brook may be confusing Helen Flavell with Anna Gibbs, whom he also cites (107, 108, 112, 114). Even so, he mentions Anna Gibbs' work without providing their titles (115). These errors could be forgivable if there does in fact exist an Anna Flavell in fictocritical academia, yet this is, to use Heather Kerr's words, a "Doubtful Category" (93). Overall, Brook's unique and renegade tone is one of bashful disregard, which is extremely idiosyncratic, and relevantly applicable to some of the creative self's pieces, but cannot be taken too seriously due to its single-mindedness. Curiously, his own name is spelt incorrectly in some citations

(*Informit Australian Public Affairs*, *Cultural Studies Review* 2002). Is this a subliminal (or overt) retaliation from fictocritics, or merely an accident? Difficult to say.

For Brook's sake, many of the pieces in Folio Four are mere opinion without context. They are less research than they are "mesearch" (Ngunjiri, Hernandez, and Chang 12), as the autoethnographers would say. Though the "narrative point" is also to self-deprecate the creative self's own work, at times sarcastically and ironically. Thematically, "Two Cents" is about a narrator proclaiming that too many people in society have an opinion that is basically irrelevant, and structurally and stylistically "Two Cents" is like this too because it has no basis in real or higher theory or critique. Other pieces in Folio Four that do this, in that they are merely prose-poetry, are pieces like "Coaxing the Ouroboros", vignettes like "Busy Bees Buzz", predominantly slices of life as in "Do the Evolution(ary Jig)", even mere song lyrics in "Solutionism" with links to a song the creative self made with Morozov's philosophies in mind. Though as a whole this section does work, and more importantly it flows fictocritically. As Amanda Nettelbeck says in her "Notes Towards an Introduction" of *The Space Between*, fictocriticism uses "intertextual echoes and analogies … of more than one way of reading … a mode of performance" (6). It is likely that Nettelbeck would be empathetic to the pieces in these creative folios. Again, perhaps not on their own, but as a whole. Her words to describe fictocriticism are "not to look for something *in* the text but to *do* something else with it" (12).

> In fictocritical writings, as suggested earlier, the 'distance' of the theorist/critic collides with the 'interiority' of the author. In other words, the identity of the author is very much at issue … The authoritative overview of the critic might be gone, but more is left than a celebration of mirror reflections, fragmentary images, surfaces; there is, after all, the presence of a powerful subjectivity, but it is one that is localised, contingent, and which says both more and less than it seems to say. (Nettelbeck 12)

Nettelbeck's opinions are somewhat idealistic in that they subscribe and support the same vagueness in 'writerly' writing that Brook describes as "monstrous" or that Robb would consider a "contamination or pollution of rational academic writing" (98).

Although Nettelbeck is incredibly visionary, her own radical, experimental and "unruly" (13) views on fictocritical writing could also be her undoing, owing to those lack of parameters and boundaries she pushes for. Of course, in 1998, when Nettelbeck and Heather Kerr were constructing the first ever (and possibly only) multi-authored fictocritical anthology in existence, this visionary attitude was totally necessary for fictocriticism's prodigious emergence in academia. Now, however, some boundaries should begin to be put into place. Boundaries and rules that, ironically, could sustain fictocriticism as a legitimate form and methodology in academia in the future. Thus, therein lies another factor in fictocriticism: *time*. *When* a fictocritical writing was made could prove to be crucial to its recognisability and categorisation. Thesis Two mentioned the change or adaptation fictocriticism underwent from more prominently female or feminist writings (Sedgwick 1993; Modjeska 1994; Kerr and Nettelbeck 1998) in the 1990s to the inclusion of more male expression (Muecke 2008; Morgan 2012; Villalobos 2014; Watkins 2014; Cholewa 2014) in the new millennium. Nettelbeck also advocates for "the critical essay that moves in the direction of the literary ... others suggest fiction that moves in the direction of the critical essay ... 'confessional' literary forms as the autobiographical ... and the journal" (13), which alludes to the positioning of more creative or more academic fictocriticism within a spectrum.

The word "journal" is important here. Many of the pieces in these folios are highly subjective, "semi-confessional ... journalistic or autobiographical" (Nettelbeck 6). Moreover, they have a distinct voice; that of a millennial first-generation Polish-Australian male. Yet their style and structure can be as fragmentary as Gibbs' "The Gift". An early version of the initial PhD project this book is based on, had been criticised for being too much like a journal entry, and not at all like fictocriticism, but this assertion is redundant when comparing the pivotal fictocritical views and examples of Gibbs, Kerr and Nettelbeck (1998). So, a compromise: let it be said that in 1998 the creative self's pieces, such as "Coaxing the Ouroboros", "Busy Bees Buzz", "Do the Evolution(ary Jig)" and "Solutionism", in a sequence or as a whole, could be fictocritical. Though now, for the sake of the evolution and development of the form, they can be sacrificed, and said to *fail* fictocritically. This may not even necessarily be true, but this text will let them be martyrised so that the form can grow. Quite a noble offering on the author's part. Sarcasm aside, it must be kept in mind at all times that this is an 'experimental' book in innovative fictocriticism. All of the creative folios are like different trials on the form. Not all succeed, because the creative self must persistently battle to (a) demonstrate expertise in the field, (b) engage with the unconventional, freeform, anarchic, rule-less and lawless methodology, whilst at the same time (c) try to innovate on fictocriticism, or create the necessary rules and foundations for it (or a new form of it) to successfully prevail and exist in academia. This is like trying to build a cabin out of burning logs, to use a crude simile.

By now this book has located, categorised, elaborated on, or at least alluded to, ample consistencies and raw energy in fictocriticism, despite the "freeform", vague and "monstrous" nature that has diluted it for so many years. These have been found in its "double-voice" (Kerr 93) and "subtext" (Rubenstein 37), its antecedence in postmodernism and "metafictional strategies" (Waugh 22), deconstruction, satire, non-conformism, opposition, and even incorrect, sarcastic or non-existent referencing, its autobiographical characteristics in memoirs (Gaita 1999), anecdotes or use of the first-person (Smith 1001-02) and storytelling narratives (Muecke and King 14, Morgan 2012), its connections to education and pedagogy (Modjeska 1994; Brewster 2013), its similarities to more established academic modes like autoethnography (Walford 2004), its phraseology (Gibbs 311; Brewster 2013), its implementation of the 'ghost' triad methodology, its "rhetorical modes (the lyrical, the elegiac, the rhapsodic, the humorous, the parodic, the satirical and so on)" as well as its potential applicability to "anthropology, ethnography, psychoanalysis and autobiography" (Gibbs 2), its need for a clear "narrative point", its narcissism, its implementation of hyperlinks (Azul 2011) and other modern, "performative" (Smith 1002) technological narrative modes that look outside of the one-dimensional text being read (Smith 2009; Naismith 2009; Watkins and Krauth 2016) and the importance of context, chronology, or *time*. Thus, the views scholars such as Brook (2002) or Robb (2013) have held in the past should now be considered dated. Fictocriticism could or should, more or less, come into its own now.

This section's folio, as in all of the previous folios, is about innovation and literary experimentation, albeit in a fragmentary or multi-voiced nature. And of course, being a probing and uninhibited exploration into deviant creative writing, the author can only plead an emotional defence for his efforts, quoting the exuberance of Watkins' and Krauth's "Radicalising the Scholarly Paper": "My heart loves writers who are academics having writers' ideas" (2). The process has been stimulating and scintillating.

CONCLUSION

I return to writing in the first-person (in)formal, for the most part. The creative and analytical selves are unified again, as the creative and analytical arcs have drawn to a close. I have changed much as a result of this adventurous exploration. Interestingly, the creative pieces became less serious and more comedic as the work progressed, rather than more serious, as I had imagined. I think a fundamental reason for this can be surmised by what Mirek says in "*Be* the Tallest Poppy" in Folio Two: that life is "just life. It's not that serious or important when compared to the grand scheme of things in the cosmos". The psychology of my creative self for much of the duration of this project was not especially healthy. The creative (and created) self in these folios, primarily written between the age of 25-30, experienced rage, abandonment, frustration, fear, despondency and an intolerable, pulverising perplexity that comes with being an often-immature person of this age bracket, like that of Ari in *Loaded*, Justine in *The River Ophelia*, and Johnny in *House of Leaves*. That vulnerability and raw (negative) human emotion, as with good fictocritical storytelling, was perpetually battered on to these pages, acting as a form of catharsis for my self. Though when this study came nearer to its end, and I left my twenties behind me, I cast aside much of that particularised anguish. Instead, I experienced hope, optimism, love and joy once again. I saw the lighter side(s) of the work; the humour, irony, ridiculousness and elation—the qualities that made my version, perspective and philosophy on certain 'truths' to be stranger than fiction. I saw a place and purpose for this kind of fictocritical storytelling and critique in the creative and academic sphere.

And now, to answer the questions posed at the beginning of my curious journey. Firstly, what is fictocritical (non-)fiction? The answer to this is best demonstrated through published examples: Kosofsky's *Tendencies*; Modjeska's *The Orchard*; the collection of works from *The Space Between*; DeLillo's *White Noise*; Byrne's *Surface Collection*; Muecke's *Joe in the Andamans*; and Danielewski's *House of Leaves* if we want to consider an even more innovative postmodern, metafictive (potentially proto-fictocritical) 'text'. These examples demonstrate what fictocritical (non-)fiction is in their ability to incorporate theory, philosophy, social commentary and critique in their writing. They also blend and hybridise multiple writing forms and genres simultaneously, which serves to challenge and probe the parameters of how writing can be delivered, read, interpreted and understood in a way that is creative, engaging for the reader, but also highly theoretical and/or academic.

Secondly, is there a definition of fictocriticism that is agreed on by all fictocritical academics? This question is an exciting one to answer, and one of the primary reasons for doing this book. For the answer is an unequivocal *no*. No one seems to agree on any single definition; there is no cluster of fictocritics nodding their heads in unison about one. I know academic writing is not usually as binary as this, but it would be nice to take a decisive plunge occasionally. Fictocriticism is simply too vague and open-ended; hence, its perpetual rise and fall in (Australian) academia. I still consider Hazel Smith's as the best definition thus far:

> fictocriticism juxta-poses creative and academic writing environments, and breaks down their separation and autonomy. Fictocritics may, for example, insert, imply, or elucidate theoretical ideas within creative work without feeling the pressure to transform those ideas into entirely fictional or poetic texts. Such texts can take many different forms, but may often be experimental and discontinuous: for example, fictional or poetic sections are juxtaposed with theoretical interjections so that they reverberate with each other. Or, fictocritical critics may attempt to disrupt the formality of the academic essay with strategies such as crossing of genres, collage, non-linearity, wordplay, anecdote, or use of the first person. (1001-02)

Gerrit Haas' thoroughly researched venture into fictocriticism in 2017 did indeed provide a "working definition" of the strategy; however, it is too engineered, scientific, mechanical and impersonal. Fictocriticism is not an automated mathematical equation! It is soulful and personal too. An eventual working definition of it will require one's head and heart for it to be properly penned down. Or it never will. It will just age, change, regress and evolve, like all words and fashions do.

Another question surrounded the fictocritical 'success' of my own writing: which of my innovative 'fictocritical' pieces were most or least successful in this experiment? I considered creating a table to methodically answer this question, but perhaps that is too scientific. I will merely state, temporarily feigning my analytical self's eye once again, which of my pieces were most successful and which, to me, were the biggest disappointments.

I believe some of the most successful ones were "The Mission Man" due to its analyses and unique integration of (very different) other writer's work(s), and its use of double-voicing in the narrative, "The Spirit of the Times" (as I was essentially trying to mimic Barthes here, whom is largely the embodiment of the fictocritical movement), "*Kwiat Dwóch Puszcz*", "Storm", "*Be* the Tallest Poppy" and "*Daj Mi Pić, Proszę Cię*" because of their social and cultural commentary told through first-person storytelling, "(Scrapped) Book: A 'Professional' Educational(?) Overview" and "An Agitation" because of their overt, yet subversive links to academia, academic practices and pedagogy, "Do the Evolution(ary Jig)", "Palahniuk's *Invisible Monsters*", "Tunnel Vision", "Repetition" (which was already published *as* fictocriticism previously), "*Idiocracy* [Film]" (though short, is self-referential), "Be Careful Though. There is such a Thing as Over-organisation", "No. In Fact, I Do Not Need, I Do Not Want. (Mantra)", "'Irony', Alanis Morissette and Me" and "The Accumulation of Demons", all due to their wariness of prevailing contemporary technological and psychological issues, social and critical commentary, diversity and breadth of form and genre, told through a distinct and incisive millennial voice.

I consider the least successful pieces as having been "A Daze to Come True", "A Sentimental Cynic", "Coast to Coast Infrequency (Part I)", "Coast to Coast Infrequency (Part II)", "Ghouls", "End of the Weekend", "Going Home", "Tiers and Towers", "Hum, Amplitude, (Being a) Focal Point", "'Big' Ideas", "Coaxing the Ouroboros", "Busy Bees Buzz", "Solutionism" (though this one could also be marked as "electric fictocriticism" as it literally has a link to an external digital source) and "Two Cents". The key reason these works failed is because (a) they were not as critical, or significantly researched/referenced to the level that, for instance, one would find in the collection of works in *The Space Between*, and (b) as innovative 'experiments' I overstretched myself immensely, trying to do too much all at once — cutting them up as vignettes, making them too vague, personal, poetic, obscure, journal-like, artistic, meandering … oh, wait. That *is* fictocriticism. But it is also *not*. Therein lies the problem(s) ensnaring it. These problems I tried to address and make very clear throughout this book.

Does fictocriticism work well within both academic and creative writing practices? Yes. Very much so. Its interdisciplinary nature shows this. But does it work in a hybridised manner? Yes again, though fictocritics argue that this is hard work. Academics and creative writers using fictocriticism need to take care so that the writing form does not become too messy, convoluted or "monstrous", as this inevitably leads to the complete dissolution of useful meaning. Perhaps this is why so many of my writings seemed to fail. Is fictocriticism a methodology that can still be innovated on though? Yes. This is visibly demonstrated in the four theses and some of the experimental folio sequences.

In that case, what did each of my theses do? Thesis One highlighted some of the dilemmas surrounding fictocriticism and contextualised *this* text in the development and (hi)story of the writing strategy.

Thesis One and Folio One bled into Thesis Two and Folio Two. Their narrative was very similar, and they were difficult to separate. Though Thesis Two took some of the context of Thesis One much further, most visibly in its discussion of postmodernism's and metafiction's connectedness to fictocriticism and in its extrapolation, and fictocriticism's autobiographical characteristics.

Thesis Three explored some of the most seminal and unambiguously fictocritical texts to discuss education and pedagogy, its similarity to other academic styles of writing and distinct characteristics in its phraseology and "narrative point". The corresponding folio work further mercilessly played with these themes, techniques and the writing form.

Thesis Four and Folio Four were different, both thematically and theoretically. They contemplated the future, of both fictocriticism and the world. They were broad, busy and ambitious, most notably in their discussion of technologies and concrete innovations regarding ("electric") fictocriticism. They also incorporated previously published work/innovations in the area of micro/flash fiction. Thesis Four was also conclusive, summarising many of the key points of the previous theses, whilst the folio work closed out the narrative arc. The biggest changes, and perhaps some of the biggest challenges, in the author (both the creative and analytical self) were seen here.

Has, or how has, fictocriticism changed over the years to become more concise and dynamic, regimented, or has it become more vague and obscure? I believe it has become clearer. And it has more distinct traits now, many of which I have tried to identify in the theses. It has also become more genderless, rather than being purely feminine, which is how it began in Australia in the 1990s with Sedgwick's *Tendencies*, Modjeska's *The Orchard* and *The Space Between*.

This research was based on my personal exploration of Australian experiences and perspectives, and thus was more *Australia*-oriented. Much of the fictocritical research I uncovered was predominantly Australian anyway. No other nation appears to dominate the field quite as much.

Which brings me to my next point: this book was, at its core, a creative writing production. It was not pure theory. Its scope and space for theoretical exploration was limited due to creative folios that were unequivocally married to theoretical theses. These two components were irretrievably linked, and could not flirt with any additional theories, ideas or concepts, without breaking the fundamental bond they had, one with the other. Another pervasive challenge was that of the diverged 'self' in fictocriticism. Finding the appropriate terminology and methodology to overcome this obstacle was an epic and prolonged struggle. The first version of this text was written entirely in the first-person, with folios and theses that were hybridised, which simply did not work as a scholarly piece. Eventually, the list of terminology was constructed to circumnavigate the issue of the 'I'. Still, though the creative and analytical selves generally remained confined to their respective roles, their eye/'I' did tend to wander, and this division was not always perfectly harmonious. Hence, the need for the list of terminology and for the allowance of the 'selves' to be merged together as one, momentarily, in the introduction and conclusion of this work. This intensely orchestrated and methodological double-voicedness may even be the biggest fictocritical innovation in this study: the literal, physical, theoretical and symbolic identification and composition of 'I' and 'self' in the folios and the theses, I believe, is fictocriticism in its most overt form, for it is two distinct, labelled voices in one document.

This study, and Flavell's *Writing-Between*, indicated the numerous categories or variations of what *could* be considered fictocriticism (*Shishōsetsu* or the 'I-novel', *fiction-théorique*, "confessional criticism", "autocritique, the new belletrism, experimental critical writing, narrative criticism ... literary non-fiction", gonzo, travel writing, writing-between, beatnik novels and autoethnography). So where can fictocriticism go from here? How can it better stand out as a form of its own? What is beyond fictocriticism, if anything? I propose these questions, and the following areas, for potential future research: further study on Canadian (and other international) fictocriticism; experimental hybridisation and formatting of the university exegesis-artefact model (and even other administrative forms of academic documentation); bridging potential inter-generational communication gaps through fictocritical writing practices; evaluating fictocriticism as a vehicle for higher theory and criticism across other social, artistic, scientific, educational, political and historical fields, including music studies (as there was originally a fifth section of work in this text relating to contemporary music, Theodor Adorno, and one of Gibbs' fictocritical-musical works that I may yet salvage and use as a potential publication in a music and/or literary journal). We shall see.

Professor Stephen Muecke's ("the wizard of fictocriticism") expertise was solicited in the final developmental stages of this book, and he once noted to me that it is not possible to define fictocriticism, rather it can only *do* things, so in this sense, this study was quite ambitious in its aim to define the form. Alas! If it in fact cannot be defined, then the experimental writings here should not be classified as experimental. They should simply be called 'fictocritical'. Though maybe I just purely cannot *do* fictocriticism, and have an in-built mental and physical block about it, like my sheer helplessness when it comes to mathematics, whistling or playing bocce. This leads to an immense frustration on my part that seeks to break down and deconstruct or reconstruct/reinvent/uncover the rules, if necessary, if only to be rid of this barrier for my own self-interest. Though if fictocriticism was clearly definable then there would be no need for these fictocritical folios and theses. But since it is not, then some latitude should be allowed for discovery and my self-interested literary manoeuvres.

All in all, I am a fictocritical optimist, but one of a new era perhaps. This exploration did not propose a 'better' phase of fictocriticism, just a different (generational) phase and conception of it. This text's goals were to legitimise the form by discussing it, rather than confining, ignoring or isolating it. I think Barthes would approve.

BIBLIOGRAPHY

ABC News. "Sydney Siege: US President Barack Obama, British Prime Minister David Cameron Briefed on Martin Place Hostage Situation". *ABC News*, 16 December 2014. http://www.abc.net.au/news/2014-12-15/world-leaders-briefed-on-hostage-situation/5967942. Web. 26 Sep. 2015.

Akujärvi, Johanna. "One and 'I' in the Frame Narrative: Authorial Voice, Travelling Persona and Addressee in Pausanias' Periegesis." *The Classical Quarterly* 62.1 (2012): 327-8.

Alanis Morissette. "Ironic." *Jagged Little Pill*. Maverick/Reprise, 1995. CD.

Albom, Mitch. *Tuesdays with Morrie: An Old Man, a Young Man, and Life's Greatest Lesson*. Hachette UK, 2009.

Alobeytha, Faisal Laee Etan. "The Use of Frame Story in Kashmira Sheth's Boys without Names." *Advances in Language and Literary Studies* 7.5 (2016): 105-11.

Anae, Nicole. ""Language Speaking the Subject Speaking the Arts": New Possibilities for Interdisciplinarity in Arts/English Education—Explorations in Three-Dimensional Storytelling." *English Teaching* 13.2 (2014): 113-40.

—. ""Creative Writing as Freedom, Education as Exploration": Creative Writing as Literary and Visual Arts Pedagogy in the First Year Teacher-Education Experience." *Australian Journal of Teacher Education* 39.8 (2014): 123-14.

—. "Chapter Six: Dialogue." *Elements of Creative Writing I (HUMT20012) Study Guide*: Central Queensland University, 2017: 1-7.

Arcade Fire. "We Used To Wait." *The Suburbs*. Mercury Records, 2010. CD.

Arnold, Josie. "The PhD in Writing Accompanied by an Exegesis." *Journal of University Teaching & Learning Practice* 2.1 (2005): 34-50.

Auslander, Philip. *Liveness: Performance in a Mediatized Culture*. Routledge, 2008.

Azul, David. "Phononostalgia: a Fictocritical Investigation into Discordant Notions of 'Voice' in Speech and Writing." *TEXT, Journal of Writing and Writing Courses* 15.1 (2011): 1-23.

Back to the Future. Dir. Robert Zemeckis. Universal Pictures, 1985. Film.

Ballard, James Graham. "Aldous Huxley: An English Intellectual by Nicholas Murray." *Guardian*, April 13, 2002.

Barnes, Kassandra, Raymond C. Marateo, and S. Pixy Ferris. "Teaching and Learning with the Net Generation." *Innovate: Journal of Online Education* 3.4 (2007): 1.

Barrett, Estelle. "What does it Meme? The Exegesis as Valorisation and Validation of Creative Arts Research." *TEXT, Journal of Writing and Writing Courses* 3 (2004): 1-7.

Barthes, Roland. *Mythologies*. Macmillan, 1972.

—. *The Pleasure of the Text*. Macmillan, 1973.

—. *Roland Barthes*. New York: Hill and Wang, 1975.

—. "The Death of the Author." *Image-Music-Text*. London: Fontana Press, 1977. 142-48.

—. *A Lover's Discourse*. New York: Hill and Wang, 1978.

Booth, David. "Nietzsche on "The Subject as Multiplicity". *Man and World* 18.2 (1985): 121-46.

Bowen, Elizabeth. "Out of a Book." *The Mulberry Tree: Writings of Elizabeth Bowen* (1946): 48-53.

Box, Dan. "Sydney Siege Inquest: Lindt Café Deaths Investigated." *The Australian*, 29 January 2015. http://www.theaustralian.com.au/in-depth/sydney-siege/sydney-siege-inquest-lindt-cafe-deaths-investi gated/storyfnqxbywy1227200443586?sv=5a2177ba498aa7bd908d26a 51619dc27. Web. 26 Sep. 2015.

Brennan, Timothy. "Running and Dodging: The Rhetoric of Doubleness in Contemporary Theory." *New Literary History* 41.2 (2010): 277-99.

Brent Jason Royster's "The Construction of Self in the Contemporary Creative Writing Workshop: A Personal Journey" (2006).

Brewster, Anne. "The Poetics of Memory." *Continuum: Journal of Media & Culture Studies* 19.3 (2005): 397-402.

Brewster, Anne. "Fictocriticism: Pedagogy and Practice." *Journal of the Association for the Study of Australian Literature* (2013): 89-92.

Brook, Scott. "Does Anybody Know What Happened to 'Fictocriticism'?: Toward a Fractal Genealogy of Australian Fictocriticism." *Cultural Studies Review* 8.2 (2002): 104-18.

Broyles, Michael. *Mavericks and Other Traditions in American Music*. Yale University Press, 2008.

Bruce, Darryl. "Fifty Years since Lashley's in Search of the Engram: Refutations and Conjectures." *Journal of the History of the Neurosciences* 10.3 (2001): 308-18.

Byrne, Denis. *Surface Collection: Archaeological Travels in Southeast Asia*. Rowman Altamira, 2007.

Caiger, George, ed. *The Australian Way of Life*. Columbia University Press, 1953.

Calvino, Italo. *If on a Winter's Night a Traveller*. Random House, 1983.

Canagarajah, A. Suresh. "Autoethnography in the Study of Multilingual Writers." *Writing Studies Research in Practice: Methods and Methodologies* (2012): 113-24.

Carnegie, Dale. *How to Win Friends and Influence People*. Sydney: Angus & Robertson, 1938.

Charters, Ann. *Kerouac: A Biography*. New York: St. Martin's Press, 1994.

Cholewa, Pawel. "The Road to 'Enlightenment' or Destruction: Drugs and Changing Perspectives in Jack Kerouac's Writing". Bachelor of Arts (Honours). Monash University, Clayton, VIC: 2012.

—. "There's a Road Train Going Nowhere". *Stoned Crows & Other Australian Icons Anthology (Meanjin)*, edited by Julie Chevalier and Linda Godfrey, Spineless Wonders, Strawberry Hills: NSW. March 2013.

—. "Repetition". *TEXT, Journal of Writing and Writing Courses* (2014).

Choromański, Michał. "A Cynical Tale." Trans. Thad Kowalski. *Ten Contemporary Polish Stories*. Ed. Edmund Ordon. Santa Barbara, CA: Greenwood. 1958, 1974. Reprint of 1958 Wayne State U P. 53-115.

Citizenfour. Dir. Laura Poitras. HBO Films, 2014. Film.

Clarke, Arthur C. *2001: A Space Odyssey*. New American Library, 1968.

Coded Bias. Dir. Shalini Kantayya. 7th Empire Media, 2020. Film.

Coghlan, Sean. "Young People 'Prefer to Read on Screen.'" *BBC News*, 16 May 2013. https://www.bbc.com/news/education-22540408. Web. 17 Nov. 2018.

Coupland, Douglas, and Marshall McLuhan. *You Know Nothing of My Work!* Atlas & Co., New York, 2010.

Courtenay, Bryce. *The Power of One*. Random House LLC, 1989.

Crew, Gary. *Voicing the Dead*. Ford Street Publishing, 2015.

Curzan, Anne. "20 Words that once Meant Something Very Different". *Ideas.Ted.Com*, 18 June 2014. http://ideas.ted.com/20-words-that-once-meant-something-very-different/. Web. 9 Aug. 2016.

Darwin, Charles. *On the Origin of Species, 1859*. Routledge, 2004.

Danielewski, Mark Z. *House of Leaves*. Random House LLC, 2000.

Dardess, George. "The Logic of Spontaneity: A Reconsideration of Kerouac's 'Spontaneous Prose Method.'" *The Oral Impulse in Contemporary American Poetry* 3 (1975): 729-46

Dawson, Paul. "A Place for the Space Between: Fictocriticism and the University." *Westerly* 47. (2002): 139. *Humanities International Complete*. Web. 5 Nov. 2013.

De Grey, Aubrey. *The Mitochondrial Free Radical Theory of Aging*. Austin, TX: RG Landes, 1999.

DeLillo, Don. *White Noise*. Penguin, 1999.

Derrida, Jacques. "Structure, Sign, and Play in the Discourse of the Human Sciences." *A Postmodern Reader* (1993): 223-42.

Dickens, Charles. *David Copperfield*. London: Bradbury and Evans, 1850.

Donne, John. *No Man is an Island: A Selection from the Prose of John Donne*. Ed. Scott Rivers. Folio Society, 2006.

Dunbar, Robin. *How Many Friends Does One Person Need? Dunbar's Number and other Evolutionary Quirks*. Cambridge, MA: Harvard University Press, 2010.

During, Simon. "Madness." *Foucault and Literature: Towards a Genealogy of Writing*. Ed. Simon During. New York: Routledge, 1992. 24-43.

Eagleton, Terry. *Literary Theory: An Introduction*. University of Minnesota Press, 1996.

Egan, Susanna. *Mirror Talk: Genres of Crisis in Contemporary Autobiography*. The University of North Carolina Press, Chapel Hill and London: 1999.

Ellis, Carolyn, and Arthur P. Bochner. "Autoethnography, Personal Narrative, Reflexivity: Researcher as Subject." (2000): 733.

Elms, Alan C. "The Woman We Didn't See." *Science Fiction Studies* 34.1 (2007): 117-28.

Ettler, Justine. *The River Ophelia*. Picador, Pan Macmillan Australia, 1995.

Fathallah, Judith May. *Fanfiction and the Author: How Fanfic Changes Popular Cultural Texts*. Amsterdam University Press, 2017. *JSTOR*, www.jstor.org/stable/j.ctt1v2xsp4.

Federico, Annette R. "'David Copperfield' and the Pursuit of Happiness." *Victorian Studies* 46.1 (2003): 69-95.

Federman, Raymond. "Imagination as Plagiarism [An Unfinished Paper...]." *New Literary History* 7.3 (1976): 563-78.

Federman, Raymond. *Double or Nothing*. New York: The Swallow Press, 1971.

Fielding, Henry. *Joseph Andrews*. Broadview Press, 2001.

—. "Tom Jones. 1749." *Book XIII* (1973).

Fitzsimmons, John. "Humanities: New Horizons." *The New Humanities: 2000 and Beyond*. CQUniversity, 20 February 1998 (Lecture).

Flavell, Helen. *Writing-Between: Australian and Canadian Ficto-criticism.* Diss. Murdoch University, 2004.

Foucault, Michel. *Discipline and Punish: The Birth of the Prison.* Vintage, 2012.

Fowler, Edward. "The Rhetoric of Confession: Shishōsetsu in Early Twentieth-Century Japanese Fiction." Review by Mary N. Layoun. *The Journal of Asian Studies* 48.1 (1989): 158-60.

French, Marilyn. "The Women's Room." *Women and Social Policy.* Palgrave, London, 1985: 109-11.

Freud, Sigmund. *Dora: An Analysis of a Case of Hysteria.* Simon and Schuster, 1997.

Frey, James. *A Million Little Pieces.* Anchor Books, 2003.

Funny People. Dir. Judd Apatow. Universal Pictures, 2009. Film.

Furphy, Joseph. *Such is Life: Text Classics.* Text Publishing, 2013.

Gaita, Raimond. *Romulus, My Father.* Text Publishing, 1999.

Gallop, Jane. "Precocious Jouissance: Roland Barthes, Amatory Maladjustment, and Emotion." *New Literary History* 43.3 (2012): 565-82.

Gibbs, Anna. "Writing and the Flesh of Others." *Australian Feminist Studies* 18.42 (2003): 309. *MasterFILE Premier.* Web. 1 Nov. 2013.

—. "Fictocriticism, Affect, Mimesis: Engendering Differences." *TEXT, Journal of Writing and Writing Courses* (2005).

Gide, André. *Les Faux-monnayeurs.* Editions Gallimard, 2012.

Gray, Christopher. "Essays from Leaving the 20th Century." *What is Situationism* (1996): 3-23.

Haas, Gerrit. *Fictocritical Strategies: Subverting Textual Practices of Meaning, Other, and Self-Formation.* transcript Verlag, 2017.

Hall, Stuart. "Introduction: Who Needs Identity?" in S. Hall & P. du Gay (eds.) *Questions of Cultural Identity,* 1.17." (1996).

—. "On Postmodernism and Articulation". Ed. Lawrence Grossberg." *Stuart Hall: Critical Dialogues in Cultural Studies. London & New York, Routledge* (1996): 131-50.

Hancox, Donna Maree, and Vivienne Muller. "Excursions into New Territory: Fictocriticism and Undergraduate Writing." *New Writing: The International Journal for the Practice & Theory of Creative Writing* 8.2 (2011): 147-58.

Haswell, Janis and Richard H. Haswell. "Gendership and the Miswriting of Students." *College Composition and Communication* 46.2 (1995): 223-54.

Head On. Dir. Ana Kokkinos. Umbrella Entertainment, 1998. Film.

Hely, Robin. *Project Neurocam: An Investigation.* Diss. Monash University, 2013.

Hemingway, Ernest. *A Moveable Feast*. Random House, 2010.

Herman, David, Jahn, Manfred, and Ryan, Marie-Laure, eds. *Routledge Encyclopedia of Narrative Theory*. Routledge, 2010.

Hodge, Bob, and Vijay Mishra. *Dark Side of the Dream: Australian Literature and the Postcolonial Mind*. Allen & Unwin, 1991.

Holloway, Wad. https://theaustralianlegend.wordpress.com/2017/10/23/author-interview-justine-ettler/. Web. 11 May. 2018.

Holt, Nicholas L. "Representation, Legitimation, and Autoethnography: An Autoethnographic Writing Story." *International Journal of Qualitative Methods* 2.1 (2003): 18-28.

Hutcheon, Linda. *Narcissistic Narrative: The Metafictional Paradox*. Waterloo: Wilfred Laurier University Press, 1980.

Huxley, Aldous. *Brave New World*. Harmondsworth: Penguin in Association with Chatto & Windus, 1955.

I Am. Dir. Tom Shadyac. Flying Eye Productions, 2010. Film.

Idiocracy. Dir. Mike Judge. 20th Century Fox, 2006. Film.

Jacobowitz, Susan. *The Holocaust at Home: Representations and Implication of Second Generation Experience*. Brandeis University, 2004.

Jameson, Fredric. "Interview with Andrea Ward." *Impulse* 13 (1987): 8-9.

Johnson, Ronna C. "You're Putting Me On": Jack Kerouac and the Postmodern Emergence." *College Literature* 27.1 (2000): 22-38.

Joyce, James. *Finnegan's Wake*. Penguin UK, 2015.

—. *Ulysses*. Jovian Press, 2017.

Jurassic Park. Dir. Steven Spielberg. Universal Pictures, 1993. Film.

Kafka, Franz. *Metamorphosis and Other Stories*. Penguin UK, 2007.

Kaplan, Fred. *Charles Dickens' Book of Memoranda*. New York: New York Public Library, 1981.

Kaprow, Allan. "The Real Experiment." *Artforum* 22.4 (1983): 37-43.

Kerouac, Jack. *On the Road*. London: Penguin Books, 2000.

—. *The Dharma Bums*. London: Penguin Books, 2007.

—. *Visions of Cody*. Penguin UK, 2012.

—. "Essentials of Spontaneous Prose." *The Portable Jack Kerouac*. Ed. Ann Charters. New York: Penguin, 1995. 484-85.

Kerr, Heather, and Amanda E. Nettelbeck, eds. *The Space Between: Australian Women Writing Fictocriticism*. UWA Publishing, 1998.

Kerr, Heather. "Fictocriticism, the 'Doubtful Category' and 'The Space Between'." *Journal of the Association for the Study of Australian Literature* (2013): 93-96.

King, Noel. "My Life Without Steve: Postmodernism, Fictocriticism and the Paraliterary." *Southern Review: Communication, Politics & Culture* 27.3 (1994): 261.

Krikelis, Lissi Athanasiou. *Postmodern Metafiction Revisited.* City University of New York, 2013.

Kroll, Jeri. "The Exegesis and the Gentle Reader/Writer." *Text, Special Issue Series* 3. April 2004. http://www.griffith.edu.au/school/art/text/.

Lang, Candice. "Autocritique." *Confession of the Critics.* H. Ed. Aram Veeser. London: Routledge, 1996. 40-54.

Lee, Jong-Eun Roselyn, et al. "Who Wants to be "Friend-Rich"? Social Compensatory Friending on Facebook and the Moderating Role of Public Self-Consciousness." *Computers in Human Behavior* 28.3 (2012): 1036-43. *Academic Search Complete.* Web. 7 Aug. 2014.

Leneghan, Sean. "The Varieties of Ecstasy Experience: An Exploration of Person, Mind and Body in Sydney's Club Culture." LAMBERT Academic Publishing, 2011.

Lilienfeld, Jane. "Contingencies of Dispersed Identity in Lydia Minatoya's" The Strangeness of Beauty". *Tulsa Studies in Women's Literature* 23.1 (2004): 91-105.

Lucy. Dir. Luc Besson. Universal Pictures, 2014. Film.

Mak, Dominik. *Kwiat Dwóch Puszcz.* Oficyna Wydawnicza "Impuls", Kraków, 2003.

Mann, Thomas. *Death in Venice and Other Stories.* Random House LLC, 2008.

Mansbach, Abraham. "Heidegger on the Self, Authenticity and Inauthenticity." *Iyyun: The Jerusalem Philosophical Quarterly* (1991): 65-91.

Mayol, Taylor. *Ozy Author.* http://www.ozy.com/acumen/who-are-the-worlds-strictest-parents/63050. Web. 1 Apr. 2016.

McCaffery, Larry, and Sinda Gregory. "Haunted House—An Interview with Mark Z. Danielewski." *Critique: Studies in Contemporary Fiction* 44.2 (2003): 99-135.

McQuail, Josephine A. "Passion and Mysticism in William Blake." *Modern Language Studies* (2000): 121-34.

McRaney, David. *You Are Not So Smart: Why Your Memory is Mostly Fiction, Why You Have Too Many Friends on Facebook and 46 Other Ways You're Deluding Yourself.* Oneworld Publications, 2012.

Méndez, Mariza. "Autoethnography as a Research Method: Advantages, Limitations and Criticisms." *Colombian Applied Linguistics Journal* 15.2 (2013): 279-87.

Michaux, Henri. *Miserable Miracle: Mescaline.* New York Review of Books, 2002.

Miller, Henry. *Tropic of Capricorn*. New York: Grove Press, 1952.

Mirolla, Michael. "Denying Labels and Identifications: A Modest Proposal on the Preservation/Prolongation of Italian-Canadian Writer Identity beyond Its Natural Life Cycle." *Proceedings of the 2008 Biennial Conference of the Association of Italian-Canadian Writers, Nov. 14-16, 2008: Envisioning Culture: Evolving Writing and Community*. Toronto: Association of Italian Canadian Writers, 2008.

Modjeska, Drusilla. *The Orchard*. Sydney: Picador, Pan Macmillan Australia, 1995.

Monforte, Javier. "What is New in New Materialism for a Newcomer?" *Qualitative Research in Sport, Exercise and Health* 10.3 (2018): 378-90.

Moorhead, Finola. *Quilt: A Collection of Prose*. Melbourne: Sybylla, 1995.

Morgan, Hamish. "What Can Fictocriticism Do?" *Altitude: An e-Journal of Emerging Humanities Work* 10 (2012).

Morozov, Evgeny. *The Net Delusion: How Not to Liberate the World*. New York: Penguin Books, 2011.

—. *To Save Everything, Click Here: The Folly of Technological Solutionism*. Public Affairs, 2013.

Muecke, Stephen and King, Noel. "On Ficto-Criticism." *Australian Book Review* 135 (1991): 13.

Muecke, Stephen. *No Road (bitumen all the way)*. Fremantle Arts Centre Press, 1997.

—. *Joe in the Andamans: And Other Fictocritical Stories*. Erskenville: Local Consumption Publications, 2008.

—. "What Is Fictocriticism?" *The Mother's Day Protest and Other Fictocritical Essays*. Rowman & Littlefield International, 2016.

Naismith, Emily, B. Comm, and Jenny Weight. "Emily Coughs: A Fictocritical Exploration of the Self via Social Media." (2009).

Nelson, Robert. "Doctoralness in the Balance: The Agonies of Scholarly Writing in Studio Research Degrees." *Text Special Issue Series* 3 (2004).

Network. Dir. Sidney Lumet. United Artists, 1976. Film.

Neuman, Shirley. "The Observer Observed: Distancing the Self in Autobiography." *Prose Studies* 4.3 (1981): 317-36.

Ngunjiri, Faith Wambura, Kathy-Ann C. Hernandez, and Heewon Chang. "Living Autoethnography: Connecting Life and Research." *Journal of Research Practice* 6.1 (2010): 1.

Noske, Catherine. "In/On/Of–The Mixed Poetics of Australian Spaces; or How I Found the Cubby. A Fictocritical Essay on White Australian (Un) Belonging." *Journal of the Association for the Study of Australian Literature* 13.2 (2013): 1-10.

O'Reilly, Nathanael David. "Between the City and the Bush: Suburbia in the Contemporary Australian Novel." Diss. Western Michigan University, 2008.

Oates, Joyce Carol. *Zombie*. Dutton, 1995.

Oldmeadow, Julian A., Sally Quinn, and Rachel Kowert. "Attachment Style, Social Skills, and Facebook Use amongst Adults." *Computers in Human Behavior* 29.3 (2013): 1142-49. *Academic Search Complete*. Web. 7 Aug. 2014.

Orlando. Dir. Christopher Sheppard. Umbrella Entertainment, 1992. Film.

Orwell, George. *Nineteen Eighty-Four*. London: Chancellor Press, 1984.

Palahniuk, Chuck. *Invisible Monsters*. Random House, 2000.

Pattinson, Elizabeth. "Discovering the Self: Fictocriticism, Flux and Authorial Identity". University of Technology, Sydney. 2013.

Pi O. *24 Hours*. Melbourne: Collective Effort Press, 1996.

Poster, M. *Cultural History and Postmodernity: Disciplinary Readings and Challenges*. New York: Columbia University Press, 1997.

Prosser, Rosslyn. "Processing Fictocriticism." Rev. of The Space Between: Australian Women Writing Fictocriticism, Ed. Heather Kerr and Amanda Nettelbeck. *TEXT, Journal of Writing and Writing Courses* (1999).

Purkes, Ian. "Is Print Media on the Decline?" *Odyssey Online*, 21 Dec 2017. https://www.theodysseyonline.com/print-media-decline. Web. 17 Nov. 2018.

Raine, Danuta. "Essaying the Self: Ethnicity, Identity and the Fictocritical Essay." *TEXT, Special Issue Series 5, The Art of the Real*. April 2009, http://www.textjournal.com.au/speciss/iss ue5/raine.htm. Web. 28 Mar. 2018.

Ranciere, Jacques. *Mute Speech: Literature, Critical Theory, and Politics (New Directions in Critical Theory)*. New York: Columbia University Press, 2011.

Rimbaud, Arthur. *A Season in Hell*. New York: Oxford University Press, 1973.

Rimmon-Kenan, Shlomith. *Narrative Fiction: Contemporary Poetics/Shlomith Rimmon-Kenan*. London: Methuen, 1983.

Robb, Simon. "Academic Divination is not a Mysticism: Fictocriticism, Pedagogy and Hypertext." *Journal of the Association for the Study of Australian Literature* (2013): 97-101.

Roberts, Gregory David. *Shantaram*. Picador Australia, 2009.

Robertson, Rachel, et al. "An Ambiguous Genre: Thoughts on Creative Non-Fiction and the Exegesis." *TEXT, Journal of Writing and Writing Courses* 44 (2017): 1-13.

Rowe, Josephine. *Tarcutta Wake: Stories.* University of Queensland Press, 2012.

Rubenstein, Roberta. "'I Meant Nothing by the Lighthouse': Virginia Woolf's Poetics of Negation." *Journal of Modern Literature* 31.4 (2008): 36-53.

Rushdie, Salman. *Midnight's Children.* Random House, 2010.

Sacks, Oliver. *The Man Who Mistook His Wife for a Hat.* Picador, 2009.

Sartre, Jean-Paul. "Existentialism and Humanism." *Philosophy: Key Texts* (1948).

—. "Being and Nothingness." Trans. Hazel E. Barnes. New York: Washington Square Press (1992).

Schlunke, Katrina, and Anne Brewster. "We Four: Fictocriticism Again." *Continuum: Journal of Media & Cultural Studies* 19.3 (2005): 393-95. Academic Search Complete. Web. 1 Nov. 2013.

Schmidt, Jan Zlotnik. "A Habit of Mind and Being: Autobiographical Creative Writing." *Kentucky English Bulletin* 39.1 (1989): 56-73.

Sciorra, Joseph. "Flash Fiction." *Voices: The Journal of New York Folklore* 38.3-4 (2012): 13.

Sedgwick, Eve Kosofsky. *Tendencies.* Duke University Press, 1993.

Sinha, Sayontan. "The Bullet Cluster (1E 0657-558) Consists of Two Colliding Galaxy Clusters in Carina. Most of the Matter in the Clusters (Blue) is Separate from the Normal Matter (Pink), Giving Evidence that all of the Matter is Dark." *Anne's Astronomy News.* http://annesastronomynews.com. Web. 26 Jun. 2014.

Smith, Hazel. "The Erotics of Gossip: Fictocriticism, Performativity, Technology." *Textual Practice* 23.6 (2009): 1001-12.

Smith, Sidonie. "Self, Subject, and Resistance: Marginalities and Twentieth-Century Autobiographical Practice." *Tulsa Studies in Women's Literature* 9.1 (1990): 11-24.

Sobolewski, Tad. "The Cruel Sunday." *Ethnic Australia* (1981): 171-3.

Spineless Wonders. "Spineless Wonders asks Josephine Rowe". *Short Australian Stories.* https://shortaustralianstories.com.au/spineless-wonders-asks-josephine-rowe/. Web. 4 Sep. 2016.

Spivak, Gayatri Chakravorty. "French Feminism in an International Frame." *Yale French Studies* 62.1 (1981): 154-84.

Sterne, Laurence. *The Life and Opinions of Tristram Shandy, Gentleman.* Wordsworth Editions, 1996.

Stewart, Kathleen. Review Excerpt on Book Cover. *The Mother's Day Protest and Other Fictocritical Essays*. Rowman & Littlefield International, 2016.

Stirling, Grant. "Neurotic Narrative: Metafiction and Object-Relations Theory." *College Literature* 27.2 (2000): 80. *Academic Search Complete*. Web. 13 Nov. 2013.

The Conversation. "State School Kids Do Better at Uni." theconversation.com/state-school-kids-do-better-at-uni-29155. Web. 17 Jul. 2014.

The National. "Vanderlyle Crybaby Geeks." *High Violet*. 4AD, 2010. CD.

"The Reverse Peephole." *Seinfeld*. Fox. 15 Jan. 1998. Television.

The Social Dilemma. Dir. Jeff Orlowski. Netflix, 2020. Film.

The Truman Show. Dir. Peter Weir. Scott Rudin Productions. Paramount Pictures, 1998. Film.

Theado, Matt. *Understanding Jack Kerouac*. Columbia: University of South Carolina Press, 2000.

This Boy's Life. Dir. Michael Caton-Jones. Knickerbocker Films, Warner Bros. Pictures, 1993. Film.

Tippet, Gary. "Heated Arguments over 'Sacred' Fire in City Park," www.theage.com.au. Web. 8 Jul. 2016.

Tolle, Eckhart. *The Power of Now: A Guide to Spiritual Enlightenment*. New World Library, 2004.

Tool. "Vicarious." *10,000 Days*. Volcano Entertainment, 2006. CD.

Torgovnick, Marianna. "Experimental Critical Writing." *Profession* (1990): 25-27.

Transcendence. Dir. Wally Pfister. Warner Bros. Pictures and Summit Entertainment, 2014. Film.

Travers, Martin. *An Introduction to Modern European Literature: From Romanticism to Postmodernism*. New York: Macmillan Press Ltd, 1998.

Trottier, Monique Louise. "If Truth be Told..." Masters thesis. University of Manitoba (Canada), 2002.

Tsiolkas, Christos. *Loaded*. Random House, 1997.

Tucker, Ian. "Interview: Evgeny Morozov: 'We are Abandoning all the Checks and Balances'". *The Guardian*. https://www.theguardian.com/technology/2013/mar/09/evgeny-morozov-technology-solutionis m-interview. 2013. Web. 21 Jun. 2018.

2001: A Space Odyssey. Dir. Stanley Kubrick. Stanley Kubrick Productions, 1968. Film.

Villalobos, Jorge. "My Name is/Mi Nombre es: Developing Internal Voices in a Quest of an Identity." 2012. Web. 3 Feb. 2014.

Volponi, Paolo. *La Macchina Mondiale*. Garzanti, 1965.

Walford, Geoffrey. "Finding the Limits: Autoethnography and Being an Oxford University Proctor." *Qualitative Research* 4.3 (2004): 403-17.

Walker, Cheryl. "Feminist Literary Criticism and the Author." *Critical Inquiry* (1990): 551-71.

Walker, Ross. *Insight Text Guide: Romulus, My Father*. Insight Publications, 2004.

Walwicz, Ania. "Look at Me, Ma—I'm Going to Be a Marginal Writer!" *Journal of the Association for the Study of Australian Literature* (2013): 162-64.

—. "horse: a psychodramatic enactment of a fairytale." Diss. Deakin University, 2016. Web. 12 Jul. 2019.

Watkins, Ross. "Bodies in Boxes: a Fictocritical Search for the Writing Process." *Text: Special Issue Website Series* 27 (2014): 1-12.

Watkins, Ross, and Nigel Krauth. "Radicalising the Scholarly Paper: New Forms for the Traditional Journal Article." *TEXT, Journal of Writing and Writing Courses* 20.1 (2016).

Waugh, Patricia. *Metafiction: The Theory and Practice of Self-Conscious Fiction*. London: Methuen, 1984.

Weeda-Zuidersma, Jeannette. "Keeping Mum: Representations of Motherhood in Contemporary Australian Literature—a Fictocritical Exploration." 2007. Web. 3 Feb. 2014.

White, Patrick. *Memoirs of Many in One*. Random House, 2011.

White, Terri-Ann, Gibbs, Anna, Jenkins, Wendy and Noel King, eds. *No Substitute: Prose, Poems, Images*. Fremantle: Fremantle Arts Centre Press, 1990.

Whitlock, Gillian, and David Carter. *Images of Australia: An Introductory Reader in Australian Studies*. UQP, 1992.

Wilding, Michael. "Marcus Clarke's Essential Recycling." *Quadrant* 55.11 (2011): 36.

Williams, Katarzyna Kwapisz. "Can "No Place" be Defined as "Our Place"? Australia as Utopia in the Writings of Post-War Polish Migrants." *Echoes of Utopia: Notions, Rhetoric, Poetics*. Eds. Klonowska B, Kolbuszewska Z, Maziarczyk G. Studies in Literature and Culture. Vol. 6. Lublin: KUL, 2012, 223-41.

—. "Life Narratives, Common Language and Diverse Ways of Belonging." *Forum Qualitative Sozialforschung/Forum: Qualitative Social Research*. 16.2 (2015).

Woodcock, Lynne. "The Comic Gothic." *The Luminary* 1 (2009).

Woolf, Virginia. *Orlando*. London: Penguin, 2006.

—. *To the Lighthouse*. Penguin, 2010.

Young, Rusty. *Marching Powder*. Pan Macmillan, 2016.

Yuan-chin, Chang. "On the Hyphenated Edge—Hyper-Existentialism, Hybridity and the Magical Hyper-Real in the Writings of Michael Mirolla." *Nebula* 7.1/2 (2010): 44-70. *Humanities International Complete*. Web. 4 Nov. 2013.

Zhang, Bo. "Through the Wormhole with Morgan Freeman." *Discover* 31.5 (2010): 23. *MAS Ultra – School Edition*.